THE COMPREHENSIVE GUIDE TO CYBERSECURITY HIRING

Strategies, Trends, and Best Practices

Dr. Jason Edwards, DMIST, CISSP

ISBN-13: 978-1-60427-203-1
e-ISBN: 978-1-60427-856-9

Printed and bound in the U.S.A. Printed on acid-free paper.

10 9 8 7 6 5 4 3 2 1

Library of Congress Cataloging-in-Publication Data can be found in the WAV
section of the publisher's website at www.jrosspub.com/wav.

Direct all inquiries to J. Ross Publishing, Inc., 151 N. Nob Hill Rd., Suite
476, Plantation, FL 33324.

Phone: (954) 727-9333
Fax: (561) 892-0700
Web: www.jrosspub.com

To my dearest Selda,

In the pages of this book, as in the chapters of our life together, your essence is interwoven with every word. Born from the beautiful lands of Turkey, your journey has brought light and joy not only into my life but into the lives of all who have the privilege of knowing you.

As a friend, you have been my steadfast companion, sharing in the laughter and tears and standing by my side through the trials and triumphs. Your unwavering support and understanding have been the bedrock upon which I have built my confidence and dreams.

As a companion, you have filled my days with love and my nights with warmth. Your wisdom, kindness, and compassion have been a guiding light, leading us through the complexities of life with grace and strength.

And as a mother, you are the embodiment of love and dedication. The care and devotion you pour into our family is a testament to the incredible person you are. Your ability to nurture, teach, and love unconditionally is a gift to our children and a legacy that will echo through generations.

Selda, this book is a small token of my immense gratitude and love for you. May it serve as a reminder of the beautiful journey we share and the endless adventures that still await us.

Tüm aşkımla,

Jason

CONTENTS

PREFACE

In an era where digital transformation is not just a trend but a necessity, cybersecurity has emerged as a cornerstone of technological progress and organizational integrity. As we delve deeper into the interconnected realms of data, networks, and cloud services, safeguarding these digital assets becomes paramount. This book is born out of the urgency and necessity to address one of the most critical aspects of cybersecurity: the human element. It is an undeniable truth that behind every robust cybersecurity infrastructure are skilled professionals who design, implement, and maintain these systems. This book aims to bridge the gap in understanding and equipping the workforce that stands on the front lines of this digital battleground, ensuring that organizations are not just technologically prepared but also strategically staffed to combat the ever-evolving cyber threats.

THE GENESIS OF THIS BOOK

The inspiration for this book emerged from my extensive experience as an educator, teaching thousands of students who were eager to forge their paths in the cybersecurity realm. Brimming with potential and ambition, these students often faced the daunting task of navigating a rapidly evolving industry. Their journeys highlighted a crucial gap in the sector—a disconnect between the burgeoning talent pool and the hiring practices of organizations. Simultaneously, my interactions with numerous talent acquisition and human resources professionals unveiled a parallel challenge. These professionals frequently sought my advice, grappling with the intricacies of identifying and recruiting cybersecurity talent. Their queries and concerns underscored a widespread need for a comprehensive resource that could demystify cybersecurity hiring. These dual perspectives—the aspiring cybersecurity professionals and the HR managers striving to recruit them—were the catalysts for this book. They underscored the necessity for a guide that simplifies the hiring process in this specialized field and bridges the understanding gap between cybersecurity requirements and talent management strategies. This book responds to those needs, aiming to harmonize the objectives of aspiring cybersecurity professionals and the organizations seeking to harness their potential.

OVERVIEW OF THIS BOOK'S CONTENT

This book is meticulously structured to guide readers through the multifaceted cybersecurity hiring process, from understanding the domain to effectively onboarding and retaining talent. It is divided into twelve comprehensive chapters, each addressing a critical aspect of the hiring process:

- **Chapter 1: Introduction to Cybersecurity Hiring** sets the stage, offering a primer on the importance and background of cybersecurity hiring and the book's objectives.
- **Chapter 2: Understanding Cybersecurity Roles and Skills** delves into the cybersecurity domain, discussing fundamental and emerging domains, key roles, and necessary skills.
- **Chapter 3: Crafting Effective Job Postings** guides readers on writing resonant job descriptions, balancing technical and soft skills, and using the correct language.
- **Chapter 4: Leveraging Professional Hiring Tools for Cybersecurity Recruitment** explores modern hiring platforms, LinkedIn strategies, and general job platforms.
- **Chapter 5: The Hiring Process** outlines planning and preparation, posting and promotion of job vacancies, and applicant tracking and management.
- **Chapter 6: Effective Interview Strategies** presents structured interview processes, questions to ask, and evaluations of candidates' technical and soft skills.
- **Chapter 7: Assessing Technical Competency** focuses on designing technical assessments and the tools and platforms for evaluation.
- **Chapter 8: Building a Cybersecurity Internship Program** covers internships' benefits, structuring, and mentorship.
- **Chapter 9: Diversity and Inclusion in Cybersecurity Hiring** emphasizes the importance of diversity, inclusive hiring strategies, and building a supportive environment.

- **Chapter 10: Onboarding and Training** discusses best practices for onboarding, training programs, and performance monitoring.
- **Chapter 11: Employee Retention and Career Development** addresses building a positive work culture, career advancement opportunities, and employee benefits.
- **Chapter 12: Future Trends in Cybersecurity Hiring** looks ahead at upcoming challenges, the role of artificial intelligence and automation, and continuous adaptation and learning.

TARGET READERSHIP

The primary beneficiaries of this book include:

1. **HR professionals:** Human resources managers and recruiters who are tasked with identifying, attracting, and hiring cybersecurity talent will find this book particularly beneficial. It gives them the insights and tools to navigate the unique recruiting challenges in this specialized field.
2. **Cybersecurity leaders and managers:** Leaders and managers within the cybersecurity domain, including Chief Information Security Officers, security managers, and team leads, will gain valuable insights into building and managing effective cybersecurity teams. This book offers guidance on understanding the skills and competencies required for various roles, aiding in better hiring decisions.
3. **Educators and trainers in cybersecurity:** Academics, trainers, and educators who are responsible for preparing the next generation of cybersecurity professionals will find this book valuable. It offers a comprehensive overview of the skills and knowledge that are in demand in the industry, enabling educators to tailor their curriculum to meet these needs better.
4. **Talent acquisition specialists:** Those specializing in talent acquisition, particularly in technology and cybersecurity-focused firms, will better understand the specific requirements and challenges in recruiting for cybersecurity roles.
5. **Career counselors and advisors:** Professionals who guide individuals who are looking to enter or advance in cybersecurity will find this book valuable for understanding cybersecurity's landscape, roles, and career paths.

THIS BOOK'S OBJECTIVE

This book equips readers with the knowledge and tools necessary to excel in cybersecurity hiring. It aims to achieve several key goals:

1. **Bridging the gap between HR and cybersecurity:** One of the foremost intentions of this book is to bridge the existing knowledge gap between human resources professionals and the technical nuances of cybersecurity. The book empowers HR professionals to make informed decisions and communicate effectively with cybersecurity teams by comprehensively understanding cybersecurity roles, skills, and industry requirements.

2. **Enhancing recruitment strategies:** This book offers in-depth guidance on developing and implementing effective recruitment strategies that are tailored explicitly to cybersecurity roles. This includes crafting compelling job descriptions, understanding the unique skill sets required in cybersecurity, and utilizing innovative recruitment tools and platforms.

3. **Developing a comprehensive understanding of cybersecurity roles:** Readers will gain a clear understanding of the various roles within the cybersecurity domain, including emerging and specialized positions. This understanding is crucial for identifying talent and aligning candidates with the appropriate roles.

4. **Improving interview and evaluation techniques:** This book provides detailed strategies for conducting compelling interviews and evaluations, ensuring that candidates are technically proficient and fit the organization's culture and values.

5. **Incorporating diversity and inclusion:** A significant focus is on developing inclusive hiring practices that promote diversity within cybersecurity teams. This is crucial for fostering innovation and reflecting organizations' diverse customer base.

6. **Fostering long-term employee engagement and retention:** Beyond hiring, this book also delves into strategies for onboarding, training, and retaining cybersecurity talent, while addressing the challenges of employee engagement and career development in this dynamic field.

CLOSING REMARKS

As I conclude this preface, I do so with a heartfelt aspiration that this book will serve as more than just a guide—that it will be a transformative tool in bridging the crucial gap between cybersecurity and human resources. I hope this book informs and inspires, leading to more robust, capable cybersecurity teams across various industries.

The journey of knowledge and improvement is continuous, and I eagerly look forward to engaging in an ongoing dialogue with readers. I invite you to join me in this conversation to share your insights, experiences, and feedback. Let's collaborate to refine and advance our approaches to cybersecurity hiring.

For more in-depth discussions, regular updates, and to connect for advisory sessions, I encourage you to follow me on LinkedIn at linkedin.com/in/jasonedwardsdmist. There, I run newsletters and offer insights beyond the scope of this book, aiming to continue contributing to the cybersecurity and HR communities.

Let's shape a future where cybersecurity talent acquisition is effective and exemplary. Your perspectives and experiences are invaluable in this shared journey toward creating safer, more secure digital environments through skilled and insightful hiring practices.

ACKNOWLEDGMENTS

As I reflect on the journey of writing this book, my heart swells with gratitude for the individuals, mentors, and organizations that have supported and inspired me. This book is not just a product of my insights but a tapestry woven from the collective wisdom and encouragement of many.

First, I sincerely thank the significant cybersecurity and human resources leaders. Your visionary perspectives and unwavering commitment to excellence have been a guiding light in navigating the complexities of this subject. Your contributions to the field have not only shaped the industry but have also profoundly influenced the content and spirit of this book.

To the wonderful friends I have made during this journey, your camaraderie and support have been invaluable. The conversations, debates, and shared experiences with you have enriched my understanding and appreciation of the diverse facets of cybersecurity hiring. You have been both confidants and catalysts for the ideas that have found their way into these pages.

A special note of gratitude goes to my family. Your endless patience, encouragement, and belief in my work have been the pillars of my strength. The sacrifices you have made and your unwavering support have been the bedrock upon which this endeavor was built.

Last but certainly not least, I extend a heartfelt acknowledgment to the survivors of the A7 program—you know who you are. Your resilience, determination, and the shared bond we have formed through our experiences are beyond words. The journey we embarked on together has inspired and reminded us of the indomitable human spirit.

To all of you who have been a part of this journey, directly or indirectly, I extend my deepest gratitude. Your contributions, in various forms, have been instrumental in bringing *The Comprehensive Guide to Cybersecurity Hiring* to fruition. Thank you for being part of this meaningful endeavor.

ABOUT THE AUTHOR

Dr. Jason Edwards has over 25 years of experience in cybersecurity and technology across various industries, including finance, insurance, and energy. He holds several credentials, such as a Certified in Risk and Information Systems Control, a Certified Information Systems Security Professional, and a Doctorate in Management, Information Systems, and Technology, specializing in Cybersecurity. He also served with the U.S. Army for 22 years, earning a Bronze Star for service during multiple tours in Iraq and Afghanistan.

Besides his professional achievements, Dr. Edwards is passionate about sharing his knowledge and expertise. He has been an Adjunct Professor of Cybersecurity at multiple universities, teaching professional and graduate-level courses. He has also authored numerous books on cybersecurity, including a children's series. He is highly active, with a large following on LinkedIn, where he is the author of the Cyber Spear educational newsletters, which offer free daily and weekly information to enhance cybersecurity awareness and build skills within the industry. Jason lives with his family in San Antonio, Texas.

 Web Added Value™

This book has free material available for download from the
Web Added Value™ resource center at *www.jrosspub.com*

At J. Ross Publishing we are committed to providing today's professional
with practical, hands-on tools that enhance the learning experience and give
readers an opportunity to apply what they have learned. That is why we offer
free ancillary materials available for download on this book and all participating Web Added Value™ publications. These online resources may include
interactive versions of material that appears in the book or supplemental
templates, worksheets, models, plans, case studies, proposals, spreadsheets
and assessment tools, among other things. Whenever you see the WAV™
symbol in any of our publications, it means bonus materials accompany the
book and are available from the Web Added Value Download Resource Center at www.jrosspub.com.

Downloads for *The Comprehensive Guide to Cybersecurity Hiring* include a
Behavioral Interview Guide for hiring managers and a career questions rubrics.

1

INTRODUCTION TO CYBERSECURITY HIRING

The contemporary business landscape is increasingly digital and with this shift comes a heightened risk of cyber threats. In an age where digital information is a critical asset, the growing incidence and sophistication of cyber threats pose a significant challenge to businesses. These threats, ranging from data breaches, ransomware attacks, and advanced persistent threats, have profound implications for a company's operational integrity, financial stability, and public reputation.

BACKGROUND AND IMPORTANCE OF CYBERSECURITY HIRING

Cybersecurity professionals are crucial in managing cyber risks, safeguarding sensitive data, and maintaining digital health. Their role is pivotal in developing cybersecurity strategies, including establishing security protocols and staying updated on cyber threats. The industry, however, faces a significant challenge: a shortage of qualified talent. This gap hinders the ability of organizations to counter sophisticated cyber threats, thereby impacting strategic planning in cybersecurity. Skilled cybersecurity teams are essential for business resilience and reputation and the ability to bounce back from incidents. The demand for these professionals is growing, but the talent scarcity poses a challenge toward maintaining a secure and stable digital business environment.

In today's digital business world, cybersecurity is a strategic function, aligning with business goals for success and sustainability. It involves tailoring cybersecurity to unique business risks and operational capabilities. Cybersecurity professionals protect data and assets, manage internal vulnerabilities, and maintain customer trust. Proactive cybersecurity strategies are critical, including regular security updates and employee training. Cybersecurity enhances competitive advantage and operational efficiency, which are integral to strategic business planning and growth.

Hiring in cybersecurity is challenging due to the industry's rapid evolution and specific skill requirements. Key challenges are identifying the right skills, bridging academic and industry gaps, adapting to evolving threats, and competing in a tight job market. Organizations must strategically recruit, focusing on adaptability, continuous learning, and innovation in order to build a resilient workforce.

Human resources (HR) plays a vital role in cybersecurity, extending beyond traditional personnel management. It involves collaborating with IT and cybersecurity departments, crafting compelling job descriptions, instilling a cybersecurity-conscious culture, and facilitating continuous learning. HR's proactive involvement is key in strengthening cybersecurity defenses and integrating HR practices into cybersecurity strategies.

The cybersecurity field is dynamic, with diverse roles adapting to new challenges and technologies. Specializations in artificial intelligence (AI), blockchain, and Internet of Things (IoT) security are emerging. The demand for cybersecurity professionals is increasing across sectors, offering vast opportunities and job security. Continuous skill development is essential to keep pace with evolving threats and technologies, making cybersecurity careers rewarding and challenging.

OBJECTIVE OF THIS BOOK

Facilitating a better understanding of cybersecurity roles is the first step in this guidance. Cybersecurity encompasses various roles, each with specific responsibilities, skill requirements, and challenges. From entry-level positions to senior management roles, knowing the nuances of each position is crucial for HR professionals. This understanding helps craft precise job descriptions, set realistic expectations, and identify suitable candidates. It involves recognizing the unique demands of roles such as network security, application security, compliance, risk management, and incident response. A comprehensive understanding of these roles allows HR managers to align their recruitment strategies with the specific needs and goals of the cybersecurity department.

Offering insights into effective recruitment strategies is another critical aspect of this guidance. The cybersecurity job market is highly competitive, and traditional recruitment approaches may not always be practical. Innovative strategies such as partnering with educational institutions, offering internships, participating in cybersecurity conferences, and utilizing social media platforms can be more effective. Additionally, understanding cybersecurity professionals' motivations and career aspirations is essential in attracting the right talent. Strategies that emphasize career growth, continuous learning opportunities, and positive work culture can be particularly effective in drawing in top candidates.

Given the high demand and limited supply of cybersecurity talent, presenting best practices for hiring and retention is essential. Best practices include thorough vetting processes, focusing on technical and soft skills like problem solving and communication. Developing an inclusive and diverse workplace is also vital because it encourages different perspectives and ideas, which are crucial in cybersecurity. Retention strategies should focus on continuous professional development, recognizing and rewarding achievements, and offering competitive compensation and benefits. Creating a work environment that values employee contributions and promotes a healthy work-life balance is equally important.

Highlighting industry trends and future directions is vital for staying ahead in cybersecurity. HR professionals must be aware of the latest developments, such as the increasing use of AI in cybersecurity, the growing importance of privacy regulations, and the shift toward cloud-based security solutions. Understanding these trends helps anticipate future skill requirements and adapt hiring strategies accordingly. It also assists in forecasting the evolution of cybersecurity roles and preparing the organization for upcoming challenges and opportunities.

Bridging the Gap Between HR and Cybersecurity

Effective communication and collaboration between HR and cybersecurity teams are the foundation of bridging this gap. Effective communication ensures that HR professionals are well-informed about the specific needs and expectations of those who hold cybersecurity roles. Regular meetings, joint workshops, and collaborative platforms can facilitate this exchange of information. Collaboration is essential in developing recruitment strategies, creating role descriptions, and setting up career development pathways. Such joint efforts lead to a more cohesive and informed approach to recruiting and managing cybersecurity talent.

Understanding the unique aspects of cybersecurity roles is crucial for HR professionals. Unlike many other fields, cybersecurity is highly dynamic, with roles often requiring a blend of technical, analytical, and strategic skills. HR teams need to comprehend the nuances of these roles, including the specific technical skills, certifications, and experience levels required. This understanding is vital in accurately assessing a candidate's fit for the role, setting realistic job expectations, and providing appropriate career development opportunities.

Developing tailored hiring processes for cyber roles is another critical aspect of bridging the gap. The traditional hiring processes may not suffice for the unique demands of cybersecurity positions. Tailoring these processes involves incorporating specific assessments to gauge technical and analytical skills, adapting interview techniques to evaluate problem-solving and critical-thinking abilities, and understanding the significance of certifications and hands-on experience. A customized approach to hiring improves recruitment quality and enhances the candidate experience, reflecting the organization's commitment to cybersecurity.

Addressing common misconceptions and challenges is essential in aligning HR practices with cybersecurity needs. Misconceptions such as overemphasizing formal education over practical experience, underestimating the importance of soft skills, or not recognizing the diversity of roles within cybersecurity can hinder effective recruitment. Challenges such as high demand and limited supply of skilled professionals, rapid technological changes, and the evolving nature of cyber threats must also be addressed. HR departments must be equipped to tackle these misconceptions and challenges through continuous learning, adapting to industry changes, and maintaining flexibility in their recruitment and retention strategies.

Bridging the gap between HR and cybersecurity is vital for building a robust cybersecurity workforce. By embracing these strategies, HR and cybersecurity departments can work in tandem to ensure the recruitment and retention of talented professionals.

Enhancing Recruitment Strategies

Leveraging technology and tools in recruitment is a crucial strategy for modernizing the hiring process. Technologies such as applicant tracking systems, AI-driven candidate screening tools, and cybersecurity-specific skill assessment platforms can significantly streamline recruitment. These tools help efficiently sort through large applications, identify candidates with the desired skills and experience, and reduce the time-to-hire. Additionally, using social media platforms and professional networking sites can aid in reaching a wider pool of potential candidates, including passive job seekers who might not actively be looking for new opportunities but are open to the right offer.

Building a talent pipeline through strategic sourcing is another important strategy. This involves identifying potential candidates well before a position becomes available. Engaging with candidates through career fairs, cybersecurity conferences, online forums, and educational institutions can help create a reservoir of potential hires. Maintaining relationships with past applicants, interns, and employees can also be beneficial. This proactive approach to sourcing ensures a ready pool of qualified candidates to tap into when a vacancy arises, thereby reducing the time and resources spent on recruitment.

Implementing practical assessment and selection methods is crucial in identifying suitable candidates for cybersecurity roles. Given the specialized nature of these roles, it is important to use assessment methods that accurately evaluate candidates' technical abilities, problem-solving skills, and adaptability. This may include practical tests, such as penetration testing or code analysis, and behavioral interviews to assess how candidates approach problems and work in a team. Such comprehensive assessment methods help ensure that the candidates have the necessary technical skills, fit well within the team, and can handle the dynamic nature of cybersecurity work.

Cultural fit refers to how well a candidate's values, beliefs, and behavior align with the organization's culture. In cybersecurity, where collaboration and a rapid response to threats are crucial, it is essential to have team members who share the organization's values and work ethos. A good cultural fit candidate is more likely to work effectively within the team, contribute positively to the work environment, and stay with the organization long-term. Hence, assessing cultural fit should be an integral part of the recruitment process.

Enhancing recruitment strategies in cybersecurity involves leveraging advanced technology and tools, building a strategic talent pipeline, implementing effective assessment methods, and understanding the importance of cultural fit. By adopting these enhanced strategies, organizations can more effectively meet their cybersecurity staffing needs, ensuring a solid defense against the ever-evolving cyber threats of the digital world.

Supporting Career Development and Retention

Strategies for nurturing talent within the organization are crucial for a cybersecurity professional's long-term success and satisfaction. This involves identifying and nurturing the strengths and potential of each employee. One practical approach is offering personalized development plans that align with the employee's career aspirations and the organization's goals. This could include opportunities for working on diverse projects, cross-training in different cybersecurity areas, and providing challenging assignments that stimulate growth and learning. Encouraging participation in cybersecurity competitions and hackathons can also benefit skill enhancement and innovation.

The importance of career progression and development in cybersecurity cannot be understated. Cybersecurity professionals often seek clear paths for advancement within their roles. Organizations should therefore establish transparent career ladders that outline the requirements and opportunities for progression. This clarity helps employees understand what they must achieve to advance and motivates them to attain the necessary skills and experiences. In addition to traditional promotions, lateral movements across different cybersecurity areas can offer valuable experiences and prevent job stagnation.

The role of mentorship and training in employee retention is significant. Mentorship programs, where seasoned professionals guide and advise less experienced staff, can be highly effective in developing skills and fostering a sense of belonging. Regular training programs, both internal and external, are also essential to keep staff updated with the latest cybersecurity trends, technologies, and best practices. Training can include workshops, certifications, webinars, or even sponsoring further education. These programs enhance skills and demonstrate the organization's commitment to its employees' professional growth, contributing to higher job satisfaction and retention rates.

Creating an engaging and supportive work environment involves cultivating a culture that values employee contributions, encourages open communication, and supports work-life balance. Recognizing and rewarding achievements through formal awards, promotions, or even informal acknowledgments can boost morale and motivation. Creating a supportive environment also means providing the necessary tools and resources for employees to perform their jobs effectively and offering support during challenging times, such as high-pressure situations or following a security breach.

Supporting career development and retention in cybersecurity requires a multifaceted approach, including nurturing talent, providing clear pathways for career progression, offering mentorship and continuous training, and creating an engaging and supportive work environment. By investing in the development and well-being of their employees, organizations not only enhance their cybersecurity capabilities but also foster a loyal and committed team.

Legal and Ethical Considerations

Navigating legal frameworks in cybersecurity hiring is essential to ensure compliance with various laws and regulations. This includes understanding and adhering to labor laws, data protection regulations, and industry-specific compliance standards. For instance, organizations must be aware of equal employment opportunity laws to avoid discriminatory practices in hiring. Additionally, with cybersecurity roles often requiring access to sensitive data, it is crucial to be aware of privacy and protection laws. Understanding these legal frameworks helps organizations structure their hiring processes to be legally compliant, avoiding potential legal issues and penalties.

Understanding ethical responsibilities in the hiring process is equally important. Ethical hiring practices in cybersecurity involve fair and unbiased recruitment processes and extend to ethical considerations specific to the cybersecurity field. This includes ensuring that candidates have a solid ethical grounding in handling sensitive information responsibly and making decisions that align with the organization's ethical standards and the broader societal implications. Assessing a candidate's ethical judgment and integrity is essential, especially in roles that deal with high-stakes data and security issues.

Ensuring diversity and inclusion in recruitment is a significant aspect of ethical hiring practices. A diverse cybersecurity workforce brings a range of perspectives, backgrounds, and problem-solving approaches, which is crucial in tackling the diverse and complex challenges in cybersecurity. Efforts to promote diversity and inclusion should encompass all stages of the hiring process, from job advertisements to candidate selection. This ensures that opportunities are accessible to various candidates, regardless of gender, race, ethnicity, or background. This enhances the team's effectiveness and contributes to a more equitable and inclusive work environment.

Balancing privacy and security in the hiring process is a delicate but crucial task, especially in the cybersecurity domain, where candidates might be privy to sensitive information as part of the recruitment process. Organizations must ensure that each applicant's personal information is handled securely and in compliance with privacy laws. This includes safeguarding the confidentiality of applicant data and being transparent about using and storing this information. Balancing these concerns requires a well-thought-out approach that respects the candidate's privacy while ensuring the security and integrity of the hiring process.

Legal and ethical considerations play a pivotal role in cybersecurity hiring. By adhering to these principles, organizations can ensure a fair, compliant, and effective hiring process, which is essential for building a trustworthy and capable cybersecurity team. This guidance is crucial for HR managers and hiring professionals in understanding and implementing practices that are both legally sound and ethically robust, fostering a responsible and inclusive approach to cybersecurity recruitment.

WHO SHOULD READ THIS BOOK?

HR managers and professionals form the primary segment of the target audience. They are often at the forefront of the recruitment process, responsible for attracting, screening, and hiring candidates. For HR professionals, this book provides valuable insights into the unique aspects of cybersecurity hiring, such as identifying the right skill sets, understanding the evolving cybersecurity landscape, and implementing effective hiring and retention strategies. This knowledge is vital for HR managers to effectively bridge the gap between the general recruitment process and the specific demands of cybersecurity roles.

Talent acquisition specialists are another key group. These specialists focus specifically on sourcing and recruiting candidates, which requires a deep understanding of cybersecurity in order to identify and attract top talent. This book offers guidance on leveraging advanced recruitment technologies, building talent pipelines, and understanding the nuances of various cybersecurity roles. This information is crucial for talent acquisition specialists to navigate the competitive market and secure the best candidates for their organizations.

The hiring managers in technology and cybersecurity fields are also a significant part of the target audience. These professionals have a more technical perspective and are often involved in the later stages of the recruitment process, such as interviewing and assessing technical skills. This book provides them with insights into effective assessment methods, the importance of cultural fit, and strategies for integrating new hires into their teams. This knowledge helps them make informed decisions when selecting candidates who are technically competent and a good fit for the team and the organization.

Executives and decision makers in IT and cybersecurity are the final segments of the target audience. These individuals are responsible for shaping the overall strategy of their departments, including workforce development and management. This book offers them a comprehensive overview of the cybersecurity hiring landscape, including legal and ethical considerations, career development and retention strategies, and insights into future industry trends. This information is critical for executives and decision makers in order to strategically align their hiring practices with organizational goals and the broader cybersecurity challenges.

Benefits for HR Professionals

For HR professionals, delving into the intricacies of cybersecurity hiring offers numerous benefits. One of the primary advantages is gaining insights into the cybersecurity field. Understanding the unique challenges, roles, and requirements of cybersecurity positions enables HR professionals to more effectively align their recruitment strategies with the specific needs of these roles. This knowledge is crucial in a field that is as specialized and dynamic as cybersecurity, where the landscape of threats and skills required evolves rapidly.

Enhancing recruitment and retention strategies is another significant benefit. Armed with a deeper understanding of cybersecurity, HR professionals can develop more targeted recruitment campaigns, craft accurate and enticing job descriptions, and implement effective assessment processes. This leads to more successful hiring outcomes. Additionally, insights into effective retention strategies, such as career development opportunities, mentorship programs, and creating a supportive work culture, are invaluable in maintaining a skilled and motivated cybersecurity workforce.

Understanding the dynamics of the cybersecurity job market is essential for HR professionals. There is a high demand for skilled professionals in the cybersecurity field and a relatively limited supply. By understanding these market dynamics, HR professionals can better navigate the competitive landscape, identify trends and opportunities, and adapt their strategies accordingly. This includes leveraging emerging recruitment channels, understanding the expectations and motivations of cybersecurity professionals, and staying informed about salary benchmarks and industry standards.

Improving collaboration with IT and cybersecurity teams is critical to successful cybersecurity hiring. HR professionals need to work closely with these teams to understand the technical requirements and nuances of cybersecurity roles. Effective collaboration ensures that the recruitment process is aligned with the cybersecurity team's specific technical and cultural needs. This collaboration also facilitates a smoother integration of new hires into the existing teams, enhances mutual understanding and respect between HR and cybersecurity professionals, and contributes to a more cohesive and effective organizational approach to cybersecurity.

For HR professionals, venturing into cybersecurity hiring brings many benefits, including gaining specialized insights, enhancing recruitment and retention strategies, understanding the job market's dynamics, and improving collaboration with IT and cybersecurity teams. These benefits are pivotal in building and maintaining a competent, efficient, and resilient cybersecurity workforce, which is essential in today's increasingly digital and security-conscious business environment.

For Cybersecurity Leaders and Managers

Cybersecurity leaders and managers stand to gain significantly from understanding and collaborating effectively with HR in the talent acquisition and management process. One of the key advantages is building effective teams with HR's support. This involves working closely with HR to ensure that the recruitment process is tailored to meet the specific needs of the cybersecurity team. By clearly communicating the technical skills, experience levels, and cultural fit required for different roles, cybersecurity leaders can assist HR in sourcing and selecting candidates who possess the necessary technical expertise and align with the team's dynamics and the organization's broader goals.

Communicating needs and expectations is another crucial aspect for cybersecurity leaders and managers. In the complex and rapidly evolving field of cybersecurity, leaders need to articulate their domain's specific requirements and challenges to HR professionals. This clarity helps HR understand the nuances of cybersecurity roles and develop recruitment strategies that address these specific needs. Clear communication also extends to defining career paths, professional development opportunities, and performance metrics, thereby aiding HR in creating a supportive and motivating environment for the cybersecurity team.

Recognizing the challenges and constraints that HR professionals must confront, such as balancing the demand for technical skills with cultural fit or navigating a competitive job market, can foster a more collaborative and effective partnership. This understanding can lead to more realistic and practical hiring strategies, ensuring that HR and cybersecurity teams work toward a common goal.

Developing a workforce strategy that is aligned with cybersecurity goals is essential for cybersecurity leaders and managers. This involves recruiting the right talent along with retaining and developing them. Collaborating with HR to design and implement strategies for professional development, career progression, and employee engagement is crucial in building a resilient and adaptable cybersecurity team.

For cybersecurity leaders and managers, collaborating with HR offers numerous benefits, including building effective teams, clearly communicating needs and expectations, understanding HR's perspective on talent acquisition, and developing a workforce strategy that aligns with cybersecurity goals. These elements create a strong, dynamic, and future-ready cybersecurity team, which is integral to the organization's overall security posture and success.

For Educators and Trainers

Educators and trainers in cybersecurity play a pivotal role in shaping the future workforce. Understanding industry needs is essential for developing relevant and practical curricula. This understanding allows educators to tailor their teaching to the current demands and future trends of the cybersecurity landscape, ensuring that the content is academically rigorous and practically applicable. Staying abreast of the latest developments, technologies, and challenges in cybersecurity helps create a current and comprehensive curriculum, thereby preparing students for the realities of the field.

Preparing students for real-world cybersecurity roles is a critical objective for educators and trainers. This involves imparting theoretical knowledge and providing practical, hands-on experience. Courses should include real-world case studies, simulations, and problem-solving exercises that mimic the challenges that students will face in their professional lives. This practical focus helps bridge the gap between academic learning and applying skills in real-world scenarios, a crucial element for students aspiring to enter the cybersecurity workforce.

While theoretical knowledge provides the foundation, practical skills are essential for success in the cybersecurity field. Integrating labs, internships, and project-based learning into the curriculum can significantly enhance students' practical skills. In addition, educators can emphasize the development of soft skills such as critical thinking, communication, and teamwork, which are equally important in the cybersecurity industry.

Fostering partnerships with industry for experiential learning will benefit both students and educators. These partnerships can provide students with valuable opportunities for internships, mentorships, and participation in industry projects. Such experiences allow students to apply their academic learning in real-world settings, gain insights into the workings of the cybersecurity industry, and develop professional networks. For educators, partnerships with industry can provide insights into evolving industry needs and trends, helping to keep the curriculum relevant and up-to-date.

For educators and trainers in cybersecurity, understanding industry needs, preparing students for real-world roles, bridging the gap between academic and practical skills, and fostering industry partnerships are all crucial tasks. These elements ensure that the education provided is aligned with industry requirements, equipping students with the skills and experience needed to succeed in cybersecurity's dynamic and challenging world.

2

UNDERSTANDING CYBERSECURITY ROLES AND SKILLS

The landscape of cybersecurity is diverse and multifaceted, encompassing several key domains that are crucial for protecting an organization's digital assets. Understanding these domains is essential for HR professionals and cybersecurity leaders in order to align roles and skills with organizational needs effectively.

OVERVIEW OF THE CYBERSECURITY DOMAIN

Cybersecurity encompasses various fundamental domains, including network security, information security, application security, and operational security, which are vital for protecting an organization's network, data, applications, and operations. Emerging and specialized domains, such as cloud security, cryptography, incident response, and forensic analysis, address specific challenges and evolving threats in the digital landscape. Cybersecurity governance and compliance ensure that practices align with legal and regulatory standards, which involves understanding regulatory requirements, risk management, and audit and compliance. The threat intelligence and analysis domains focus on identifying and understanding cyber threats for proactive defense and informed decision making. Cybersecurity needs differ across sectors, with each industry facing unique threats, compliance standards, and challenges requiring tailored strategies and solutions. Understanding these various aspects is critical for cybersecurity hiring and management, enabling adequate protection against cyber threats and compliance with legal obligations.

Fundamental Domains in Cybersecurity

There are four domains of cybersecurity. Network security focuses on protecting an organization's network infrastructure. This includes safeguarding against unauthorized access, misuse, malfunction, modification, destruction, or improper disclosure. Network security professionals work to ensure the integrity and availability of network and data services by implementing various security measures such as firewalls, intrusion detection systems, and network access controls. Their role is critical in preventing attacks that can disrupt or cripple an organization's network operations.

Information security is concerned with safeguarding data integrity and confidentiality. It encompasses strategies and practices to protect sensitive information from unauthorized access or alterations, both in transit and at rest. Professionals in this domain are responsible for developing policies and procedures for data protection, conducting risk assessments, and implementing data encryption and other security measures. Their work is crucial in ensuring that confidential information, such as customer data, financial records, and intellectual property, is secure from breaches and leaks.

Application security focuses on securing software and applications from threats. This domain involves identifying and fixing vulnerabilities in software applications to prevent attacks such as a Structured Query Language injection, cross-site scripting, and buffer overflows. Application security specialists work closely with developers to incorporate security measures in the software development life cycle, conduct security testing, and monitor applications for emerging threats. Their role is vital in protecting applications from exploitation as cyberattack entry points.

Operational security (OpSec) involves managing and protecting data assets. This domain deals with the processes and decisions for handling and protecting data, including the procedures for storing, processing, and transmitting data. OpSec professionals ensure that operational procedures align with security policies and regulatory requirements. They protect an organization's data assets from internal and external threats and maintain a business operation's continuity and efficiency.

These fundamental domains in cybersecurity—network security, information security, application security, and operational security—form the cornerstone of an organization's cybersecurity efforts (see Figure 2.1). An understanding of these domains is crucial for those who are involved in cybersecurity hiring and management because it allows for the identification of specific skills and roles required to protect an organization's digital infrastructure and assets effectively.

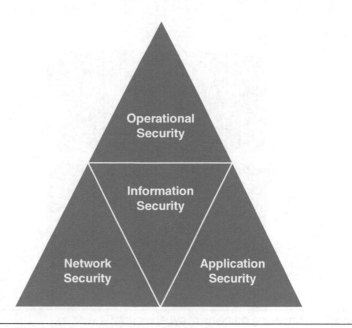

Figure 2.1   Fundamental domains of cybersecurity.

Emerging and Specialized Domains

The cybersecurity landscape continually evolves, with new domains emerging as technology advances. Understanding these specialized areas is crucial for effective cybersecurity management and recruitment (see Figure 2.2).

Cloud security is a rapidly growing domain that is driven by the increasing adoption of cloud-based systems and services. This area focuses on protecting cloud environments from threats and vulnerabilities, ensuring the security of data that is stored and processed in the cloud. Professionals in cloud security are responsible for developing and implementing security policies and controls that are specific to the cloud, such as managing access, protecting against data breaches, and ensuring compliance with various regulations. As more organizations move their operations to the cloud, the demand for expertise in cloud security continues to rise.

Cryptography is a foundational domain in cybersecurity, playing a critical role in securing communications and information. It involves creating and analyzing algorithms and protocols to prevent unauthorized access to sensitive information. Cryptography ensures the confidentiality and integrity of data by encrypting it, thereby making it inaccessible to unauthorized users. Specialists in cryptography are involved in designing encryption systems,

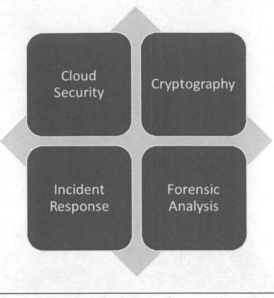

Figure 2.2   Emerging domains of cybersecurity.

developing secure communication protocols, and safeguarding data against tampering and interception. Their work is vital in securing communications, data protection, and digital transactions.

Incident response is a crucial domain, focusing on handling and mitigating cybersecurity incidents. Incident response teams manage the situation when a security breach or cyberattack occurs. This includes identifying the extent of the breach, containing the threat, eradicating the cause of the incident, and recovering any compromised systems. Incident response professionals must be skilled in rapid problem solving, crisis management, and communication to navigate and mitigate the aftermath of cybersecurity incidents effectively.

Forensic analysis is the domain that is concerned with investigating and analyzing cybercrimes. Forensic analysts work on uncovering the trail of digital evidence left by cyberattacks. Their role involves collecting, preserving, and analyzing data from various digital sources to trace the source of cyberattacks, understand the methods used, and assist in preventing future incidents. This domain requires a meticulous approach and a thorough understanding of various technologies and legal considerations since the findings often contribute to legal actions against cybercriminals.

These emerging and specialized domains—cloud security, cryptography, incident response, and forensic analysis—represent the advanced frontiers of cybersecurity. Mastery in these areas is increasingly sought after as organizations strive to counter sophisticated cyber threats and adapt to the changing digital landscape. For human resources (HR) and cybersecurity leaders, an awareness of these domains is essential to identify the talent and skills needed to address the complex cybersecurity challenges of today and tomorrow.

Cybersecurity Governance and Compliance

Cybersecurity governance and compliance are domains that ensure that an organization's cybersecurity practices align with legal and regulatory requirements and internal policies and standards.

Understanding regulatory requirements and standards is a foundational aspect of cybersecurity governance. This involves staying informed about national and international laws, regulations, and data protection and cybersecurity standards. These may include frameworks like the General Data Protection Regulation, the Health Insurance Portability and Accountability Act (HIPAA), and the Payment Card Industry Data Security Standard (PCI DSS), among others. Professionals in this domain must interpret these regulations and understand their implications for the organization's cybersecurity strategies and practices. This knowledge is essential to ensure that an organization's data handling and security measures comply with legal and regulatory obligations.

Implementing policies and procedures for compliance is another critical area. This involves developing and enforcing internal policies and procedures that align with the aforementioned regulatory requirements. Cybersecurity governance professionals work on creating comprehensive policies that cover aspects like data privacy, network security, incident response, and employee cybersecurity conduct. They also ensure that these policies are effectively communicated across the organization and that employees understand their roles and responsibilities in maintaining cybersecurity.

Risk management in cybersecurity involves identifying, assessing, and mitigating risks that are associated with cyber threats and vulnerabilities. This domain is key for the proactive management of potential cybersecurity issues. Risk management professionals conduct regular risk assessments to identify potential security weaknesses, evaluate their impact, and develop mitigation strategies. This proactive approach is vital in preventing cybersecurity incidents and minimizing potential organizational damage.

Audit and compliance are essential for ensuring adherence to laws, regulations, and internal policies. This area regularly audits an organization's cybersecurity practices and systems to verify compliance with external and internal standards. Audits can reveal gaps in compliance and security that might otherwise go unnoticed. Compliance professionals are responsible for keeping abreast of changes in laws and regulations, updating policies accordingly, and ensuring that the organization meets all necessary cybersecurity standards.

Cybersecurity governance and compliance ensure that an organization's cybersecurity practices are legally sound and practical. This domain encompasses understanding and implementing regulatory requirements, managing risks, and conducting audits to ensure ongoing compliance. A deep understanding of these areas is essential for professionals hiring and managing cybersecurity talent to ensure that the organization protects itself against cyber threats and adheres to legal and regulatory obligations.

Threat Intelligence and Analysis

Threat intelligence and analysis is a critical domain in cybersecurity that focuses on proactively identifying and understanding potential cyber threats. This area is pivotal for developing effective defense strategies and informed decision making.

Monitoring and analyzing cyber threats is the cornerstone of threat intelligence. This process involves continuously scanning the digital landscape to identify emerging threats, vulnerabilities, and attack trends. Professionals in this field use various tools and techniques to gather information about potential threats, including malware analysis, network traffic analysis, and social media monitoring. The goal is to understand the nature of threats, their potential impact, and the methods used by attackers. This continuous monitoring is crucial for the early detection of threats, allowing organizations to respond swiftly and effectively to mitigate risks.

Based on the insights gathered from monitoring activities, cybersecurity professionals devise strategies to prevent or minimize the impact of cyberattacks. This includes recommending security enhancements, developing incident response plans, and advising on best practices for digital hygiene. Proactive defense is about staying one step ahead of cybercriminals by anticipating their moves and strengthening the organization's defenses accordingly.

Utilizing intelligence for informed decision making involves leveraging the insights from threat intelligence to guide cybersecurity policies and strategies. This intelligence informs decisions at various levels, from technical decisions about security controls and software updates to strategic decisions about cybersecurity investments and policy development. Effective use of threat intelligence ensures that these decisions are based on current and comprehensive information, leading to a more robust cybersecurity posture.

Collaborating with external entities for information sharing is an increasingly important aspect of threat intelligence. Cybersecurity is not an isolated field; threats often impact multiple organizations and sectors. Therefore, sharing information about threats, vulnerabilities, and attacks with other organizations, industry groups, and government entities is vital for a collective defense strategy. This collaboration can take the form of sharing indicators of compromise, tactics used by attackers, and effective defense strategies. Such collaboration helps individual organizations and strengthens the overall cybersecurity resilience of the wider community.

Threat intelligence and analysis is a dynamic and critical domain in cybersecurity, encompassing the monitoring and analysis of cyber threats, the development of proactive defense strategies, the utilization of intelligence for decision making, and collaboration for information sharing. Understanding this domain is crucial for cybersecurity professionals and those who are involved in cybersecurity hiring and management because it plays a crucial role in protecting organizations against the ever-evolving landscape of cyber threats.

Cybersecurity in Different Sectors

Cybersecurity needs and challenges can vary significantly across different industries, each with its unique landscape of threats, compliance standards, and technological advancements. Understanding these sector-specific nuances is crucial for developing targeted cybersecurity strategies and solutions.

Variances in cybersecurity needs across industries are primarily due to the different types of data that are being handled, the nature of operations, and the specific threats faced by each sector. For example, the financial sector deals with confidential financial data and is frequently targeted by cybercriminals for financial gain. In contrast, the healthcare sector handles sensitive health information, making patient privacy and data integrity paramount. Similarly, the manufacturing sector, increasingly reliant on interconnected systems and Internet of Things (IoT) devices, faces distinct challenges in securing its operational technology. Each industry requires a tailored approach to cybersecurity that addresses its particular risks and regulatory environment.

Sector-specific challenges and solutions highlight the need for a nuanced approach to cybersecurity. For instance, protecting customer data and transaction information is a crucial challenge in the retail sector, necessitating robust encryption and secure payment processing systems. Securing critical infrastructure against potential disruptions is a primary concern in the energy sector. Solutions in each sector must be customized to address these unique challenges effectively by leveraging industry-specific knowledge and technologies.

The importance of industry-specific compliance standards is a critical aspect of sector-based cybersecurity. Many industries are subject to specific regulatory requirements that dictate how data should be protected. Healthcare organizations, for example, must comply with HIPAA regulations, while standards like the Gramm-Leach-Bliley Act and the PCI DSS govern financial institutions. Understanding and adhering to these compliance standards is a legal requirement for maintaining customer trust and safeguarding the organization's reputation.

Trends and advancements in sector-based cybersecurity reflect the ongoing evolution of threats and the continuous development of new technologies and strategies to counteract them. For instance, the increasing use of artificial intelligence (AI) and machine learning in cybersecurity provides enhanced threat detection and response capabilities across various sectors. Additionally, cloud security has become a crucial focus area in many industries as cloud computing becomes more prevalent. Keeping abreast of these trends and advancements is essential for cybersecurity professionals to stay ahead of potential threats and effectively leverage the latest tools and strategies.

Cybersecurity in different sectors involves understanding each industry's unique needs, challenges, and compliance requirements. Tailoring cybersecurity strategies to these sector-specific nuances is crucial for adequate protection against threats. Additionally, staying informed about the latest trends and technological advancements in sector-based cybersecurity is essential for maintaining a robust and responsive cybersecurity posture across diverse industries.

KEY ROLES AND JOB TITLES

In the ever-evolving cybersecurity landscape, various entry-level to advanced roles play critical parts in protecting digital assets. Security analysts and IT security specialists form the core of cybersecurity teams, focusing on monitoring threats and maintaining IT security infrastructure. Cybersecurity consultants provide expert advice on digital asset protection, while junior penetration testers proactively identify system vulnerabilities. Mid-level roles like security engineers, cybersecurity managers, incident responders, and compliance officers build and manage secure systems, oversee security operations, respond to incidents, and ensure regulatory compliance. Advanced positions like chief information security officers and security architects lead strategic cybersecurity initiatives and design comprehensive security systems. Forensic experts investigate cybercrimes and risk managers handle cybersecurity risks organization-wide. Specialized roles, such as ethical hackers, cryptographers, security software developers, and cloud security specialists, address specific areas in cybersecurity, highlighting the need for specialized skills. The field is marked by continuous learning and adaptation, with emerging roles like AI security specialists and IoT security experts reflecting new technological challenges. The future of cybersecurity will likely see roles like quantum computing security analysts and cyber-legal consultants, emphasizing the importance of interdisciplinary skills in addressing sophisticated cyber threats. This dynamic domain requires a blend of technical acumen, strategic thinking, and adaptability to combat evolving cybersecurity challenges effectively.

Selected Entry-Level Positions

Security analysts are integral to an organization's cybersecurity team, tasked with continuously monitoring and analyzing security breaches and potential threats. Their role extends beyond mere observation; they are responsible for actively scrutinizing network traffic, identifying anomalous activities, and interpreting various threat intelligence sources. A security analyst's job is to provide an early warning system for potential security incidents. They analyze the nature and scope of detected breaches, assess the potential impact, and formulate response strategies. Additionally, they play a crucial role in maintaining security monitoring tools and often update and refine security policies and protocols based on their findings.

IT security specialists are the technical backbone of an organization's cybersecurity infrastructure. Their role involves a hands-on approach to securing IT systems and networks. This includes installing, configuring, and maintaining various security measures like firewalls, antivirus programs, and intrusion detection systems. They regularly conduct system audits to ensure compliance with security policies and standards and work to identify and remediate vulnerabilities. Furthermore, IT security specialists are often involved in user education, such as helping staff understand and adhere to security best practices. They must stay abreast of the latest cybersecurity trends and technologies, ensuring that the organization's defenses remain robust.

Cybersecurity consultants operate at the intersection of technology and strategy, offering expert advice to clients on safeguarding their digital assets. They conduct thorough security assessments, identify vulnerabilities in the client's cybersecurity posture, and develop tailored solutions to mitigate these risks. Their role often involves creating and implementing comprehensive cybersecurity strategies, including technical solutions and policy and governance frameworks. Cybersecurity consultants must possess a broad understanding of various cybersecurity domains, excellent problem-solving skills, and the ability to communicate complex security concepts to nontechnical stakeholders. They must also stay updated on industry trends and regulatory changes to provide relevant and practical advice.

Junior penetration testers—often called ethical hackers—play a critical role in proactive cybersecurity defense. They conduct controlled cyberattacks on their organization's systems to uncover vulnerabilities that malicious actors could exploit. This role requires a deep understanding of attack methodologies and the ability to think like a hacker. Junior penetration testers must methodically document their findings, recommend remediation strategies, and often assist in implementing these solutions. They collaborate closely with other cybersecurity team members to reinforce the organization's defenses. Continuous learning is crucial to this role since they must keep pace with the latest hacking techniques and emerging security threats.

Entry-level positions in cybersecurity serve as the foundational layer of an organization's cybersecurity efforts. Each role, from security analysts to junior penetration testers, contributes uniquely to the overall security posture, requiring a blend of technical expertise, analytical skills, and continuous learning.

Selected Mid-Level Roles

Security engineers are pivotal in the design and construction of secure systems. Their role encompasses many responsibilities—from the initial design phase of systems and networks to their implementation and ongoing maintenance. Security engineers are tasked with ensuring that all aspects of IT infrastructure are robust against cyber threats. This involves conducting vulnerability assessments, developing security protocols, and integrating protective measures like firewalls and encryption technologies. They work closely with other IT professionals to ensure that security considerations are embedded in all technology projects and initiatives. Security engineers must possess a deep understanding of both hardware and software security, and they are often involved in troubleshooting security issues and providing technical guidance on security matters.

Cybersecurity managers play a strategic role in overseeing an organization's security operations. They are responsible for the overall direction and management of cybersecurity initiatives. This role involves planning and executing security strategies, managing cybersecurity teams, and coordinating with other departments to ensure a cohesive approach to security across the organization. Cybersecurity managers also play a crucial role in incident management, coordinating responses to security breaches and ensuring that lessons are learned to prevent future incidents. They need strong leadership and communication skills to manage their teams effectively and articulate complex security concepts to other stakeholders. Additionally, staying informed about the latest cyber threats and industry best practices is crucial for cybersecurity managers to safeguard their organizations effectively.

Incident responders are the first line of defense when a cybersecurity breach occurs. Their primary role is to quickly and effectively respond to and mitigate the impact of cyberattacks. This involves identifying the nature and scope of the breach, containing the threat, eradicating the cause of the breach, and recovering compromised systems. Incident responders work under high-pressure conditions and are adept at making quick decisions. They also play a crucial role in post-incident analysis, helping to understand how the breach occurred and what can be done to prevent similar incidents. This role requires technical expertise, problem-solving skills, and the ability to communicate effectively during crises.

Compliance officers in the cybersecurity realm are responsible for ensuring that an organization adheres to all relevant laws, regulations, and internal policies. Their work involves understanding the complex landscape of cybersecurity regulations, which can vary greatly depending on the industry and type of data the organization handles. Compliance officers develop and implement policies and procedures that meet these regulatory requirements, conduct regular compliance audits, and work to remediate any identified issues. They also play an educational role by training staff on compliance requirements and best practices. Given the ever-changing nature of cybersecurity threats and regulatory landscapes, compliance officers must continuously update their knowledge and adapt the organization's compliance strategies accordingly.

Mid-level roles in cybersecurity—including security engineers, cybersecurity managers, incident responders, and compliance officers—are crucial for effectively implementing and managing cybersecurity strategies within an organization. These roles require a deep understanding of technical aspects and skills in strategic planning, leadership, crisis management, and regulatory compliance. They are central to building and maintaining a secure and resilient digital environment in the face of evolving cyber threats.

Advanced and Leadership Roles

The chief information security officer (CISO) is a senior-level executive who leads an organization's cybersecurity strategy. The CISO is responsible for the overall direction of all cybersecurity initiatives within the organization.

This role requires a strategic mindset and the ability to align cybersecurity strategies with the organization's goals and objectives. A CISO oversees the development and implementation of security policies and procedures, manages the cybersecurity team, and ensures that the organization is prepared to respond to any cybersecurity incidents. They also play a crucial role in educating other executives and board members about cybersecurity risks and strategies. The CISO must stay abreast of the latest cybersecurity trends and threats and be adept at communicating complex security issues to nontechnical stakeholders.

A security architect is a specialized role that is focused on developing comprehensive security architectures. Security architects design and implement complex security systems that protect an organization's IT infrastructure from cyber threats. This role involves a deep understanding of hardware and software security solutions and requires thinking strategically about long-term security needs. Security architects must evaluate and implement advanced security protocols and technologies, ensure that new IT projects comply with security standards, and often lead teams in developing security solutions. They also play a crucial role in continuously assessing and improving the organization's security posture.

Forensic experts play a critical role in the investigation of cybercrimes. Forensic experts specialize in identifying, collecting, and analyzing digital cyberattack evidence. Their work is important to understanding how a breach occurred, who was responsible, and the extent of the damage. This role requires a meticulous approach and a thorough understanding of various technologies and legal considerations. Forensic experts often work closely with law enforcement agencies and legal teams, and their findings can be pivotal in legal proceedings against cyber criminals. This role demands technical expertise and strong problem-solving and communication skills.

A risk manager in cybersecurity oversees the organization's overall approach to managing cybersecurity risks. This involves identifying potential security threats, assessing their likelihood and impact, and developing mitigation strategies. Risk managers ensure that cybersecurity risks are managed within the acceptable levels defined by the organization. They develop risk management policies and procedures, conduct regular risk assessments, and recommend appropriate mitigation measures. Risk managers must have a broad understanding of cybersecurity threats and the ability to balance risk with business objectives. They also play a crucial role in promoting a risk-aware culture within the organization.

Advanced and leadership roles in cybersecurity, such as CISOs, security architects, forensic experts, and risk managers, are essential for guiding and securing an organization's digital assets. These roles require deep technical knowledge, strategic planning, leadership skills, and the ability to communicate effectively with various stakeholders.

Specialized and Niche Roles

Ethical hackers, also known as penetration testers, play a critical role in cybersecurity by actively testing systems for vulnerabilities. They simulate cyberattacks to identify weaknesses in an organization's network and systems before malicious hackers can exploit them. This role requires a deep understanding of hacking techniques and the ability to think like an attacker. Ethical hackers must be proficient in various cybersecurity tools and methodologies and often specialize in certain types of systems or attack techniques. Their work is essential for proactive security because they provide valuable insights that help organizations strengthen their defenses against real cyber threats. Additionally, ethical hackers must adhere to strict ethical guidelines, ensuring that their activities are authorized and will not cause unintended harm.

Cryptographers specialize in developing encryption technologies, a cornerstone of modern cybersecurity. They work on creating and analyzing algorithms that secure data by converting it into a format that can only be read by intended recipients with the correct decryption key. This role requires a strong background in mathematics and computer science and an understanding of current cryptographic techniques and potential vulnerabilities. Cryptographers protect sensitive information such as financial transactions, personal data, and classified communications. Their work secures and ensures the integrity and confidentiality of digital information in various applications.

Security software developers are responsible for creating software solutions that enhance an organization's cybersecurity. They design, develop, and test various security software, including antivirus programs, firewalls, and intrusion detection systems. This role involves a deep understanding of both software development and cybersecurity principles. Security software developers must be proficient in coding and software design and be fully aware of cybersecurity threats and trends. Their work is crucial in developing tools to protect against and respond to cyberattacks effectively. They often work closely with other cybersecurity professionals to ensure that their software meets the organization's security needs.

Cloud security specialists focus specifically on cloud-related security, a rapidly growing area in cybersecurity. As more organizations move their operations to cloud environments, the need for specialized security in this area has increased significantly. Cloud security specialists secure cloud infrastructure, applications, and data. This includes implementing security measures in cloud environments, ensuring compliance with regulatory standards, and managing access controls. They must thoroughly understand cloud technologies and the unique security challenges that cloud computing poses. Their work is vital in ensuring that cloud services are used securely and that sensitive data stored in the cloud is protected from unauthorized access and breaches.

Specialized and niche roles in cybersecurity, such as ethical hackers, cryptographers, security software developers, and cloud security specialists, address specific areas within the broader field of cybersecurity. These roles require specialized knowledge and skills and are essential for addressing the diverse and complex security challenges of modern organizations. The work of these professionals is integral to maintaining the integrity, confidentiality, and availability of digital information in an increasingly interconnected world.

The Evolving Nature of Roles

The cybersecurity landscape is continually influenced by emerging technologies, leading to an evolution in the nature and scope of roles within the field. The advent of technologies like AI, machine learning, and the IoT has introduced new complexities and opportunities in cybersecurity. These technologies have created new threats that need to be addressed and have also led to the development of advanced tools and techniques for cybersecurity professionals. As a result, roles such as AI security specialist or IoT security expert are becoming more prevalent, reflecting the need for expertise in these specific areas.

Given the rapid pace at which cyber threats and technologies change, professionals must commit to lifelong learning to stay relevant and practical. This continuous education might involve acquiring new certifications, attending workshops and conferences, or participating in online courses and webinars. The ability to adapt and evolve with the changing landscape differentiates successful cybersecurity professionals. This adaptability applies to technical skills and staying informed about changes in regulations, industry standards, and best practices.

Future trends in cybersecurity are likely to introduce potential new job titles and roles. With the increasing interconnectivity of devices and systems, roles like quantum computing security analyst or autonomous systems security engineer may emerge. These roles would address specific challenges associated with these advanced technologies. Additionally, the growing importance of data privacy might give rise to roles like privacy strategy consultant, reflecting the need for expertise in navigating the complex landscape of data privacy regulations and practices.

Cross-functional skills and interdisciplinary roles are becoming increasingly important in cybersecurity. Addressing cyber threats requires a blend of skills from different domains as they become more sophisticated. For example, a cybersecurity data analyst might need to combine data science and cybersecurity skills to effectively analyze threat patterns and vulnerabilities. Similarly, roles like cyber-legal consultant could emerge, requiring a mix of legal and cybersecurity knowledge to navigate the complexities of cyber law. The future of cybersecurity lies in professionals who can bridge the gap between traditional cybersecurity skills and other disciplines.

The evolving nature of cybersecurity roles is characterized by the impact of emerging technologies, the necessity for continuous learning and adaptation, the emergence of future trends and new job titles, and the increasing importance of cross-functional and interdisciplinary skills. This dynamic landscape demands professionals who are technically proficient, versatile, adaptable, and capable of effectively integrating knowledge from various fields to combat future cybersecurity challenges.

NECESSARY SKILLS AND COMPETENCIES

In cybersecurity, a comprehensive skill set is essential and includes technical proficiencies such as mastery of security tools, understanding of networking and system administration, coding knowledge, and familiarity with cloud infrastructure. Analytical and problem-solving abilities are crucial for interpreting complex data, identifying vulnerabilities, and devising innovative solutions. Soft skills, including effective communication with diverse stakeholders, leadership, mentoring, negotiation, and conflict resolution, play a vital role. Business acumen is critical to effective cybersecurity management, including understanding business operations and aligning security strategies with organizational goals. Furthermore, continuous learning and adaptability are indispensable since professionals must stay abreast of emerging technologies, pursue ongoing education, and remain flexible in the rapidly evolving cybersecurity landscape. This diverse skill set ensures that cybersecurity professionals are well-equipped to protect organizations against current and future cyber threats.

Technical Skills

In cybersecurity, specific technical skills are fundamental to the effectiveness and success of professionals in this field. Proficiency in security tools and technologies is essential. This includes a thorough understanding of tools for network security monitoring, intrusion detection systems, firewalls, antivirus software, and more. Cybersecurity professionals must be adept at using these tools to detect, prevent, and respond to security threats. They should also be capable of configuring and maintaining them to ensure optimal performance and security.

A firm understanding of networking and system administration is what forms the backbone of cybersecurity. Professionals must be well-versed in the principles of network design, operations, and the administration of systems. This includes knowledge of protocols, network architecture, and network services. They should understand how different network components interact and can be exploited by attackers and how to secure them against such threats. Additionally, system administration skills, such as managing and configuring operating systems, servers, and other IT infrastructure, are a must.

Knowledge of coding and scripting languages is increasingly important in cybersecurity. While not all roles require deep programming expertise, a basic understanding of how software is built and operates is beneficial. Familiarity with languages like Python, JavaScript, or PowerShell, for instance, enables professionals to automate tasks, analyze data, and potentially identify and exploit vulnerabilities in software. Coding skills also allow a better understanding of cyberattacks, enabling more effective defense strategies.

As more organizations migrate to cloud environments, cybersecurity professionals must understand the security challenges and best practices for cloud computing. This includes knowledge of cloud service models (infrastructure as a service, platform as a service, and software as a service), cloud storage security, and managing cloud-based resources. Professionals should be proficient in securing cloud environments and understanding the unique risks and vulnerabilities of cloud services.

The necessary technical skills for cybersecurity professionals encompass proficiency in security tools and technologies, a solid understanding of networking and system administration, basic to intermediate knowledge of coding and scripting, and familiarity with cloud services and infrastructure. These skills form the technical foundation to safeguard information and systems effectively.

Analytical and Problem-Solving Skills

Analytical and problem-solving skills are crucial in cybersecurity, where professionals are constantly required to interpret complex data, identify vulnerabilities, devise solutions, and strategize for long-term security.

Cybersecurity professionals must sift through vast amounts of data from security systems such as firewall logs, intrusion detection systems, and network traffic. Analyzing this data requires a keen eye for detail and the ability to discern patterns and anomalies that may indicate a security threat. This skill involves understanding the data and determining the potential implications and necessary actions.

Cybersecurity is often about thinking like an attacker to anticipate and identify vulnerabilities in systems and networks. Professionals must critically evaluate their organization's security posture, understanding where weaknesses exist and how they could be exploited. This process requires a thorough understanding of current cybersecurity threats, an awareness of the organization's specific risk factors, and the ability to think outside the box.

These professionals must be able to think creatively to find practical solutions to complex security challenges. This often involves devising innovative ways to defend against attacks, such as developing unique security protocols, implementing unconventional defense mechanisms, or creatively using existing tools and resources. Creative problem-solving is particularly important in responding to new or evolving cyber threats that may not have standard or established mitigation techniques.

Strategic planning for long-term security measures is also a critical competency. Cybersecurity is not just about responding to immediate threats but also about planning and implementing long-term strategies to enhance the overall security posture. This involves understanding the broader cybersecurity landscape, anticipating future trends and challenges, and developing comprehensive plans to strengthen security over time. Strategic planning requires a balance between technical knowledge, understanding of business objectives, and foresight to prepare for future challenges.

Analytical and problem solving skills are critical in cybersecurity, encompassing the ability to analyze complex data, think critically to identify vulnerabilities, employ creative problem solving in threat mitigation, and engage in strategic planning for long-term security. These skills enable cybersecurity professionals to effectively protect organizations against a wide range of cyber threats, both current and emerging.

Soft Skills and Communication

In addition to technical expertise, soft skills and effective communication are essential for cybersecurity professionals, enabling them to interact successfully with various stakeholders, lead teams, mentor others, and navigate complex interpersonal dynamics.

Effective communication with both technical and nontechnical stakeholders is crucial. Cybersecurity professionals often need to explain complex technical issues to individuals who may not have a technical background, such as company executives or employees in non-IT departments. This requires the ability to translate technical jargon into clear, understandable language. It is also essential for these professionals to communicate cybersecurity risks and strategies effectively, ensuring that all stakeholders understand the significance of cybersecurity measures and policies.

Leadership and team management abilities are fundamental for those in supervisory or managerial roles within cybersecurity. These skills involve directing and coordinating cybersecurity efforts and inspiring and motivating team members. Effective leadership in cybersecurity includes fostering a positive team environment, setting clear goals and expectations, and managing resources efficiently. It also involves making tough decisions quickly, particularly in high-pressure situations like responding to a security breach.

Teaching and mentoring for skill development is essential to cybersecurity, especially given the field's rapidly evolving nature. Senior cybersecurity professionals are often expected to mentor junior staff, sharing knowledge and experience to help them develop their skills. This includes technical training and imparting best practices, ethical guidelines, and professional development advice. Teaching and mentoring can extend beyond the immediate team, including training sessions or workshops for nontechnical staff to raise cybersecurity awareness organization-wide.

Negotiation and conflict resolution skills are essential, particularly in situations where cybersecurity measures may impact other business operations or where there may be differing opinions on addressing security issues. Cybersecurity professionals must be able to negotiate effectively to balance security needs with business objectives, finding solutions that satisfy all parties. This includes being adept at conflict resolution, as they may need to mediate disputes or disagreements regarding cybersecurity strategies or implementations that arise within teams or between departments.

Soft skills and communication are vital for cybersecurity professionals. Practical communication skills enable them to convey complex information clearly and build understanding among various stakeholders. Leadership and team management skills are crucial for guiding teams and driving cybersecurity initiatives. Teaching and mentoring abilities help develop the next generation of cybersecurity talent. Negotiation and conflict resolution skills are vital to harmonizing different interests and perspectives, ensuring cohesive and effective cybersecurity strategies.

Business Acumen and Knowledge

In cybersecurity, possessing business acumen and a solid understanding of business operations is as vital as technical expertise. This comprehensive knowledge enables cybersecurity professionals to align security strategies with organizational goals, understand industry-specific challenges, and efficiently manage resources.

Understanding business operations and goals is essential for cybersecurity professionals. They need to comprehend how the different business units function and how they contribute to the organization's overall objectives. This understanding helps to identify critical assets that need protection and to assess how cybersecurity threats can impact various aspects of the business. By understanding the business context, cybersecurity professionals can prioritize security efforts in a way that supports and enhances business operations rather than hindering them.

The alignment of security strategies with business objectives is critical for the success of any cybersecurity program. Cybersecurity measures should not be implemented in isolation but should be considered integral to achieving the organization's broader goals. This involves working closely with business leaders to ensure that the security strategies support business growth, enable operational efficiency, and protect the organization's reputation. It also means being able to justify security investments in terms of their value to the business, whether through risk reduction, compliance with regulatory requirements, or enhancing customer trust.

Awareness of industry-specific challenges and solutions is essential because cybersecurity threats vary significantly across different industries. For instance, the financial sector faces different cyber threats and regulatory requirements than the healthcare sector. Understanding these nuances allows cybersecurity professionals to tailor their strategies to address their specific industry's unique challenges and compliance needs. This industry-specific knowledge is crucial for developing effective security measures that are both robust and relevant.

Cybersecurity professionals, especially those in leadership roles, must be able to allocate and manage resources effectively to maximize security coverage while staying within budget constraints. This involves strategically deciding where to invest cybersecurity tools, personnel, and training. It also includes tracking and demonstrating the return on investment of cybersecurity initiatives, which is crucial for securing ongoing support and funding from business leaders.

Business acumen and knowledge are critical competencies for cybersecurity professionals. Understanding business operations and goals, aligning security strategies with these objectives, being aware of industry-specific challenges, and managing budgets and resources effectively are all essential for integrating cybersecurity practices seamlessly into the broader business context. These skills enable cybersecurity professionals to contribute not only to the security but also to the overall success and sustainability of the organization.

Continuous Learning and Adaptation

In the fast-paced and ever-evolving field of cybersecurity, continuous learning and adaptation are beneficial and essential for professionals to stay adequate and relevant. This commitment to ongoing education and adaptability is critical in keeping pace with the rapidly changing nature of cyber threats, technologies, and industry best practices.

New technologies can introduce both novel opportunities and unprecedented challenges. Cybersecurity professionals must stay informed about advancements, such as AI, blockchain, IoT, and quantum computing, because these technologies shape the future of cyber threats and defenses. This involves not only understanding the technical aspects of new technologies but also recognizing their potential security implications and the evolving tactics of cyber adversaries.

Pursuing certifications and ongoing education is a concrete way for cybersecurity professionals to continually enhance their knowledge and skills. The field offers a range of professional certifications that cater to various specializations within cybersecurity, such as Certified Information Systems Security Professional, Certified Ethical Hacker, and Computer Technology Industry Association Security+. These certifications often require professionals to keep up with continuing education credits, thereby ensuring they stay current in their knowledge. Additionally, attending conferences, workshops, and webinars is an excellent way to learn about cybersecurity's latest research, tools, and strategies.

Adaptability to evolving cybersecurity landscapes is a key attribute of successful cybersecurity professionals. The cyber-threat environment is dynamic, with new attacks emerging frequently. Professionals must be able to quickly adapt their strategies and techniques to counter these evolving threats. This adaptability extends to various aspects of their role, including adjusting to new regulatory requirements, adopting new technologies, and modifying organizational security policies in response to changing threat landscapes.

Given the field's complexity and the continuous development of new threats and technologies, a commitment to lifelong learning is essential for professional success and growth. This ongoing learning journey involves formal education, training, and self-directed learning, such as reading industry publications, engaging in professional forums, and experimenting with new technologies and tools. A mindset geared toward continuous improvement and curiosity is invaluable in staying ahead in cybersecurity.

3

CRAFTING EFFECTIVE
JOB POSTINGS

In the rapidly evolving field of cybersecurity, attracting top talent is a critical challenge for organizations. This requires a deep understanding of what cyber professionals look for in a job opportunity and how they perceive potential roles. Crafting effective job postings is not just about listing responsibilities and requirements; it is about resonating with cybersecurity experts regarding their aspirations, values, and skills. The key lies in developing job descriptions that not only detail the roles and responsibilities but also emphasize growth opportunities, highlight the unique challenges of cybersecurity positions, and align with the career aspirations of potential candidates.

Moreover, integrating career development opportunities into job postings is essential. This includes outlining pathways for advancement, training programs, mentorship, and a focus on skill enhancement. Balancing the technical and soft skill requirements is also crucial when it comes to attracting a diverse range of applicants with the right mix of qualifications and interpersonal abilities.

Emphasizing the company's culture, values, and achievements in cybersecurity further enhances the appeal of the job postings. A well-crafted job posting should include a clear job title and summary, detailed responsibilities, and specifics about qualifications and skills. It is essential to detail compensation, benefits, and the application process while maintaining a tone and language that is inclusive, clear, and reflective of the company's culture.

The correct language and terminology, tailored to the target audience, are instrumental in attracting suitable candidates. This involves balancing professionalism and approachability, avoiding common pitfalls like clichés and buzzwords, and ensuring the job posting remains current with industry trends. Regular feedback and iterations based on input from cybersecurity team members and candidate comments can significantly improve the effectiveness of job postings. This comprehensive approach to crafting job postings is essential for attracting and retaining the best talent in the field of cybersecurity.

WRITING JOB DESCRIPTIONS THAT RESONATE WITH CYBER PROFESSIONALS

Creating job descriptions that genuinely resonate with professionals in the field is both an art and a science. This section delves into understanding the unique perspective of cyber professionals, focusing on what they seek in their career paths, including growth opportunities, challenges, and alignment with their professional aspirations. It guides us through the intricacies of detailing roles and responsibilities, ensuring that every aspect of the job is clearly defined and relevant to the organizational goals. Furthermore, it emphasizes the importance of incorporating career development opportunities and balancing technical and soft skills. It also highlights how company culture and values play a crucial role in attracting cybersecurity talent. The start of this process is shown in Figure 3.1.

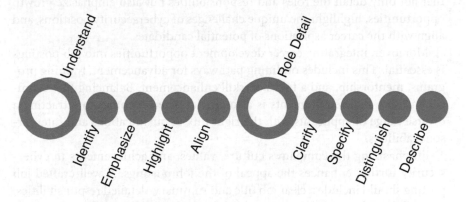

Figure 3.1   Crafting cybersecurity job descriptions.

Understanding the Cyber Professional's Perspective

In order to create job postings that effectively attract cyber professionals, it is crucial to understand their mindset and what they look for in a job. This understanding shapes job descriptions, ensuring that they resonate with the target audience.

Identifying what cyber professionals seek in a job is the first step. These individuals often seek roles that challenge them intellectually and offer a sense of purpose. They are typically motivated by opportunities to combat evolving cyber threats and protect sensitive information. Many are attracted to roles where they can deploy their skills in innovative ways to make a tangible impact on the organization's cybersecurity posture. Understanding these desires is crucial in crafting job descriptions that appeal to the ideal candidates.

Emphasizing growth opportunities and challenges in the job description is crucial. Cybersecurity professionals are generally career-driven and seek continuous professional development. Highlighting opportunities for advancement, upskilling, and working on cutting-edge projects can be very appealing. It is essential to convey how the role will challenge them and contribute to their professional growth. This could include exposure to the latest technologies, involvement in high-profile projects, or opportunities to lead initiatives.

Highlighting the unique aspects of the cybersecurity role within your organization can differentiate your job posting from others. This might involve detailing the specific technologies they will work with, the impact of their role on business operations, or the unique cybersecurity challenges that your organization faces. Describing the work environment, company culture, and how the role fits into the broader organizational mission can also help candidates visualize themselves in the role.

Cybersecurity professionals often have specific career goals, such as becoming an expert in a particular domain, leading a cybersecurity team, or innovating in areas like threat intelligence or incident response. Tailoring job descriptions to reflect how the role aligns with these aspirations can make the position more attractive. This involves understanding the typical career paths in cybersecurity and clearly articulating how the role can be a stepping-stone to achieving their professional objectives.

Understanding the perspective of cyber professionals is crucial in crafting effective job postings. Organizations can create compelling job descriptions that attract the right talent by identifying what they seek in a job, emphasizing growth and challenges, highlighting the unique aspects of the role, and aligning with their career aspirations. This approach ensures that the job postings draw in qualified candidates and resonate with those who are a good fit for the role and the organization's culture.

Detailing Roles and Responsibilities

To attract suitable candidates for cybersecurity positions, it is crucial to detail the roles and responsibilities in the job postings with clarity and precision.

This includes clearly defining the role, specifying tasks and objectives, distinguishing between essential and desirable responsibilities, and describing the team and organizational structure.

Clearly defining the role and its importance to the organization is the first step. The job description should articulate the position's primary function and how it contributes to the organization's broader objectives. This could involve explaining how the role fits into the company's cybersecurity framework, its impact on protecting company assets, or its contribution to maintaining regulatory compliance. Making the significance of the role clear helps candidates understand the value and purpose of the job, which can be a significant motivating factor for potential applicants.

Specifying daily tasks and long-term objectives provides candidates with a concrete job idea. The description should list critical daily activities like monitoring network traffic, responding to security alerts, or conducting vulnerability assessments. It should also outline the long-term goals or projects the candidate would be expected to contribute to or lead. This dual focus on immediate tasks and long-term objectives helps candidates gauge the scope of the role and assess how it aligns with their skills and career aspirations.

Distinguishing between essential and desirable responsibilities is vital for setting realistic expectations. Essential responsibilities are the nonnegotiable aspects of the job, the tasks, and the skills that are crucial for the role. On the other hand, desirable responsibilities may include additional skills or experiences that would be beneficial but are not critical for the role. Differentiating these helps candidates self-assess their suitability for the role and understand the areas where there is room for growth or development.

Describing the team and organizational structure helps candidates understand the working environment and their place within it. This could include information about the size and composition of the team, the reporting structure, and the interaction with other departments or teams within the organization. This insight helps candidates visualize how they would fit into and contribute to the team and understand the dynamics and collaboration required in the role.

Detailing roles and responsibilities clearly and comprehensively is crucial in attracting suitable candidates for cybersecurity positions. By clearly defining the role and its importance, specifying daily tasks and long-term objectives, distinguishing between essential and desirable responsibilities, and describing the team and organizational structure, organizations can provide potential applicants with a clear and realistic picture of what the job entails and how it fits into the larger organizational context.

Incorporating Career Development Opportunities

A key aspect of attracting top talent in cybersecurity is to showcase the career development opportunities that come with the role. Detailing training programs, advancement pathways, mentorship availability, and a focus on professional growth can significantly enhance the appeal of a job posting.

Cybersecurity professionals place a high value on updating and expanding their skills. Job descriptions should detail the organization's available training programs, workshops, or courses. This could include sponsored certifications, access to online learning platforms, or attending industry conferences and seminars. Emphasizing a commitment to ongoing professional development demonstrates that the organization invests in its employees' growth and stays current with the latest cybersecurity trends and technologies.

Potential candidates often seek roles that show a clear trajectory for moving upward or expanding their expertise. Job postings should describe potential career paths, including opportunities for promotion, lateral moves into different cybersecurity specializations, or leadership roles. This information gives candidates a sense of the long-term career possibilities and growth they can expect within the organization.

Mentioning mentorship and support structures is beneficial. Many professionals in the field look for environments where they can learn from experienced colleagues and gain insights into different aspects of cybersecurity. Highlighting the availability of mentorship programs, peer learning groups or collaborative team structures can be attractive. This shows that the organization values knowledge sharing and provides a supportive personal and professional development environment.

Focusing on professional growth and skill enhancement in the job description appeals to candidates' desire for continual improvement and mastery of their craft. Emphasize how the role enhances technical and soft skills, such as leadership, communication, and strategic thinking. Detailing how the organization supports its employees in acquiring new skills and keeping up with the evolving cybersecurity landscape can make the role more attractive to ambitious candidates.

Incorporating career development opportunities in job postings is a powerful strategy for attracting skilled cybersecurity professionals. By outlining training and learning opportunities, highlighting career advancement pathways, mentioning mentorship and support structures, and focusing on professional growth, organizations can appeal to candidates who are not only looking for a job but also a place where they can evolve, learn, and succeed in their cybersecurity careers.

Balancing Technical and Soft Skill Requirements

In crafting effective job postings for cybersecurity roles, balancing technical and soft skill requirements is crucial. This balance ensures that the candidates are technically proficient and capable of thriving in a collaborative and dynamic work environment.

Listing essential technical skills and qualifications is fundamental to the job description. This should include specific technical competencies required for the role, such as proficiency in specific cybersecurity tools, knowledge of network security protocols, experience with certain coding languages, or familiarity with specific security frameworks and standards. Clearly outlining these requirements helps potential candidates assess whether their technical skills align with the role's demands. Being precise about the skills that are necessary to perform the job effectively is essential.

Stressing the importance of soft skills like communication and teamwork is equally important. In the field of cybersecurity, the ability to communicate complex concepts clearly to both technical and nontechnical stakeholders is invaluable. Additionally, teamwork skills are critical since cybersecurity professionals often work in collaborative environments, dealing with cross-functional teams. Highlighting the need for problem solving, adaptability, and ethical judgment may also attract well-rounded candidates who can contribute positively to the workplace culture.

Distinguishing between mandatory and preferred skills helps set realistic expectations for candidates. Mandatory skills are nonnegotiable and essential for the role. In contrast, preferred skills might include additional qualifications or experiences that would enhance a candidate's fit for the role but are not critical for job performance. This distinction helps candidates understand the minimum requirements and the additional skills that could give them a competitive edge.

Encouraging a diverse range of applicants is important for fostering an inclusive work environment and tapping into a vast talent pool. This can be achieved by using inclusive language in the job description and explicitly stating that candidates from diverse backgrounds are encouraged to apply. Emphasizing the organization's commitment to diversity and inclusion can attract candidates who might otherwise feel discouraged from applying, ensuring a more comprehensive range of perspectives and experiences in the candidate pool.

Balancing technical and soft skill requirements in job postings is critical to attracting the right talent for cybersecurity roles. Listing essential technical skills and qualifications, stressing the importance of soft skills, distinguishing between mandatory and preferred skills, and encouraging diversity in applicants are all strategies that contribute to creating effective and inclusive job postings. This approach helps find candidates with the right technical expertise and those who align with the organization's culture and values.

Emphasizing Company Culture and Values

In attracting the right cybersecurity talent, it is essential to emphasize the company culture and values in job postings. This approach helps candidates determine if they align with the organization's ethos and working environment, which is crucial for long-term job satisfaction and success.

Describing the company's mission and values gives potential applicants a sense of the organization's overarching goals and principles. This might involve explaining the company's commitment to innovation, integrity, customer service, or social responsibility. It is beneficial to articulate how cybersecurity roles contribute to the broader mission of protecting the company's digital assets and ensuring data privacy. By aligning the job description with the company's mission and values, candidates can better understand the purpose behind their potential work and the ethical framework within which the company operates.

Showcasing the work environment and team dynamics helps paint a picture of the day-to-day experience within the company. This could include details about the collaborative nature of the teams, the company's approach to work-life balance, or the nature of the workspaces (such as open-plan offices or remote working options). For cybersecurity roles, explaining how the team fits into the more extensive IT department or the company can provide insights into how cross-functional collaboration occurs within the organization.

Highlighting company achievements in cybersecurity can be particularly attractive to candidates. This might include awards, recognitions, or successful projects demonstrating the company's cybersecurity commitment and capabilities. Such achievements showcase the company's strengths and suggest a forward-thinking and competent environment where professionals can work on impactful and cutting-edge projects.

Promoting diversity, equity, and inclusion (DEI) initiatives is increasingly essential in job postings. Candidates often look for workplaces where diversity is valued and inclusive practices are evident. Highlighting the company's efforts in promoting a diverse workforce and an inclusive culture—such as employee resource groups, diversity training programs, or specific diversity hiring goals—can make the job more appealing to a broad range of candidates.

It demonstrates the company's commitment to creating a welcoming and supportive environment for all employees.

Emphasizing company culture and values in job postings is a crucial strategy for attracting cybersecurity talent. Describing the company's mission and values, showcasing the work environment and team dynamics, highlighting achievements in cybersecurity, and promoting DEI initiatives help potential candidates gauge whether or not they would thrive in the organization. This approach attracts candidates with the right skills and those who share the company's values and are likely to contribute positively to the workplace culture.

KEY COMPONENTS OF A JOB POSTING

This section focuses on the key components of a job posting that make it practical and appealing. Crafting a precise and engaging job title and summary sets the tone for the entire posting, thereby aligning it with the organization's goals. This section delves into outlining detailed responsibilities, ensuring clarity about the role's impact and daily activities, and aligning these with industry standards. It also covers the importance of clearly stating qualifications and skills, including technical proficiencies and soft skills, and differentiating between essential and preferred qualifications. Furthermore, it highlights the significance of detailing compensation, benefits, and unique company offerings, along with guiding applicants through the application process and providing clear contact information, making the job posting informative and inviting.

Job Title and Summary

The job title and summary are the first contact points between a potential candidate and a job posting. They play a critical role in attracting the right talent by providing a snapshot of the role. It is important to craft these elements thoughtfully, in order to ensure that they accurately represent the position and appeal to the desired candidates.

The job title should reflect the nature and level of the position and resonate with the target audience. It should be specific enough to be meaningful and recognizable to professionals in the field. For example, a *senior cybersecurity analyst* title is more descriptive and appealing than a generic title like *IT staff*. The title should also align with industry standards to ensure that it is easily searchable and understandable by potential candidates.

Providing a concise overview of the role in the summary is crucial. This brief paragraph should give candidates a clear idea of the position and its importance within the organization. The summary should include critical aspects of the job, such as main responsibilities, the position's primary focus, and how it contributes to the larger objectives of the cybersecurity team and the organization. This overview sets the stage for the detailed information in the job posting.

The role's objectives should be linked to the organization's overall goals. This alignment helps candidates understand the broader context of the position and how their work would impact the organization. It also demonstrates that the organization has a clear vision and direction, which can attract candidates seeking purposeful and impactful work.

Setting the tone for the entire posting with the job title and summary is critical. These elements should be crafted to inform, engage, and excite potential candidates. The tone should reflect the company's culture—formal, innovative, collaborative, etc. An inviting and positive tone can make the job more appealing and encourage candidates to read further into the posting details.

An accurate and appealing job title, a concise overview of the role, alignment with organizational goals, and setting the right tone are all essential in attracting suitable candidates. These components set the stage for the rest of the job posting and play a significant role in drawing in potential applicants.

Detailed Responsibilities

Providing a detailed and explicit enumeration of responsibilities in a job posting is crucial for setting accurate expectations and attracting suitable candidates. This section should be comprehensive, outlining specific duties and how the role contributes to the organization.

Enumerating specific job duties and expectations is the first step in detailing responsibilities. This involves listing the essential tasks that the candidate will be expected to perform. For a cybersecurity role, this might include conducting regular system audits, implementing security measures, responding to security incidents, or developing security policies. Being specific about these duties helps candidates assess whether their skills and experience align with the role's requirements. It also prevents misunderstandings about the nature of the work involved.

Clarifying the role's impact on the organization helps candidates understand the significance of the position. This could involve explaining how the role contributes to the organization's overall security posture or how it supports business objectives. For example, a job description for a network security engineer might detail how the role is crucial for maintaining the integrity and reliability of the company's network infrastructure, which is vital for the smooth operation of business processes.

Describing typical day-to-day activities gives candidates a glimpse into what a regular day might look like in the role. This can include routine tasks, the types of projects they might work on, and the everyday challenges they may encounter. For instance, the description could outline a typical day for a cybersecurity analyst, from monitoring network activities and analyzing security alerts to collaborating with other IT staff and reporting the findings.

Aligning responsibilities with industry standards ensures that the role aligns with professional norms and expectations. This means that the responsibilities listed should be relevant and standard for the role in the cybersecurity industry. For example, the responsibilities of a chief information security officer (CISO) should align with what is generally expected of a CISO in terms of leadership, strategy development, and security management. This alignment ensures that the role is attractive to professionals who are already in or are aspiring to be in similar positions in the industry.

Detailing responsibilities in a job posting requires enumerating specific duties, clarifying the role's impact, describing day-to-day activities, and aligning these responsibilities with industry standards. This thorough detailing helps potential candidates to clearly understand what the job entails and how it fits into the larger context of the organization and the cybersecurity industry. It aids in attracting candidates who are well-suited for the role and prepared for its responsibilities.

Qualifications and Skills

Clearly outlining the required qualifications and skills in a job posting is vital to attracting capable and well-suited candidates for the cybersecurity role. As is highlighted in Figure 3.2, it is important to identify the necessary educational background, certifications, technical proficiencies, and soft skills while distinguishing between essential and desired qualifications.

Outlining necessary education, certifications, and experience includes specifying the minimum educational requirements, such as a bachelor's degree in computer science, cybersecurity, or a related field. Additionally, listing required or preferred certifications (such as Certified Information Systems Security Professional, Certified Information Security Manager, Certified Ethical Hacker, etc.) helps attract candidates with a certain level of professional recognition. Experience requirements should also be clearly stated, whether

EDUCATION   TECHNICAL SKILLS   SOFT SKILLS

Figure 3.2   Qualifications and skills.

the role calls for an entry-level candidate or someone with several years of experience in specific areas of cybersecurity.

Specifying technical and software proficiencies tailors the job posting to candidates with the right technical background. This should include detailed knowledge of specific security tools, programming languages, network protocols, or operating systems that are relevant to the role. For example, a security engineer role may require proficiency in firewall management, intrusion detection systems, and experience with Linux/Windows operating systems. Being specific about technical requirements helps candidates self-assess their suitability for the role.

Soft skills like problem solving and adaptability are crucial for success in dynamic and challenging cybersecurity environments. Highlighting the need for strong analytical skills, excellent communication abilities, and a capacity for creative thinking can attract well-rounded candidates. Skills such as teamwork, leadership, and ethical judgment are also highly valued in cybersecurity roles since they contribute significantly to the effectiveness of security operations and team dynamics.

Differentiating between essential and desired qualifications helps in setting realistic expectations. Essential qualifications are nonnegotiable—the absence of which would disqualify a candidate. On the other hand, desired qualifications may include additional skills or experiences that would be beneficial but are not critical for the role. This distinction allows candidates to understand their minimum requirements and the additional attributes that could enhance their application.

Outlining qualifications and skills in a job posting requires a detailed description of the necessary education, certifications, experience, technical and software proficiencies, and soft skills. Differentiating between essential and desired qualifications is also vital. This approach ensures that the job posting attracts candidates who are technically competent and equipped with the necessary soft skills and professional attributes to excel in the cybersecurity role.

Compensation and Benefits

An effective job posting in the cybersecurity realm should also clearly detail the compensation and benefits offered. This not only helps to attract quality candidates but also demonstrates the organization's recognition of the value and demand for these specialized roles.

Cybersecurity roles are often compensated higher than other technology roles due to their specialized nature and high demand, so it is essential to be transparent about the salary range. A clear compensation structure, including base salary, bonuses, and performance-related pay, helps candidates gauge whether the offer aligns with their expectations and industry standards.

It is beneficial to acknowledge in the job posting that cybersecurity roles are typically well-compensated due to their critical importance in safeguarding organizational assets, the specialized skills required, and the often high-pressure nature of the work. This understanding reinforces the value that the organization places on these roles and can be a key attraction point for top talent.

In addition to a competitive salary, comprehensive benefits packages are often vital for job seekers. Detailing the healthcare options, retirement benefits such as 401(k) plans, and any bonus structures or profit-sharing arrangements can make the role more attractive. These benefits demonstrate the organization's commitment to the overall well-being and financial security of its employees.

Mentioning work-life balance perks, such as flexible hours and remote work options, is increasingly important. Cybersecurity work can sometimes demand irregular hours due to the need to respond to incidents or complete critical projects. Offering flexible working arrangements or the ability to work remotely can be a significant draw, particularly for candidates who value a healthy work-life balance. These perks can also testify to the organization's modern and employee-centric approach to work.

Including unique benefits that are specific to the company can further enhance the attractiveness of the role. These could include professional development opportunities such as funding for further education or certifications, unique wellness programs, team-building retreats, or even stock options in the company. Unique benefits that reflect the company's culture and values can help differentiate the organization from other employers and attract candidates who are looking for a workplace that aligns with their personal and professional goals.

Clearly outlining the salary and compensation structure, acknowledging the typically higher pay in cyber careers, highlighting standard and unique benefits, and emphasizing work-life balance perks are all strategies that can attract skilled professionals. These elements demonstrate the organization's commitment to offering competitive and comprehensive packages, which is crucial for recruiting top talent in the cybersecurity field.

Application Process and Contact Information

A clear and straightforward application process encourages potential candidates to apply and provides them with the necessary information to do so effectively. This section should guide applicants through the submission process, provide contact details for further inquiries, set expectations about the recruitment timeline, and encourage a diverse range of applicants.

Guiding applicants through the submission process involves detailing the steps they must take to apply for the position. This might include instructions on how to apply, what documents are required (such as a resume, cover letter, or certifications), and any specific details that need to be included. For example, if the application needs to be submitted through an online portal, provide a direct link and any necessary instructions for using the portal. Clear guidance can streamline the application process and prevent confusion or frustration.

Providing precise contact details for inquiries is essential. This might include an email address or phone number where candidates can reach out with questions about the role, the application process, or the organization. Having a point of contact for potential applicants can be crucial in maintaining their interest in the role, especially if they need clarification on certain aspects of the job posting.

Setting the recruitment timeline helps manage candidates' expectations. This includes information on when applications will be reviewed, when interviews are likely to occur, and an estimated timeline for when a decision will be made. Being transparent about the timeline can help candidates plan accordingly and reduce uncertainty about the process.

Encouraging candidates to apply regardless of meeting every criterion can attract a broader range of applicants, including those who might be an excellent fit for the role but are hesitant to apply because they do not meet every listed qualification. This approach promotes diversity and can uncover talented individuals with relevant skills and experiences, even if they don't perfectly match the job description. It's essential to convey that the organization values potential and a willingness to learn as much as it does existing skills and experiences.

The application process and contact information section of a job posting should provide clear instructions on applying, offer contact details for further inquiries, set expectations about the recruitment timeline, and encourage a wide range of candidates to apply. This approach facilitates a smoother application process and ensures that the organization attracts a diverse pool of qualified candidates.

USING THE RIGHT LANGUAGE AND TERMINOLOGY

The art of using the correct language and terminology in job postings is crucial for connecting with the desired candidates in the field of cybersecurity. This section explores how to effectively use industry-specific jargon and keywords that resonate with professionals while avoiding overly technical language that may deter qualified applicants. It emphasizes the importance of balancing professionalism with approachability and adopting a tone that reflects the company's culture. This section also stresses the need for clarity and inclusivity in language, avoiding ambiguity, and promoting diversity. Tailoring the language to suit different levels of expertise and addressing specific candidate concerns ensures that the posting appeals directly to the intended audience. Additionally, this section is a guide to avoiding common pitfalls like clichés and unnecessary details, while underscoring the importance of being mindful of unconscious biases in language choices. Including regular updates to reflect current trends and seeking feedback for continuous improvement ensures that job postings remain practical and relevant.

Industry-Specific Jargon and Keywords

Effectively utilizing industry-specific jargon and keywords in a cybersecurity job posting is crucial for attracting suitable candidates. This includes using terminology that is familiar to professionals in the field, incorporating relevant keywords, ensuring the language is accessible, and maintaining a balance between professionalism and approachability.

Utilizing terminology that is familiar to cybersecurity professionals helps in resonating with the target audience. This involves using terms and phrases that are commonly understood in the cybersecurity community. For instance, mentioning specific security protocols, types of cyber threats, or cybersecurity frameworks can immediately signal to a professional that the job is relevant to their expertise. Using familiar terminology helps attract candidates who are well-versed in the specific areas the role requires.

Incorporating keywords that are relevant to the specific role and necessary skills is essential for two reasons. First, it ensures that the job posting is easily discoverable through search engines or job search platforms. Including keywords—such as *network security, penetration testing, or risk assessment*—or listing specific tools and technologies that are relevant to the role can improve the visibility of the posting. Second, it helps candidates to quickly identify whether their skills and experience align with the role's requirements.

While it is essential to include specific terms and jargon, the language should not be so technical that it becomes inaccessible or intimidating to potential candidates who might possess the broader skills and potential for the role. The goal is to attract candidates with the right expertise without making the position seem unapproachable or excessively niche.

Balancing professionalism with approachability in the job posting helps create a positive first impression. While professional and industry-specific language establishes credibility and seriousness, ensuring a welcoming and inclusive tone is equally essential. This can involve using clear, concise language and a friendly tone that invites candidates from diverse backgrounds to apply. A job posting that is both professional and approachable will appeal to a broader range of candidates and make them feel more comfortable in applying.

Using industry-specific jargon and keywords in a cybersecurity job posting should be strategic. It is important to use terminology and keywords that resonate with the target professional audience while ensuring that the language remains accessible and the tone approachable.

Tone and Clarity

The tone and clarity of a job posting are pivotal in attracting suitable candidates and accurately reflecting the company's culture and values. A well-crafted job posting should adopt a tone that resonates with the company culture, ensures clarity and ease of reading, avoids ambiguity in role descriptions and expectations, and uses inclusive language that promotes diversity.

Adopting a tone that reflects company culture helps attract candidates who will fit well within the organization. A more casual and energetic tone may be appropriate if the company culture is dynamic and innovative.

Conversely, if the organization has a more formal and structured environment, a professional and straightforward tone might be more suitable. The tone of the posting can give potential candidates insights into what it might be like to work at the company and help attract those who align with the company's ethos.

The posting should be well-organized and easy to read, with clear headings and concise language. Avoiding jargon that is not widely understood outside of specific circles and explaining any necessary technical terms can make the posting more accessible. A clear and well-structured job description helps potential applicants quickly understand the role and its requirements, making it easier for them to decide whether to apply.

The responsibilities and requirements of the role should be explicitly stated to avoid any confusion or misinterpretation. This includes being specific about the skills and experience required, the scope of the role, and any key performance indicators or targets associated with the position. Unambiguous descriptions help attract candidates who are confident in their ability to meet the job requirements and align with the role's expectations.

Using language that promotes inclusivity and diversity is increasingly essential in job postings. This involves using gender-neutral language, avoiding cultural biases, and explicitly stating that candidates from diverse backgrounds are encouraged to apply. An inclusive job posting reflects well on the company's commitment to diversity and equal opportunity and widens the pool of potential applicants. This approach helps create a diverse and inclusive workforce, bringing a broader range of perspectives and ideas to the organization.

The tone and clarity of a job posting are critical in attracting suitable candidates and setting the stage for a successful recruitment process. A job posting that reflects the company culture is straightforward to read, avoids ambiguity, and uses inclusive language. It is more likely to attract a diverse range of qualified candidates who are well-suited to the role and the organization.

Tailoring Language to the Target Audience

Effectively tailoring the language of a job posting to the target audience is a critical strategy in attracting suitable candidates for cybersecurity roles. It involves adjusting the language to suit different levels of expertise, focusing on aspects most appealing to the intended applicant pool, emphasizing what makes the role unique, and proactively addressing potential candidate concerns or questions.

For entry-level positions, the language should focus more on learning opportunities, foundational skills, and company growth potential. For mid-level or senior roles, the language should shift to emphasize advanced skills, leadership opportunities, and the impact of the role on the organization's cybersecurity posture. Understanding the target audience's experience level helps craft a message that resonates with their specific career stage and aspirations.

Focusing on what matters most to the intended applicant pool is critical to a compelling job posting. For cybersecurity professionals, this might include working on challenging projects, the opportunity to use cutting-edge technology, or contributing to significant cybersecurity initiatives. Understanding the motivations and priorities of the target audience helps highlight the aspects of the role that are most likely to attract their interest. This could involve unique benefits offered by the company, the chance to work in a particularly innovative or impactful domain within cybersecurity, or the company's reputation in the industry. Emphasizing these unique selling points can make the role stand out to potential candidates who are looking for more than a standard job offer.

Addressing potential candidate concerns or questions in the job posting can also be a strategic move. This might include clarifying aspects of the role that are typically ambiguous in the industry and providing reassurance about everyday concerns such as work-life balance, opportunities for remote work, or paths for career progression within the company. Proactively addressing these points can help alleviate doubts and make the job more attractive to candidates who are considering multiple options.

Tailoring the language of a job posting to the target audience is essential in attracting suitable candidates for cybersecurity roles. By adjusting the language to suit different levels of expertise, focusing on the priorities of the intended applicants, highlighting unique aspects of the role, and addressing potential concerns, organizations can create job postings that not only attract a high volume of applicants but also resonate with the most qualified and suitable candidates for the role.

Avoiding Common Pitfalls

Crafting a job posting for a cybersecurity role requires careful consideration to avoid common pitfalls that can detract from its effectiveness. Steer clear of clichés and buzzwords, avoid an overload of unnecessary details, be mindful of unconscious bias in language, and regularly update the posting.

While specific industry-specific terms are necessary, relying too heavily on buzzwords or jargon can make the job posting seem vague and insubstantial. Phrases like *rockstar coder* or *cyber ninja* are often seen as clichés and may not be taken seriously by seasoned professionals. Instead, the language should be clear, direct, and specific to the skills and responsibilities that are relevant to the role. This approach ensures that the posting is professional and resonates more authentically with experienced candidates.

Not overloading the job posting with unnecessary details is essential for maintaining clarity and focus. While providing enough detail about the role and its requirements is crucial, excessive information can be overwhelming or distracting. The job description should be concise and focused on the most important aspects of the role, including key responsibilities, required qualifications, and unique selling points of the position and the company.

Language in the job posting should be gender-neutral and free from phrases that unwittingly reflect biases or stereotypes. For example, terms like *aggressive* might inadvertently signal a preference for a specific type of candidate. Focusing on inclusive language helps ensure that the job appeals to a broad and diverse pool of candidates.

Regularly update postings to reflect the latest trends, skills, and technologies that are relevant to the role. This not only ensures that the role remains attractive to candidates who are up-to-date with current developments but also demonstrates that the organization is forward-thinking and adaptive to changes in the industry.

Avoiding common pitfalls in job postings for cybersecurity roles involves clarifying clichés and buzzwords, avoiding unnecessary details, being mindful of unconscious bias, and regularly updating the content. By adhering to these guidelines, organizations can create effective, clear, and inclusive job postings that attract a diverse range of qualified candidates and accurately reflect the demands and dynamics of the role.

Feedback and Iteration

Implementing a process of feedback and iteration is essential for continually improving the quality and effectiveness of cybersecurity job postings. This involves seeking input from current cybersecurity team members, utilizing candidate feedback, monitoring the effectiveness of different language styles, and continuously updating the postings in line with industry developments.

Seeking input from cybersecurity team members can provide valuable insights into what makes a role attractive and how best to communicate the job's requirements and benefits. Team members who are already in similar roles can offer a perspective on what initially attracted them to the position and what aspects of the job might appeal to potential candidates. Their first-hand experience can be invaluable in crafting a realistic and engaging job description.

Feedback from applicants, especially those who participated in the interview process but perhaps were not selected or declined the offer, can reveal a lot about the strengths and weaknesses of the job posting. Candidates can provide insights into what attracted them to the role, what parts of the job description were unclear, and what factors influenced their decision. This feedback can be instrumental in refining the language and content of future postings.

Monitoring the effectiveness of different language styles can help identify what resonates best with the target audience. This could involve experimenting with different tones, structures, and formats to see which yields the best response regarding the quality and quantity of applicants. Analyzing the performance of various job postings can provide data-driven insights into which approaches are most effective in attracting qualified candidates.

As new threats emerge and new technologies are developed, the skills and experiences required for cybersecurity roles can change. Keeping job postings up-to-date with these developments ensures that they remain relevant and attractive to top talent. Regularly revisiting and updating job descriptions can also demonstrate to candidates that the organization is committed to staying at the forefront of cybersecurity.

Feedback and iteration are critical to crafting effective cybersecurity job postings. Seeking input from team members, using candidate feedback, monitoring language effectiveness, and continuously updating postings with industry developments are all strategies that create dynamic and compelling job descriptions.

4

LEVERAGING PROFESSIONAL HIRING TOOLS FOR CYBERSECURITY RECRUITMENT

In today's fast-paced cybersecurity sector, the strategic use of professional hiring tools is more crucial than ever. This chapter delves into the varied landscape of hiring platforms, shedding light on their unique features and how they cater to the nuanced needs of cybersecurity recruitment. From understanding the distinct advantages of general and niche platforms to navigating the sophisticated functionalities of modern hiring tools, this chapter sets the stage for an in-depth exploration of effective recruitment strategies. It emphasizes the importance of aligning these tools with organizational goals and the evolving landscape of cybersecurity talent acquisition. It sets a foundation for a deeper understanding of leveraging technology to attract top-tier cybersecurity professionals.

INTRODUCTION TO HIRING PLATFORMS

In the dynamic field of cybersecurity recruitment, understanding and leveraging the proper hiring platforms is crucial. This encompasses a range of platforms, from general to niche, each with unique benefits and limitations. It provides insights on selecting the most appropriate one, based on specific hiring needs. It highlights the advanced features of modern hiring tools such as automated candidate screening, communication enhancements, and human resources (HR) system integration, coupled with best practices for creating compelling employer profiles and ensuring data security. Additionally, this section touches upon emerging trends in recruitment technology, including artificial intelligence (AI) and machine learning (ML), and offers criteria for platform selection, focusing on aspects like reach, cost-effectiveness, user experience, and alignment with organizational goals. This consolidation offers a holistic view of the strategic use of hiring platforms in cybersecurity talent acquisition.

Understanding Different Types of Hiring Platforms

Understanding different types of hiring platforms is crucial in cybersecurity recruitment because each platform offers unique opportunities and challenges. General hiring platforms like LinkedIn, Indeed, and Monster are widely used across various industries. Their extensive user bases make them ideal for reaching a broad audience of potential candidates. These platforms are particularly effective for roles that require a more comprehensive set of skills or for targeting candidates who may not be active on specialized forums. The primary advantage of these general platforms is their reach; however, the vastness can also mean that the pool of applicants may include many who do not possess the specialized skills required for cybersecurity roles.

On the other hand, niche hiring platforms are specifically tailored to the cybersecurity industry. Examples include CyberSecJobs.com and InfoSec Jobs, which focus exclusively on roles in the cybersecurity domain. These platforms attract professionals dedicated to and specialized in cybersecurity, ensuring a more focused and relevant candidate pool. The specialized nature of these platforms means that job postings are likely to reach an audience with the specific skills and experience required for the role. However, the limitation is in their reach, as they may have a smaller user base than general platforms.

Selecting the right platform based on hiring needs is a critical step. General platforms can be beneficial for broader roles or when seeking a diverse range of applicants. In contrast, niche platforms are more suitable for specialized positions or to find candidates with specific cybersecurity expertise. The choice of platform should align with the specific requirements of the role and the desired profile of the candidate.

Integrating multiple platforms for a comprehensive approach can maximize the recruitment process's effectiveness. Combining general and niche platforms can strike a balance between reaching a broad audience and targeting specialized professionals. This integrated approach ensures a diverse range of applicants while still focusing on the specialized skills that are crucial for cybersecurity roles. Additionally, leveraging multiple platforms can enhance the visibility of the job posting and increase the chances of finding the ideal candidate for the role.

Understanding and utilizing different types of hiring platforms is critical to effective recruitment in cybersecurity. A strategic approach that considers the specific requirements of the role and utilizes both general and niche platforms can lead to a more prosperous and efficient hiring process. This comprehensive approach ensures reaching the right mix of candidates, from a vast talent pool to those with highly specialized cybersecurity skills.

Features of Modern Hiring Tools

Modern hiring tools have become essential for streamlining the hiring process, particularly in specialized fields like cybersecurity. These tools come equipped with various features designed to enhance efficiency and effectiveness. Key features of these modern hiring tools, as shown in Figure 4.1, include automated candidate screening and matching, communication tools for engaging applicants, integration with HR management systems, and customizable job posting and application features.

Automated candidate screening and matching is a significant feature of modern hiring tools. These systems use algorithms and ML to scan resumes and applications in order to identify candidates who best match the job requirements. This automation can significantly reduce the time spent on the initial screening process, thereby allowing hiring managers to focus on the most promising candidates. For cybersecurity roles, where specific skills and qualifications are crucial, this feature ensures that the candidates who advance in the hiring process have the necessary technical competencies and experiences.

Communication tools for engaging applicants are another essential feature. These tools can range from automated email responses to more sophisticated systems that manage ongoing communication with candidates. They facilitate timely and consistent interactions with applicants, informing them about their application status and next steps. Effective communication is critical to maintaining candidate interest and engagement throughout the hiring process, particularly for in-demand cybersecurity professionals who may have multiple job prospects.

Integration with HR management systems is vital for a seamless recruitment process. Modern hiring tools offer integration capabilities with existing HR software, such as an applicant tracking system (ATS), payroll, and performance management systems. This integration allows for a more streamlined

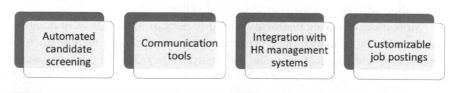

Figure 4.1   Features of modern hiring tools.

workflow, thus reducing the administrative burden and ensuring that candidate information is easily accessible and manageable throughout the recruitment life cycle. For cybersecurity roles, where rapid onboarding and alignment with ongoing projects might be necessary, this integration can expedite the transition from candidate to team member.

Customizable job postings and application features are crucial for attracting suitable candidates. Modern hiring tools often provide options to customize job postings and application processes to suit specific roles and company branding. This customization can include specific questions related to cybersecurity skills, scenarios, or problem-solving exercises that are relevant to the role. A tailored application process enhances the candidate experience and helps filter applicants to ensure a better fit with the role's requirements.

Modern hiring tools with features like automated candidate screening, practical communication tools, integration with HR systems, and customizable job postings are essential in the current recruitment landscape, particularly for specialized fields like cybersecurity. These features streamline the hiring process and enhance the quality of candidate engagement and selection, leading to more efficient and successful recruitment outcomes.

Best Practices for Platform Use

Effectively utilizing recruitment platforms requires a strategic approach that includes creating compelling employer profiles, streamlining the recruitment process, ensuring data security and privacy, and actively engaging with the platform's community and resources. These best practices are crucial in optimizing the recruitment process, particularly in a field as specialized as cybersecurity.

Creating compelling employer profiles is the first step to making the most of recruitment platforms. An employer profile should not only list basic company information but also showcase the company's culture, values, and vision. This can include details about the work environment, company achievements, employee testimonials, and specific initiatives or projects. For cybersecurity roles, highlighting the company's commitment to innovation and technology and showcasing notable cybersecurity projects or achievements can be particularly appealing. A strong employer profile helps attract skilled candidates who align with the company's culture and values.

Most modern hiring platforms offer a variety of tools that were designed to simplify and enhance the recruitment process. This can include an ATS, automated communication tools, and analytics to track the performance of job postings. Utilizing these tools can significantly improve efficiency, allowing for quicker and more effective candidate screening, communication, and selection. For cybersecurity roles, where timely recruitment is often critical, leveraging these tools can expedite the process without compromising the quality of hires.

Data security and privacy compliance are essential when recruiting for cybersecurity roles. This involves safeguarding candidate information and adhering to data protection regulations. Choosing platforms that comply with privacy laws and have robust security measures is essential. Internal protocols for handling candidate data should also be established to ensure confidentiality and compliance throughout the recruitment process.

Engaging with the platform's community and resources can significantly enhance the recruitment effort. Many platforms offer forums, webinars, articles, and other resources that can provide insights into industry trends, candidate preferences, and recruitment strategies. Participating in these communities can also increase the company's visibility among potential candidates. For cybersecurity roles, engaging in discussions about the latest security challenges, technology advancements, or industry best practices can position the company as a thought leader and an attractive employer in the field.

Best practices for using recruitment platforms include creating compelling employer profiles, utilizing platform tools to streamline recruitment, ensuring data security and privacy, and engaging with the platform's community and resources. These practices attract top talent, ensure efficient and compliant recruitment processes, and enhance the company's reputation as a desirable employer.

Trends and Future Developments

Staying abreast of trends and future developments in recruitment technology is crucial for maintaining an effective hiring strategy. As shown in Figure 4.2, this involves keeping up with evolving recruitment technologies, anticipating changes in job seeker behavior, adapting to new platform features and algorithms, and leveraging advanced technologies like AI and ML for enhanced recruitment efficiency.

Recruitment technologies continuously advance, offering new tools and features to streamline hiring. For instance, in recruitment, virtual reality and augmented reality are on the rise, providing immersive job previews or interviews. Staying updated with these technological advancements ensures that the recruitment process remains modern, efficient, and appealing to tech-savvy candidates, which is crucial in cybersecurity.

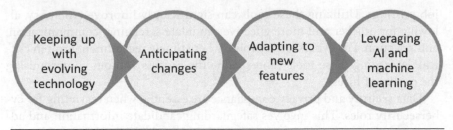

Figure 4.2 Trends and future developments.

Anticipating changes in job seeker behavior is critical to aligning recruitment strategies with candidate preferences. How job seekers search for and apply for jobs constantly evolves, influenced by technological advancements and shifting cultural norms. For example, there is an increasing preference for mobile-friendly application processes and platforms that offer a seamless, user-friendly experience. Understanding these evolving preferences is crucial for attracting top talent, particularly younger candidates who are more likely to use mobile devices and social media in their job search.

As platforms update their algorithms and introduce new features, the job posting and candidate engagement strategies may need to be adjusted. For instance, using SEO (search engine optimization) strategies in job postings can be crucial for visibility on algorithmic sorting platforms. Keeping abreast of these changes ensures that job postings remain effective and visible to suitable candidates.

Leveraging AI and ML for recruitment efficiency is an emerging trend that can significantly enhance the hiring process. AI can automate routine tasks such as resume screening, candidate matching, and initial candidate communications. ML algorithms can analyze patterns in successful hires to refine the screening process over time. These advanced technologies can save time, reduce the administrative burden, and help identify the most suitable candidates based on data-driven insights.

Understanding and adapting to trends and future developments in recruitment technology is vital for effective hiring in the cybersecurity sector. Keeping up with evolving technologies, anticipating changes in job seeker behavior, adapting to new platform features, and leveraging AI and ML are critical strategies for maintaining an efficient and modern recruitment process. These approaches ensure that organizations can effectively attract and engage with top talent in an increasingly competitive and technologically advanced job market.

Platform Selection Criteria

Choosing the right recruitment platform is a critical decision in the hiring process, especially for specialized roles in cybersecurity. The selection should be based on criteria that ensures the chosen platform aligns with the organization's recruitment goals and needs. These criteria include assessing the reach and relevance of different platforms, considering cost-effectiveness and return on investment (ROI), evaluating user experience and support services, and aligning platform capabilities with organizational needs.

Assessing the reach and relevance of different platforms involves determining how well a platform can connect the organization with the desired candidate pool. For cybersecurity roles, it is essential to consider whether professionals with the specialized skills and experience required actually frequent a specific platform. General job platforms may offer a broader reach but may not have the concentration of specialized talent that niche cybersecurity job boards offer. The choice depends on whether the priority is to cast a wide net or to target a specific subset of the job market.

Considering cost-effectiveness and ROI is essential in any recruitment strategy. Different platforms have varying cost structures, such as pay-per-post, subscription models, or additional fees for premium features. The decision should be based on carefully evaluating the cost relative to the potential benefits. For instance, a more expensive niche platform might offer higher quality candidates and a better hit rate for filling specialized roles, providing a better ROI than a cheaper but less targeted platform.

Evaluating user experience and support services ensures a smooth recruitment process. This includes the ease of posting jobs, managing applications, and communicating with candidates. A good user experience on the platform can streamline recruitment and improve efficiency. Additionally, the level of support services offered by the platform, such as customer service, technical support, or assistance with optimizing job postings, can significantly impact the overall effectiveness of the recruitment effort.

Aligning platform capabilities with organizational needs means choosing a platform that complements the organization's specific recruitment strategies and goals. This involves considering factors like the organization's size, the hiring volume, the level of expertise required for the roles, and any specific features or tools that would be particularly beneficial. For example, a large organization with high-volume recruitment might benefit from a platform with advanced AI-driven screening tools. At the same time, a smaller company might prioritize a platform with more personalized customer support.

Selecting the right recruitment platform for cybersecurity roles involves carefully considering several criteria. The platform's reach and relevance, its cost-effectiveness and ROI, the user experience and support services it offers, and how well its capabilities align with the organization's needs are all crucial factors in making an informed decision. By evaluating these criteria, organizations can choose a platform that meets their recruitment needs and supports their long-term talent acquisition strategies.

LINKEDIN STRATEGIES FOR CYBERSECURITY HIRING

In the context of cybersecurity hiring, LinkedIn emerges as a powerful platform with specific strategies to enhance recruitment effectiveness. Optimizing company profiles on LinkedIn involves creating compelling and informative pages that showcase a company's cybersecurity initiatives and culture, using rich media to engage candidates, and building a robust industry network. Effective job posting on LinkedIn includes crafting standout job descriptions, targeting the right audience with platform-specific tools, utilizing sponsored posts for broader reach, and encouraging employee engagement in sharing and endorsing postings.

The platform's specialized recruitment tools, such as LinkedIn Recruiter and Talent Insights, offer advanced candidate search capabilities and data-driven decision making. Networking and relationship building are crucial, with strategies including active participation in relevant LinkedIn groups, establishing connections with industry professionals, and using the platform for brand building and thought leadership.

Finally, monitoring and analytics play a vital role in strategy refinement, tracking the performance of job postings and campaigns, analyzing engagement and applicant quality, and adjusting strategies based on data insights to understand the metrics for successful LinkedIn recruitment. This consolidated approach provides a comprehensive framework for leveraging LinkedIn effectively in cybersecurity hiring strategies.

Optimizing Company Profiles

In the competitive landscape of cybersecurity recruitment, optimizing company profiles on hiring platforms and professional networks is a strategic move to attract top talent. A compelling and informative company profile not only showcases the organization's strengths and values but also serves as a tool to engage and build relationships with potential candidates. Critical aspects of optimizing company profiles include creating detailed and attractive company pages, showcasing cybersecurity initiatives and culture, utilizing rich media and regular updates for engagement, and building a network of industry connections and followers.

The company profile should comprehensively overview the organization's history, mission, and values. It is essential to articulate what sets the company apart from others, such as innovative projects, cutting-edge technology, or a unique approach to cybersecurity. The goal is to present a narrative that resonates with cybersecurity professionals, highlighting aspects of the company that align with their career aspirations and values.

Showcasing cybersecurity initiatives and culture is particularly important in this field. This could involve detailing specific cybersecurity projects, highlighting awards or recognitions, and describing the cybersecurity team's impact within the company. Additionally, portraying the company's culture, such as its approach to teamwork, innovation, work-life balance, and ongoing learning opportunities, can make the organization more attractive to prospective candidates who are not just looking for a job but a place where they can thrive.

Using rich media and updates to engage potential candidates can significantly enhance a company's profile. Including videos, images, and infographics about the company, its work environment, and its employees can provide a more dynamic and engaging portrayal of the organization. Regular updates, such as news about recent achievements, participation in industry events, or insights into current cybersecurity trends, keep the profile active and relevant, thereby increasing visibility and engagement with potential candidates.

Building a network of industry connections and followers is essential for extending the reach of the company's profile. This can be achieved through active participation in relevant industry groups and forums, sharing insightful content, and engaging with the content of others in the field. Networking efforts should aim to build genuine relationships within the cybersecurity community, positioning the company not only as an employer but also as a contributor to industry dialogue.

Optimizing company profiles on hiring platforms is an essential strategy in cybersecurity recruitment. Creating a comprehensive and engaging company page, showcasing cybersecurity initiatives and culture, using rich media for engagement, and building a network in the industry are critical steps in attracting top cybersecurity talent. These efforts help create a strong employer brand that resonates with professionals in the field, making the organization an attractive place to work and grow.

Effective Job Posting on LinkedIn

LinkedIn, a premier professional networking platform, offers unique opportunities for employers who are seeking to recruit top talent, especially in specialized fields like cybersecurity. To maximize the effectiveness of job postings on LinkedIn, it is crucial to craft standout job descriptions, target the right audience using LinkedIn's tools, leverage sponsored posts for extended reach, and encourage employee engagement with the postings.

Crafting job descriptions that stand out is essential on LinkedIn, where numerous job listings compete for attention. A standout job description should be concise yet comprehensive; it should highlight the critical aspects of the role, including responsibilities, qualifications, and unique selling points of the company and the position. Using engaging language and a clear structure can help draw attention. Including specific keywords related to cybersecurity will also ensure that the job posting is easily discoverable by candidates who are searching for relevant roles.

Targeting the right audience with LinkedIn tools is a strategic approach to ensure that suitable candidates see suitable job postings. LinkedIn offers advanced targeting tools based on factors such as industry, job function, seniority level, and geographic location. These tools can be used to tailor the visibility of the job posting to professionals with backgrounds and experiences that align with the cybersecurity role. This targeted approach helps reach candidates who are more likely to be interested and qualified for the position.

Utilizing sponsored posts for greater reach can significantly enhance the visibility of the job posting. Sponsored posts on LinkedIn are promoted beyond the company's immediate network, reaching a broader audience. This can be particularly useful for highly specialized roles in cybersecurity, where the ideal candidates might not be actively seeking new opportunities but could be enticed by an attractive job proposition. Investing in sponsored posts can increase the likelihood of the job posting reaching these passive candidates.

Encouraging employees to share and endorse postings leverages the power of personal networks and adds credibility to the job posting. Employees can share the job posting on their LinkedIn profiles, extending the post's reach and providing a personal endorsement of the company as a great workplace. This peer-to-peer sharing can be particularly effective in attracting candidates who value insights from current employees. Additionally, it fosters a sense of employee involvement and pride in their workplace.

Effective job posting on LinkedIn for cybersecurity roles involves crafting detailed and engaging job descriptions, using LinkedIn's targeting tools to reach the right audience, leveraging sponsored posts for broader visibility, and encouraging employees to share and endorse the postings. By utilizing these strategies, employers can significantly enhance the effectiveness of their recruitment efforts on LinkedIn, attracting a pool of qualified and interested candidates for their cybersecurity roles.

Leveraging LinkedIn's Recruitment Tools

LinkedIn offers specialized recruitment tools to enhance the hiring process, which is especially useful for sourcing top talent in cybersecurity. These tools, including LinkedIn Recruiter, Talent Insights, InMail, and various networking features, provide recruiters with advanced capabilities for finding, engaging, and managing potential candidates.

LinkedIn Recruiter allows for precisely targeting candidates based on specific criteria such as skills, experience, education, and location. For cybersecurity roles, recruiters can use this tool to search for candidates with particular technical skills or experiences in the cybersecurity domain. This advanced search capability enables recruiters to efficiently identify and reach out to potential candidates who closely match the job requirements.

Implementing LinkedIn Talent Insights for data-driven decisions enhances the recruitment strategy by providing valuable analytics and market data. Talent Insights offers real-time data on talent pools, hiring trends, and competitive intelligence. Recruiters can use this information to understand the availability of cybersecurity talent in specific regions, industry hiring trends, and how their company's employer brand compares to competitors. This data-driven approach allows for more strategic decision making in the recruitment process.

Engaging candidates through InMail and LinkedIn groups is an effective way to connect with potential applicants. InMail allows recruiters to send personalized messages directly to candidates, even those not actively seeking new opportunities. This can be particularly effective for engaging passive candidates who fit the role but might not respond to traditional job advertisements. Additionally, participating in LinkedIn groups that are related to cybersecurity and technology can help recruiters build relationships with potential candidates, understand their interests and concerns, and promote job openings in a more informal and engaging setting.

Building a talent pipeline and nurturing prospects is crucial for long-term recruitment success. LinkedIn's tools enable recruiters to create a pool of potential candidates who may be a good fit for future roles, even if they are not currently looking for a job. Recruiters can stay in touch with these prospects, share relevant content and updates about the company, and engage with them periodically to keep the company top-of-mind. This approach ensures that when a suitable role opens up, there is already a pool of engaged and interested candidates to draw from.

Leveraging LinkedIn's recruitment tools, such as LinkedIn Recruiter, Talent Insights, InMail, and networking features, can significantly enhance the recruitment process for cybersecurity roles. These tools provide advanced search capabilities, valuable market insights, direct engagement opportunities with candidates, and the ability to build and nurture a talent pipeline. Utilizing these resources enables recruiters to make more informed decisions, engage effectively with potential candidates, and ultimately source the best talent for their cybersecurity needs.

Networking and Relationship Building

Effective networking and relationship building are crucial to a successful recruitment strategy. LinkedIn, with its vast network of professionals, provides an ideal platform for these activities. Engaging in relevant groups, connecting with industry professionals, using the platform for brand building and thought leadership, and engaging with potential candidates are vital strategies.

Participating in relevant LinkedIn groups and discussions can significantly enhance a recruiter's presence in the cybersecurity community. These groups are often frequented by professionals who share insights, discuss industry trends, and seek career opportunities. Actively contributing to discussions, sharing relevant content, and providing valuable insights can help establish a recruiter's credibility and expertise. This participation increases visibility and helps understand cybersecurity professionals' interests and concerns, which can inform recruitment strategies.

Establishing connections with industry professionals is another important aspect of networking on LinkedIn. Recruiters should actively seek to connect with a wide range of individuals in the cybersecurity field, including potential candidates, industry experts, and other recruiters. These connections can provide valuable insights into the talent market, potential referral opportunities, and updates on industry developments. Personalized connection requests and follow-up messages can foster stronger relationships and create a network of contacts that can be leveraged for future recruitment needs.

Using LinkedIn for brand building and thought leadership is a powerful tool in attracting top talent. Recruiters and their organizations can share content that showcases their expertise, company culture, and contributions to the cybersecurity field. This might include articles, white papers, case studies, or company achievements and initiatives updates. Establishing the company as a thought leader in cybersecurity enhances its reputation and makes it more attractive to potential candidates looking for employers at the forefront of the industry.

Maintaining ongoing engagement with potential candidates is crucial for building a talent pipeline. This involves regular communication with individuals who have shown interest in the company or might be a good fit for future roles. Recruiters can engage with these prospects by sharing relevant job postings, updates about the company, and industry news. Keeping potential candidates informed and interested ensures they are more likely to consider opportunities with the company when they arise.

Networking and relationship building on LinkedIn are critical to a successful recruitment strategy in cybersecurity. Participating in relevant groups, establishing connections with industry professionals, using the platform for brand building and thought leadership, and maintaining engagement with potential candidates are effective ways to build a strong presence and attract top talent. These strategies help create a network of contacts, enhance the company's reputation, and ensure a pool of engaged candidates for future recruitment needs.

Monitoring and Analytics

Monitoring and analyzing the performance of job postings and recruitment campaigns on LinkedIn is essential for optimizing strategies and ensuring successful outcomes. The effective use of analytics involves tracking various metrics to assess the performance, analyzing engagement and the quality of applicants, making data-driven adjustments to recruitment strategies, and understanding the key metrics that indicate successful recruitment on LinkedIn.

Tracking the performance of job postings and campaigns is the first step in leveraging analytics. This involves monitoring how many views, clicks, and applications each job posting receives. LinkedIn provides tools that allow recruiters to see the performance of their postings in real time. This data can reveal the effectiveness of the job title, description, and how well the role resonates with the target audience. Understanding these metrics helps identify which aspects of the posting are working well and which may need tweaking.

Analyzing engagement and applicant quality is crucial in understanding the effectiveness of the recruitment strategy. Engagement metrics include the number of applications received and the level of interaction with the posting, such as likes, comments, and shares. Analyzing the quality of applicants is equally essential; this involves assessing how well the candidates' skills and experiences align with the job requirements. High engagement but low-quality applicants may suggest adjusting the job description or the targeting criteria.

If specific job postings are underperforming, the data can indicate whether the issue lies in the job description, incorrect targeting, or the compensation package's lack of appeal. Recruiters can use these insights to make informed adjustments, such as rewording the job description, changing the targeting parameters, or even reevaluating the role's requirements. This iterative process, guided by data, enhances the chances of attracting suitable candidates.

Understanding the metrics for successful LinkedIn recruitment involves knowing which data points most indicate success. Key metrics might include the number of qualified applicants, the conversion rate from viewer to applicant, and the engagement rate with the posting. Additionally, metrics such as time to fill and the quality of hire (assessed post-hire) are essential in evaluating the overall effectiveness of the recruitment strategy on LinkedIn.

Monitoring and analytics play a crucial role in the success of LinkedIn recruitment campaigns, particularly for specialized fields like cybersecurity. Recruiting can continually refine their strategies by tracking and analyzing the performance of job postings, engagement levels, and applicant quality and making data-driven adjustments. Understanding and focusing on critical metrics enables recruiters to optimize their LinkedIn recruitment efforts, ensuring that they attract and hire the best talent.

UTILIZING INDEED AND OTHER GENERAL JOB PLATFORMS

Utilizing Indeed and other general job platforms effectively is a critical strategy in cybersecurity recruitment, offering a broad reach and diverse talent pool. Job posting strategies on these platforms focus on crafting clear and compelling listings, using keywords and SEO for better visibility, differentiating postings in a competitive market, and providing detailed information about the company and its role. Applicant filtering and screening are streamlined through practical screening questions, automated tools for initial candidate filtering, and managing the flow and communication with applicants, ensuring a balance between the volume and quality of candidates.

Engagement with a broader audience is achieved by showcasing company culture and tailoring messages to appeal to a wide range of job seekers while utilizing platform analytics to understand applicant demographics. Cost-effective recruitment involves budgeting for job postings, measuring cost per hire and ROI, and exploring the free and premium features of these platforms. Additionally, integrating recruitment processes with HR systems, such as an

ATS, streamlines the workflow, ensures data consistency, and enhances the overall candidate experience, making these general job platforms an invaluable tool in the recruitment arsenal.

Job Posting Strategies on General Platforms

When posting job listings for cybersecurity roles on general platforms, it is vital to employ strategies that ensure the postings stand out and reach suitable candidates. This involves crafting clear and compelling job listings, utilizing keywords and search engine optimization (SEO), differentiating postings in a competitive market, and providing detailed information about the company and its role.

The job description should be concise yet detailed, clearly outlining the role's responsibilities, required qualifications, and any unique aspects of the job. It is essential to convey not just the technical requirements of the role but also what makes it exciting and rewarding. The goal is to create a listing that captures the essence of the role and the company culture, thus enticing suitable candidates to apply.

Utilizing keywords and SEO ensures that the job listing is discoverable by candidates who are searching for specific roles. This includes incorporating relevant terms that professionals in the cybersecurity field are likely to use when searching for job opportunities. Keywords could relate to specific skills, technologies, certifications, or industry jargon. SEO strategies also involve structuring the job listing to enhance its visibility on search engines and job search platforms, thereby increasing its reach.

Differentiating postings in a competitive market is crucial, especially in cybersecurity, where demand for talent often outstrips supply. This can involve highlighting what sets the company apart, such as innovative projects, career development opportunities, company culture, or benefits. The aim is to make the job posting stand out among numerous others and resonate with the specific type of candidate the company seeks.

The job posting should include a thorough description of the company, its mission and values, and detailed information about the role. This consists of the day-to-day responsibilities, technical requirements, and insights into how the role contributes to the organization's broader objectives. Clear and detailed information helps candidates assess their fit with the role and the company, making them more likely to apply if they see a good match.

Effective job posting strategies on general platforms involve crafting clear and compelling listings, strategically using SEO and keywords, differentiating the postings from others in the market, and providing comprehensive information about the company and the role. These strategies help attract the right talent by making the postings more visible, appealing, and informative to potential candidates.

Applicant Filtering and Screening

In the recruitment process for cybersecurity roles, efficient applicant filtering and screening are crucial steps to identify the most suitable candidates. This involves setting up practical screening questions, using automated tools for initial candidate filtering, managing the flow of applicants and communications, and striking a balance between the volume and quality of applicants.

Setting up practical screening questions is integral to the initial filtering process. These questions should be designed to quickly ascertain whether an applicant meets the essential criteria for the cybersecurity role. Practical screening questions might include queries about specific technical skills, certifications, years of experience in the field, or familiarity with specific cybersecurity tools and practices. The aim is to create a set of questions that can effectively weed out candidates who do not meet the basic requirements for the role.

Using automated tools for initial candidate filtering can significantly enhance the efficiency of the screening process. Many recruitment platforms and the ATS offer features that automatically filter candidates based on responses to screening questions or specific keywords in their resumes. This automation saves valuable time by reducing the number of applications that need to be reviewed manually. It ensures that the recruitment team focuses on candidates who have met specific essential criteria.

Managing applicant flow and communications is critical to maintaining an organized recruitment process. This involves tracking the status of each application, ensuring timely responses to candidates, and keeping candidates informed about their progress in the recruitment process. Effective applicant flow management helps create a positive candidate experience, which is crucial for maintaining the organization's reputation as a desirable employer and is significant in competitive fields like cybersecurity.

While having a large enough pool of candidates to choose from is essential, it is equally important to ensure that the candidates are of high quality and closely match the role's requirements. This might involve refining job postings, screening questions, or sourcing strategies to attract a more targeted group of applicants. The goal is to strike an optimal balance where the recruitment team has sufficient qualified candidates to consider without being overwhelmed by the volume of applications.

Effective applicant filtering and screening in cybersecurity recruitment involves setting up targeted screening questions, utilizing automated tools for initial filtering, managing the flow of applicants and communications efficiently, and balancing the volume and quality of applicants. These strategies help ensure that the recruitment process is efficient, organized, and successful in attracting and identifying the most suitable candidates for cybersecurity roles.

Engaging with a Broader Audience

Engaging with a broad and diverse talent pool in cybersecurity recruitment is essential for finding the best candidates. This requires reaching out to a broad audience, showcasing the company culture, tailoring recruitment messages, and using platform analytics to understand the demographics of applicants.

Reaching diverse and broad talent pools involves expanding recruitment efforts beyond traditional channels. This can include posting job listings on diverse job boards, participating in career fairs or industry conferences that attract a wide range of participants, and using social media platforms to reach a broader audience. It may also be effective for cybersecurity roles to engage with educational institutions, hacker communities, or online forums where diverse cybersecurity talent may be present. Diversifying the recruitment channels helps tap into various job market segments, increasing the chances of finding suitable candidates.

Showcasing company culture to a general audience is crucial in attracting many candidates. The company's values, mission, work environment, and employee experiences should be communicated in a way that resonates with a broad audience. This can include highlighting initiatives that demonstrate the company's commitment to diversity, work-life balance, professional development, and innovation. An intense portrayal of the company culture can attract candidates with the required skills and align with the company's values and ethos.

Tailoring messages for a broader range of job seekers means adapting recruitment communications to appeal to different groups. This includes creating inclusive job postings and marketing materials that resonate with a diverse audience. The language should be free of industry jargon that might intimidate newcomers and must avoid stereotypes that could inadvertently exclude certain groups. Messaging should emphasize the company's openness to diverse backgrounds and experiences; this is especially valuable in cyber-security, where diverse perspectives can greatly enhance problem solving and innovation.

Utilizing platform analytics to understand applicant demographics is a data-driven approach to refining recruitment strategies. Many job posting platforms offer analytics tools that provide insights into the demographics of the people who view and apply for job postings. This data can include information on each applicant's location, education level, previous job roles, and other demographic factors. Analyzing this data helps reveal the reach of recruitment efforts and can guide adjustments to ensure that job postings are effectively reaching the intended audience.

Engaging with a broader audience in cybersecurity recruitment involves reaching diverse talent pools, showcasing the company culture, tailoring messages to appeal to a wide range of job seekers, and utilizing platform analytics to understand applicant demographics. These strategies help attract diverse candidates, ensuring that recruitment efforts are inclusive and effective in finding the best talent.

Cost-Effective Recruitment

Implementing a cost-effective recruitment strategy is crucial, especially in cybersecurity, where the demand for skilled professionals can make recruitment expensive. This involves careful budgeting for job postings, measuring cost per hire and ROI, exploring both free and premium features on recruitment platforms, and comparing performance across different platforms to ensure the most efficient use of resources.

Budgeting for job postings and sponsored listings involves allocating financial resources effectively to maximize the visibility and reach of the job postings. Since sponsored listings often have a higher visibility than standard postings, they can be a worthwhile investment. However, it is essential to balance the use of sponsored listings with the budgetary constraints of the recruitment campaign. A well-planned budget should consider the costs associated with different platforms, the number of advertised roles, and the duration and frequency of the postings.

Measuring cost per hire and ROI is essential in evaluating the effectiveness of the recruitment strategy. Cost per hire includes all expenses related to the recruitment process, such as advertising, recruitment platform fees, and internal HR costs. Conversely, ROI assesses the value that the new hire brings to the organization relative to the cost of hiring them. Monitoring these metrics helps with understanding the most cost-effective recruitment strategies and contributes to making informed decisions about future recruitment investments.

Exploring free and premium features on recruitment platforms can help maximize the recruitment budget. Many platforms offer a range of free features, such as primary job postings, access to a limited pool of resumes, and simple applicant tracking tools. While more costly, premium features often provide greater visibility, advanced search and filtering capabilities, and more sophisticated applicant tracking and analytics tools. Balancing the use of free and premium features based on the specific needs and budget of the recruitment campaign can enhance cost-effectiveness.

Comparing performance across different platforms is crucial in determining the most effective channels for recruitment. This involves evaluating the number and quality of candidates that each platform yields, the platform's cost, and the overall user experience. Regularly assessing the performance of various platforms can provide insights into where to allocate resources more effectively and which platforms offer the best value for recruitment needs.

Cost-effective recruitment in cybersecurity involves careful budgeting for job postings, measuring cost per hire and ROI, strategically using free and premium platform features, and comparing the performance across different platforms. These practices help ensure that recruitment efforts are effective in attracting qualified candidates and efficient in resource utilization and budgetary expenditure.

Integrating with HR Systems

In recruiting for cybersecurity roles, integrating recruitment efforts with HR systems, notably an ATS, is crucial for streamlining and optimizing the hiring process. This integration involves syncing with an ATS, refining the recruitment workflow, ensuring data accuracy, and enhancing the candidate experience.

An ATS is designed to manage the recruitment process effectively, from posting job listings to handling applications and facilitating communication with candidates. Organizations can centralize their recruitment efforts by integrating job postings on various platforms with an ATS, making tracking and managing applicant data easier. This synchronization allows for efficient monitoring of applications across different platforms and ensures that all candidate information is captured and stored in a single system.

Streamlining the recruitment workflow through system integration is critical to efficiency. Integration with an ATS can automate various aspects of the recruitment process, such as filtering applications based on predefined criteria, scheduling interviews, and generating reports. This streamlining reduces the administrative burden on HR and recruitment teams, allowing them to focus more on engaging with candidates and evaluating their fit for the role. A well-integrated system can facilitate better communication and collaboration among recruitment team members.

Ensuring data consistency and accuracy is another significant benefit of integrating recruitment with HR systems. Having a single, centralized system for all applicant data reduces the risk of errors or inconsistencies from managing data across multiple platforms. This ensures that the recruitment team can access accurate, up-to-date information at all times, which is crucial for making informed decisions throughout the hiring process.

Improving the candidate experience through system integration is an often-overlooked advantage. A seamless integration between job posting platforms and an ATS can lead to a more streamlined application process for candidates, thereby minimizing complications and delays. For instance, candidates might benefit from features like easy application processes, timely updates on their application status, and efficient scheduling of interviews. A positive application experience can enhance the employer's brand and increase the likelihood of top candidates accepting job offers.

Integrating recruitment efforts with HR systems, particularly an ATS, is crucial for optimizing the recruitment process for cybersecurity roles. This integration helps sync applicant data, streamline the recruitment workflow, ensure data accuracy, and improve the candidate experience.

MAXIMIZING VISIBILITY AND RESPONSES

Maximizing visibility and eliciting responses in recruitment demands a strategic, multipronged approach. To enhance job posting visibility, it is essential to use SEO techniques for optimizing job descriptions, actively engaging in social media promotion, leveraging employee advocacy, and forging partnerships with educational and industry organizations. Regularly updating and refreshing job postings are crucial tasks for maintaining relevance and attractiveness. Simultaneously, encouraging candidate engagement is critical and can be achieved by crafting compelling calls to action (CTAs) in job postings, simplifying the application process, presenting clear and appealing employer value propositions, and ensuring prompt and effective responses to inquiries and applications.

Analytically, leveraging metrics and data is vital for optimizing recruitment strategies. This includes tracking views, applications, and engagement metrics, identifying successful channels and tactics, and continually adjusting strategies based on performance data. Experimentation with different posting times and formats can also yield valuable insights. At the same time, building a strong employer brand is critical and involves clear communication of the company's mission, values, and culture; showcasing employee testimonials and success stories; highlighting the unique benefits of working there; and consistently promoting this brand across platforms. Enhancing the candidate experience through feedback and continuous improvements while fostering a respectful and responsive reputation are also integral to successful recruitment efforts, especially in specialized fields like cybersecurity.

Strategies for Increased Job Posting Visibility

In a competitive job market, especially in fields like cybersecurity, increasing the visibility of job postings is crucial for attracting top talent. Effective strategies to enhance the visibility of job postings include utilizing SEO techniques, engaging in social media promotion and employee advocacy, partnering with educational institutions and industry organizations, and regularly updating and refreshing job postings.

Utilizing SEO techniques involves incorporating relevant keywords and phrases that potential candidates will likely use when searching for cybersecurity jobs. This could include specific skills, tools, certifications, and job titles related to the role. By optimizing job descriptions with these keywords, the postings are more likely to appear in search engine results, thereby reaching a larger audience of potential applicants.

Engaging in social media promotion and employee advocacy can significantly increase the visibility of job postings. Social media platforms like LinkedIn, Twitter (now X), and Facebook are practical tools for sharing job postings and reaching a broader audience. Encouraging employees to share job openings on their networks can further amplify this reach. Employee advocacy extends the job posting's visibility and adds a layer of credibility and personal endorsement, which may appeal to potential candidates.

Partnering with educational institutions and industry organizations is another effective way to increase job posting visibility. Collaborating with universities, technical colleges, cybersecurity boot camps, and professional organizations can provide access to a pool of emerging talent and established professionals. These partnerships might involve participating in career fairs, guest lecturing, sponsoring events, or posting job openings on institution-specific job boards. Such partnerships increase visibility and establish the company as an active participant and employer of choice within the cybersecurity community.

Regularly updating and refreshing job postings is essential to maintain visibility. Over time, job postings can become buried under newer job boards and search engine listings. By regularly updating the content (even with minor changes) and reposting, job listings can maintain a higher ranking in search results. Additionally, regular updates ensure that the job postings reflect the latest requirements and are aligned with current cybersecurity trends and needs.

Encouraging Candidate Engagement

To encourage candidate engagement, employers should focus on crafting compelling CTAs in job postings, simplifying the application process, presenting clear and appealing employer value propositions, and ensuring prompt and effective responses to inquiries and applications.

A CTA is a statement or phrase designed to prompt an immediate response or encourage an immediate reaction from the reader. In the context of job postings, this could be an invitation to apply, learn more about the company, or contact the recruitment team. Effective CTAs should be clear, direct, and create a sense of urgency or excitement. For example, a CTA like "Join our innovative cybersecurity team and make a real-world impact" can be more engaging than a generic "Apply now."

Simplifying the application process is essential to maintain candidate interest. A complex or lengthy application process can significantly deter potential applicants. Streamlining this process involves reducing the number of steps to apply, minimizing the need for repetitive information entry, and ensuring that the application can be completed on various devices, including mobile phones. Making the application process as straightforward and user-friendly as possible encourages more candidates to complete their applications.

Providing clear and appealing employer value propositions (EVPs) is critical. An EVP is a unique set of offerings and values that an employer provides to its employees, differentiating it from its competitors. The EVP should resonate with the target audience's desires and expectations, highlighting aspects such as career development opportunities, company culture, benefits, work-life balance, and the impact of the work. A strong EVP can attract candidates who are not only skilled but also an excellent cultural fit for the organization.

Responding promptly and effectively to inquiries and applications maintains candidate interest and builds a positive reputation as an employer. This includes acknowledging the receipt of applications, informing candidates about their application status, and promptly providing feedback or next steps. Prompt and clear communication throughout the recruitment process can enhance the candidate experience, increase engagement, and improve the overall perception of the company as an employer of choice.

Leveraging Analytics for Optimization

In recruitment, particularly for specialized fields like cybersecurity, leveraging analytics is essential for optimizing job postings and strategies. Utilizing data effectively involves tracking various metrics, identifying the most successful channels and tactics, adjusting strategies based on performance data, and experimenting with different posting times and formats.

Tracking views, applications, and engagement metrics is the first step in leveraging analytics. This involves monitoring how many people view the job postings, how many apply, and the level of interaction (likes, shares, comments) with the postings on various platforms. These metrics provide valuable insights into the visibility and appeal of the job postings. For example, many views but low application rates could indicate that the job description is not compelling enough or that the application process is too cumbersome.

Identifying successful channels and tactics through analytics is crucial for efficient resource allocation. By analyzing where the most qualified applicants are, recruiters can identify which platforms and recruitment tactics are yielding the best results. This might include professional networking sites like LinkedIn, job boards, social media platforms, or referrals. Understanding which channels are most effective allows recruiters to focus their efforts and budget on the platforms that provide the highest ROI.

Adjusting strategies based on performance data is critical to continuous improvement. If specific job postings are underperforming, the data can help pinpoint whether the issue is with the job description, the chosen platforms, or the targeting criteria. Recruiters can use these insights to make informed adjustments, such as rewording the job description, changing the platforms where the job is posted, or altering the candidate profile being targeted. This iterative process, which is data-driven, enhances the chances of attracting suitable candidates.

Experimenting with different posting times and formats can also be informed by analytics. The effectiveness of job postings can vary depending on the time of day or week they are posted and the format used. For example, certain platforms may have higher user activity during specific hours, or some formats (like video or infographics) may effectively engage specific audience segments. Experimenting with these variables and analyzing the resulting data can help identify the most effective strategies for job postings.

Building a Strong Employer Brand

A strong employer brand communicates the company's mission, culture, and values effectively; showcases employee testimonials and success stories; highlights unique benefits and aspects of working at the company; and maintains consistency in brand promotion across various platforms.

Communicating the company's mission, culture, and values is fundamental to building a strong employer brand. This involves clearly articulating what the company stands for, its goals, and the principles guiding its operations and employee relationships. For instance, a cybersecurity company might emphasize its commitment to innovation, digital security, and creating a positive impact in the tech world. This communication helps potential employees understand what the company is about and whether their personal and professional aspirations align with the organization's ethos.

Showcasing employee testimonials and success stories is a powerful way to build an employer brand. Employee stories and testimonials provide a genuine look into the company's work environment and culture. These narratives can be shared through various platforms, such as the company's career website, social media, and professional networking sites. Highlighting diverse employee experiences, career growth stories, and team achievements can be particularly effective in portraying the company as an employer that values and supports its staff.

Highlighting the benefits and unique aspects of working at the company is also crucial. This goes beyond just listing the standard benefits; it is about showcasing what makes working at the company particular. This could include unique professional development opportunities, innovative work on cutting-edge cybersecurity projects, a collaborative and supportive work environment, flexible work arrangements, or unique health and wellness programs. These aspects can make the company stand out as an attractive workplace.

Consistently promoting the employer brand across platforms ensures a unified and coherent message. Whether it is on the company's career page, social media, job boards, or recruitment campaigns, the messaging about the company's culture, mission, and values should be consistent. Consistent branding helps in building recognition and a strong reputation as an employer, making the company more attractive to potential candidates and reinforcing the company's image as an employer of choice.

Candidate Experience and Feedback

The candidate experience plays a crucial role in attracting and retaining top talent. Ensuring a positive and informative application process, gathering and utilizing feedback from applicants, making continuous improvements, and fostering a reputation for respect and responsiveness are critical elements of this strategy.

A positive and informative application process is essential for a suitable candidate experience. This involves creating a straightforward, user-friendly application process that respects the candidate's time and effort. Clear instructions, timely communication about the process and status, and a system that is easy to navigate contribute to a positive experience. Additionally, providing information about the role, the company culture, and what candidates can expect during the recruitment process helps set clear expectations and demonstrates the company's professionalism.

Gathering feedback from applicants and candidates is vital in understanding the effectiveness of the recruitment process. This can be done through post-application surveys, feedback forms after interviews, or informal conversations. Feedback should cover various aspects of the application and interview process, including the ease of application, clarity of communication, and overall experience. This feedback provides valuable insights into what works well and what areas need improvement.

Making continuous improvements based on feedback ensures that the recruitment process is consistently evolving to better meet the needs of candidates. This could involve streamlining specific steps in the application process, improving communication timelines, or adjusting interview techniques. Using candidate feedback to refine the recruitment strategy demonstrates a commitment to creating a positive experience for potential employees.

Fostering a reputation for respect and responsiveness is critical in building a strong employer brand. Regardless of the outcome, candidates should feel respected and valued throughout the recruitment process. Prompt responses to inquiries, respectful communication, and providing feedback to candidates after interviews contribute to a respectful candidate experience. A reputation for being a responsive and considerate employer can significantly enhance the company's ability to attract top talent since candidates are more likely to apply to and accept offers from companies that treat them well during the recruitment process.

ANALYTICS AND PERFORMANCE MEASUREMENT

Understanding and effectively managing recruitment analytics is essential for measuring and enhancing the performance of hiring strategies. Important aspects involve identifying crucial metrics and key performance indicators (KPIs) that define recruitment success, utilizing platform-specific analytics tools, interpreting data to refine recruitment approaches, and benchmarking against industry standards and competitors. Measuring job posting performance is also critical, which includes tracking views, clicks, and application rates; analyzing the quality of applicants and conversion rates; assessing the effectiveness of job descriptions and requirements; and making necessary adjustments to improve performance.

ROI and budget management form a significant part of recruitment analytics. This involves calculating the ROI for various recruitment activities, budgeting across different channels and tools, balancing cost efficiency with the quality of hires, and making data-driven decisions for optimal budget allocation. Additionally, focusing on candidate sourcing and pipeline analytics includes monitoring sources of top candidates, analyzing the talent pipeline and flow, identifying bottlenecks, and strategizing to build a sustainable talent pipeline. Continuous improvement and adaptation in recruitment is a never-ending cycle, necessitating regular reviews and updates to strategies, staying informed about market and industry changes, adapting to technological advancements in recruitment analytics, and fostering a culture of continuous learning and improvement within the recruitment process.

Understanding Recruitment Analytics

Understanding and leveraging recruitment analytics is crucial for refining strategies and achieving success in cybersecurity recruitment. This involves identifying key metrics and KPIs for recruitment, utilizing platform-specific analytics tools, interpreting data to inform recruitment strategies, and benchmarking against industry standards and competitors.

Identifying key metrics and KPIs for recruitment success is the first step. These metrics might include time to fill, cost per hire, quality of hire, applicant source effectiveness, and candidate conversion rates. Time to fill measures the time taken to fill a position, which is crucial in fast-paced fields like cybersecurity. Cost per hire encompasses all costs that are associated with the recruitment process, while quality of hire evaluates the performance and retention of new hires. Understanding which sources (job boards, social media, referrals) bring in the most qualified candidates and the conversion rate of applicants to hires are also key metrics. These KPIs provide a quantitative basis for assessing the effectiveness of recruitment strategies.

Utilizing platform-specific analytics tools is essential for gathering and analyzing recruitment data. Most job posting platforms and an ATS offer built-in analytics tools that provide insights into the performance of job postings and the behavior of applicants. These tools can track metrics such as the number of views, applications, and shares that a job posting receives, along with more detailed data like applicant drop-off points and engagement rates. Leveraging these tools can help recruiters understand how well their job postings perform and where improvements can be made.

Interpreting data to inform recruitment strategies involves analyzing the collected metrics to make informed decisions. This could mean identifying the most effective channels for job postings, understanding the characteristics of successful hires, or pinpointing areas in the recruitment process that need improvement. For example, suppose data shows that a significant number of applicants drop off at the application stage. In that case, it might indicate that the process is too complex or lengthy, prompting a need for simplification.

Benchmarking against industry standards and competitors helps contextualize the organization's recruitment performance. This involves comparing the company's recruitment metrics with industry averages and competitors' performance. Benchmarking can reveal areas where the company is excelling or underperforming compared to others in the industry. It also helps set realistic goals and expectations for recruitment and identify best practices that could be adopted or adapted.

Measuring Job Posting Performance

In cybersecurity recruitment, measuring the performance of job postings is vital to understanding their effectiveness and making necessary adjustments. Key aspects of this measurement include tracking views, clicks, and application rates, analyzing the quality of applicants and conversion rates, assessing the effectiveness of job descriptions and requirements, and making adjustments to improve performance.

Tracking views, clicks, and application rates provides fundamental indicators of a job posting's reach and initial appeal. The number of views and clicks can give insights into how many potential candidates see the posting and whether the title or initial description is compelling enough to warrant further action. The application rate, or the number of applications received relative to views or clicks, can indicate how appealing and precise the job opportunity is to potential candidates. Low application rates relative to many views might suggest that the job posting is not sufficiently engaging or clear.

Analyzing the quality of applicants and conversion rates is crucial for understanding the effectiveness of the job posting beyond just initial interest. This involves evaluating whether the applicants meet the desired qualifications and how many of those applicants move forward in the recruitment process. A high number of applicants but a low conversion rate to interviews or hires might indicate that while the job posting attracts interest, it may not attract suitable candidates.

Assessing the effectiveness of job descriptions and requirements is essential. This includes reviewing the clarity, comprehensiveness, and appeal of the job description and ensuring that the requirements are realistic and aligned with industry standards. It also involves ensuring that the descriptions and requirements accurately reflect the role and the company's needs. Feedback from candidates, particularly those who decline job offers or drop out of the process, can provide valuable insights into how the job posting is perceived.

Adjusting postings for improved performance is an ongoing process. Based on the insights gained from tracking and analysis, recruiters should continuously refine their job postings. This might involve tweaking the language to make it more engaging, adjusting the requirements if they are too narrow or too broad, or reevaluating the benefits and opportunities highlighted in the posting. Regular adjustments ensure that the job posting remains relevant, attractive, and effective in attracting suitable candidates.

ROI and Budget Management

Effective management of ROI and budget is critical in cybersecurity recruitment, where the demand for specialized talent often leads to competitive hiring scenarios. Critical aspects of ROI and budget management include calculating the ROI for recruitment activities, budgeting for various channels and tools, balancing cost efficiency with the quality of hires, and making data-driven decisions regarding budget allocation.

Calculating ROI for recruitment activities is fundamental to understanding the effectiveness of these efforts. ROI in recruitment can be measured by evaluating the costs involved in the hiring process (including advertising, recruiter fees, and time spent by internal staff) against the benefits brought in by the new hire (such as their contributions to the company, performance, and impact on team productivity). This calculation helps determine which recruitment strategies and channels yield the most value for the investment.

The budget should be allocated across different channels, such as job boards, social media, recruitment agencies, and career fairs, depending on their effectiveness and the specific needs of the role. It is essential to consider both traditional and innovative recruitment methods and allocate funds to explore diverse sources of talent. This budgeting should also factor in recruitment tools and technology costs to streamline the hiring process and improve candidate quality.

Balancing cost efficiency with the quality of hires is a critical aspect of recruitment budget management. While minimizing costs is essential, it is crucial not to compromise on the quality of hires, especially in a field as critical as cybersecurity. Investing in high-quality recruitment processes can lead to better candidate matches, higher employee retention, and more value to the organization. This balance requires careful evaluation of how cost-cutting measures might impact the overall quality and effectiveness of the recruitment process.

Making data-driven decisions for budget allocation involves using data and analytics to inform where and how the recruitment budget is spent. By analyzing the performance of past recruitment efforts, including the cost per hire, time to fill, and success rates of different recruitment channels, organizations can make informed decisions on how to allocate their budget effectively. This approach ensures that recruitment spending is targeted toward strategies and channels that have proven to be most effective, optimizing the use of resources for better outcomes.

Candidate Sourcing and Pipeline Analytics

Effectively managing candidate sourcing and pipeline analytics is crucial in the recruitment process. This involves monitoring the sources of top candidates, analyzing the talent pipeline and flow, identifying bottlenecks and areas for improvement, and strategizing to build a sustainable talent pipeline.

Monitoring sources of top candidates is essential for understanding which recruitment channels and strategies are most effective. Organizations can identify the most fruitful sourcing strategies by tracking where the most qualified and successful candidates are sourced from, whether it is job boards, social media, referral programs, or recruitment events. This information helps in optimizing recruitment efforts and allocating resources more effectively.

Analyzing the talent pipeline and flow involves examining each candidate's journey from initial contact to hiring. This analysis can reveal insights into the effectiveness of the recruitment process at each stage, such as the initial application, screening, interviewing, and final selection. Understanding the flow of candidates through the pipeline helps identify stages where candidates are most likely to drop out or where delays typically occur.

Identifying bottlenecks and areas for improvement streamline the recruitment process. Bottlenecks could occur at various stages, such as lengthy application processes, slow response times, or inefficient interviewing schedules. Identifying these issues allows for targeted interventions to improve the process. For instance, simplifying the application form or enhancing communication with candidates can significantly reduce drop-off rates.

Strategizing for building a sustainable talent pipeline is critical for long-term recruitment success. This involves filling current vacancies and planning for future hiring needs. Building relationships with potential candidates, creating talent pools for critical roles, and engaging with passive candidates can ensure a steady flow of qualified applicants.

Continuous Improvement and Adaptation

In a rapidly evolving job market and industry like cybersecurity, continuous improvement and adaptation in recruitment strategies are essential. This involves regularly reviewing and updating recruitment practices, staying informed about market and industry changes, adapting to technological advancements, and fostering a culture of continuous learning and improvement.

Regularly reviewing and updating recruitment strategies ensures that they remain adequate and relevant. This could involve reassessing job descriptions, refining candidate sourcing strategies, or updating the selection criteria. Regular reviews allow for adjustments in response to feedback, changes in the job market, or shifts in organizational needs.

Staying informed about market and industry changes includes keeping up with the latest trends in cybersecurity skills and technologies, understanding changes in the job market, and being aware of shifts in candidate expectations and behaviors. This knowledge helps tailor recruitment strategies to attract and retain the best talent.

Adapting to technological advancements in recruitment analytics involves leveraging the latest tools and technologies to enhance recruitment. This might include using an AI-powered ATS, data analytics tools, or advanced candidate sourcing platforms. Staying abreast of and incorporating these technological advancements can significantly improve the efficiency and effectiveness of recruitment efforts.

Fostering a culture of continuous learning and improvement in recruitment is vital for sustained success. This involves encouraging feedback from candidates and hiring managers, learning from successful and unsuccessful hires, and continuously seeking ways to enhance the recruitment process. A culture that values learning and adaptation ensures that recruitment strategies evolve with industry best practices and organizational needs.

5

THE HIRING PROCESS

The hiring process in cybersecurity starts with meticulous planning and preparation, which includes defining organizational needs, developing a recruitment plan, creating job descriptions, and setting up a solid recruitment infrastructure. This stage involves assessing cybersecurity gaps, determining the scope of positions, aligning hiring with business objectives, and consulting with team leaders for role-specific requirements. Developing a comprehensive recruitment plan is crucial; it includes setting clear timelines, allocating resources, deciding on candidate sourcing channels, and establishing a cross-functional hiring team. This stage is vital to drafting accurate job descriptions, ensuring legal and diversity compliance, implementing an Applicant Tracking System (ATS), and preparing tools for candidate assessment. Additionally, engaging department heads, training interviewers, and establishing clear evaluation criteria will ensure a cohesive and efficient hiring process.

The next phase focuses on posting and promoting job vacancies, effective job posting techniques, and leveraging promotional strategies. This includes crafting compelling job advertisements, using search engine optimization (SEO) for better online visibility, selecting appropriate platforms for posting, and regularly refreshing postings. Employer branding highlights the company's culture, values, and achievements and showcases career development opportunities. Adapting strategies for remote hiring and addressing location-specific nuances is essential for a global talent pool. The process also involves responsive communication with applicants, acknowledging applications, maintaining transparency, and providing feedback. Applicant tracking and management through ATS, screening and shortlisting candidates, structuring interviews, and ensuring a fair and consistent interview process are critical. The final decision making involves collecting feedback, comparing candidates against job requirements, and post-interview engagement, including extending offers, conducting reference checks, and ensuring a positive candidate experience throughout the hiring journey. The full process is shown in Figure 5.1.

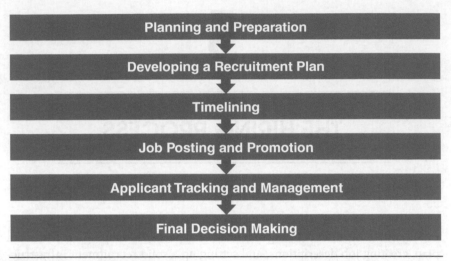

Figure 5.1 The hiring process.

PLANNING AND PREPARATION

The planning and preparation phase of the hiring process in cybersecurity is comprehensive, beginning with defining specific organizational needs, assessing gaps, and aligning hiring with business objectives and cybersecurity strategies. This involves consulting with team leaders for role-specific requirements, setting clear timelines, allocating resources, and deciding on candidate sourcing channels, all integral to developing an effective recruitment plan. Creating detailed job descriptions, outlining necessary skills and qualifications, and ensuring compliance with legal and diversity standards are vital steps. The infrastructure for recruitment is set up by implementing or updating the ATS, establishing structured interview frameworks, preparing assessment tools, and coordinating logistics for interviews. This phase also encompasses stakeholder involvement, where department heads and team leaders are engaged, hiring managers and interviewers are trained on best practices, and clear roles and responsibilities within the hiring team are established to ensure alignment on evaluation criteria and decision-making processes.

Defining the Hiring Needs

In the cybersecurity realm, defining precise hiring needs is pivotal for aligning talent acquisition with organizational goals and effectively bridging cybersecurity gaps. This process begins with a thorough assessment of the organization's cybersecurity posture, identifying areas that require strengthening or new capabilities that must be developed. It is crucial to understand the organization's specific cybersecurity challenges and whether they are related to network security, data protection, threat intelligence, or another area. This assessment helps pinpoint the types of roles and expertise needed to fortify the cybersecurity framework.

Following the assessment, determining the scope and level of positions to be filled is essential. This involves deciding whether the organization needs entry-level analysts, mid-level managers, or senior strategists and then defining the specific responsibilities and expectations for these roles. The alignment of hiring with overall business objectives and the broader cybersecurity strategy ensures that each new hire contributes effectively to the organization's security posture. Consulting with cybersecurity team leaders and other key stakeholders is crucial for understanding the technical and soft skills that are required for specific roles. Their insights ensure that the hiring process targets candidates who have the necessary technical expertise and fit well within the existing team dynamics and the company's culture.

Developing a Recruitment Plan

Creating a robust recruitment plan is a cornerstone of successful hiring in cybersecurity. This process involves setting clear timelines and milestones, which are crucial for navigating the hiring process from job posting to finalizing a hire. These timelines ensure that each recruitment phase follows an organized and efficient schedule, including sourcing, screening, interviewing, and offering. Alongside this, allocating appropriate resources and budget is essential. This allocation covers various aspects of recruitment, such as advertising on job platforms, utilizing recruitment agencies, and investing in tools and technologies for efficient candidate screening and communication.

The recruitment plan also entails deciding on the most effective channels and methods for sourcing candidates. This decision is based on where potential candidates are likely to be found, such as professional networking sites, industry-specific job boards, or referral programs. Additionally, establishing a cross-functional hiring team is vital for a holistic recruitment approach. This team, typically comprising members from human resources (HR), cybersecurity, and other relevant departments, brings diverse perspectives. Their collective expertise ensures a comprehensive evaluation of candidates by assessing technical skills and cultural fit, which will ultimately lead to more informed and effective hiring decisions.

Creating Job Descriptions and Personal Specifications

As mentioned in the previous chapter, creating detailed and accurate job descriptions is critical to the recruitment process, especially in cybersecurity. These descriptions should comprehensively outline the role's responsibilities, necessary skills, qualifications, and the specific experience required. This clarity helps attract candidates who are capable and a good fit for the role. Including information about critical responsibilities, day-to-day tasks, and any unique aspects of the position or the working environment is essential. Additionally, job descriptions should detail the technical and soft skills needed, along with any specific certifications or educational qualifications that are essential for the role.

Alongside the technical requirements, identifying vital personal attributes and competencies that align with the company culture and the specific demands of the role is essential. This might include problem-solving abilities, adaptability, teamwork, and communication skills. It is also crucial to ensure that job descriptions comply with legal standards—particularly nondiscrimination—and reflect the organization's commitment to diversity and inclusion. This helps attract a diverse range of applicants and ensures adherence to ethical and legal recruitment standards. Including personal attributes and compliance with diversity standards plays a significant role in shaping the pool of candidates and ensuring the recruitment process aligns with broader organizational values and legal requirements.

Setting up Recruitment Infrastructure

Implementing or updating the ATS is a foundational step in establishing an adequate recruitment infrastructure and is particularly vital in the streamlined hiring of cybersecurity professionals. An ATS automates various aspects of the recruitment process, from posting job openings to managing candidate data and tracking the progress of applications. This system not only enhances efficiency but also helps in maintaining organization and consistency throughout the hiring process. It is essential to ensure that the ATS is up-to-date and equipped with features that cater to the specific needs of recruiting for cybersecurity roles, such as advanced candidate filtering capabilities and integration with other HR management tools.

Alongside technological infrastructure, establishing a structured and consistent interview framework is crucial for evaluating candidates effectively. This framework should include a standardized set of interview questions or assessments that are aligned with the specific requirements for cybersecurity roles. Effective tools and resources for candidate assessment may include technical tests, problem-solving exercises, or situational judgment tests. These tools aid in objectively assessing a candidate's skills and fit for the role. Additionally, coordinating logistics for interviews, whether remote or in person, is an important aspect. This involves scheduling interviews, ensuring that all necessary technology for remote interviews is available, and creating a comfortable and conducive environment for in-person interviews. Effective coordination and interview preparation will help provide a smooth and professional experience for candidates, which will reflect positively on the organization.

Stakeholder Involvement and Training

Engaging with department heads and team leaders is a crucial aspect of the recruitment process, especially in specialized fields like cybersecurity. Involving these stakeholders ensures that the recruitment strategy aligns with each department's specific needs and expectations. Their insights are invaluable in defining the precise skills and competencies that are required for cybersecurity roles, thereby contributing to more accurate job descriptions and more targeted candidate evaluations. This collaboration also facilitates a deeper understanding of the role's impact within the team and the broader organization, enabling a more holistic assessment of candidates.

Furthermore, training hiring managers and interviewers on best recruitment practices is fundamental to ensuring a fair, effective, and legally compliant hiring process. This training should cover aspects such as unbiased interviewing techniques, understanding diversity and inclusion principles, and familiarity with the competencies required for cybersecurity roles. Establishing clear roles and responsibilities within the hiring team is essential to maintaining a structured and efficient recruitment process. Each team member should have a defined role in sourcing candidates, conducting interviews, or making final hiring decisions. Ensuring alignment on evaluation criteria and the decision-making process is critical to achieving consistency and fairness in candidate assessments. This alignment helps make objective decisions based on predefined criteria, reducing the influence of unconscious biases and ensuring that the best candidates are selected based on their skills, experiences, and fit with the company culture.

POSTING AND PROMOTION OF JOB VACANCIES

The posting and promotion of job vacancies in cybersecurity recruitment encompasses several vital strategies. Effective job posting involves crafting compelling and clear job advertisements, utilizing SEO strategies for enhanced online visibility, and selecting the most appropriate platforms for posting, including niche sites, general job boards, and social media. These postings are regularly updated to maintain relevance. Promotional strategies include leveraging social media and professional networks, engaging current employees in referral programs, collaborating with industry associations and educational institutions, and utilizing targeted advertising and recruitment events. Employer branding is critical, highlighting the company's culture, values, achievements, career development opportunities, and commitment to diversity, equity, and inclusion initiatives. Content is tailored to resonate with cybersecurity professionals. For global and remote hiring, strategies are adapted to accommodate a global talent pool, address location-specific regulations and cultural nuances, and tailor messages for remote or hybrid work opportunities, including implementing virtual recruitment and onboarding processes. Finally, responsive communication throughout the process is vital, acknowledging applications, maintaining transparency, providing clear timelines and expectations, offering feedback to candidates, and keeping communication lines open and professional.

Effective Job Postings

Crafting compelling and clear job advertisements is a critical component in attracting the right talent. A well-crafted job posting should concisely convey the essential responsibilities and requirements of the role while highlighting what makes the company a unique and desirable workplace. It should speak directly to the desired candidates, clearly outlining what the job entails and the qualifications needed, without being overly technical or jargon-heavy. This clarity helps attract applicants who are qualified, genuinely interested in the role, and aligned with the company's values.

SEO strategies also ensure that job postings are easily discoverable online. This includes integrating relevant keywords related to cybersecurity, specific skills, tools, or certifications that potential candidates might use in their job search. Choosing the right platforms for posting is also crucial; this could include niche job boards specializing in cybersecurity roles, general platforms for a wider reach, and social media channels for more targeted or passive candidate engagement. Regularly updating and refreshing job postings is essential to keep them relevant and visible. Updated postings are more likely to appear in search results and catch the attention of active job seekers, ensuring that the opportunities reach suitable candidates promptly.

Promotional Strategies

Leveraging social media and professional networks is an essential promotional strategy in modern recruitment, particularly for specialized fields like cybersecurity. Utilizing platforms such as LinkedIn, Twitter (now X), and other industry-specific forums allows companies to post job openings and actively showcase their culture, technological advancements, and achievements. This approach extends beyond traditional job advertising by building a brand presence that resonates with potential candidates. Engaging on these platforms, sharing content that is relevant to cybersecurity, and participating in industry conversations can attract active job seekers and passive candidates who may be enticed by attractive opportunities.

Another effective strategy involves engaging current employees in referral programs. With their firsthand experience of the company culture and understanding of the job requirements, employees can be excellent sources for attracting suitable candidates. Encouraging them to refer professionals from their networks often leads to more engaged and fitting candidates. Collaborating with industry associations and educational institutions for career fairs, seminars, and workshops can tap into emerging talent and those who are looking for career transitions. Utilizing targeted advertising and participating in recruitment events that are focused on cybersecurity can also help reach a more tailored audience, ensuring that individuals with the specific skills and interests that are relevant to the roles see the job openings.

Employer Branding

Employer branding involves highlighting the company's culture, values, and achievements, which are essential in differentiating the organization in the competitive job market. Showcasing the company's unique attributes, such as its commitment to innovation, ethical practices, or contributions to groundbreaking cybersecurity projects, helps attract candidates who align with these values. This aspect of branding is about more than just the benefits offered; it is about painting a picture of the company's ethos and how it operates daily.

In addition, showcasing career development opportunities and employee testimonials can significantly enhance employer branding. Prospective candidates are often attracted to companies that invest in their employees' growth and professional development. Highlighting training programs, opportunities for advancement, and real stories from current employees about their growth and success within the company can be powerful. Furthermore, actively promoting diversity, equity, and inclusion initiatives demonstrates a commitment to creating a welcoming and supportive work environment. Finally, creating content that is specifically tailored to resonate with cybersecurity professionals, such as insights into the company's cybersecurity projects, technological advancements, or thought leadership, further strengthens the employer brand among the target professional community.

Global and Remote Hiring Considerations

Global and remote hiring considerations are increasingly important in today's interconnected world, especially in cybersecurity, where talent can be sourced worldwide. Adapting recruitment strategies for a global talent pool involves recognizing and valuing the diversity of international candidates. This means looking for the best skills and experiences and understanding and accommodating different cultural perspectives and work styles. In this approach, job postings and recruitment messages should be tailored to appeal to a global audience, highlighting the company's inclusiveness and ability to support a diverse workforce.

Another critical aspect is addressing location-specific regulations and cultural nuances. This includes being aware of and compliant with employment laws in different countries, understanding visa and work permit requirements, and being sensitive to cultural differences that might affect the recruitment and working experience. For remote or hybrid work opportunities, it is essential to communicate clearly about the nature of these arrangements. This involves outlining expectations regarding work hours, collaboration across time zones, and the balance between remote and in-office work, if applicable. Implementing virtual recruitment and onboarding processes is also crucial in this digital era. This includes conducting interviews via video conferencing, utilizing online assessment tools, and developing an effective virtual onboarding process to ensure that new hires feel welcomed, informed, and integrated into the team, regardless of their physical location.

Responsive Communication

Responsive communication is a fundamental aspect of a successful recruitment process, particularly in cybersecurity, where the competition for top talent is intense. Acknowledging the receipt of applications is the first step in establishing a rapport with candidates. It is essential to maintain transparency throughout the hiring process by informing applicants of their status and what the next steps are. This approach demonstrates respect for the time and effort that candidates put into their applications and helps build a positive perception of the company.

Candidates appreciate knowing the estimated time frames for review processes, interviews, and final decisions. This clarity helps manage their expectations and reduces uncertainty, which is a significant source of applicant anxiety. Offering constructive feedback to unsuccessful candidates is another crucial element of responsive communication. This feedback should be specific and helpful, offering insights into areas for improvement, which can be valuable for the candidate's professional development. Finally, keep communication lines open and maintain a professional attitude at all stages of the recruitment process.

APPLICANT TRACKING AND MANAGEMENT

Applicant tracking and management in cybersecurity recruitment is an important process that starts with implementing an ATS to enhance efficiency. An ATS is used for candidate tracking and management, automating repetitive tasks, securely organizing and storing candidate information, and streamlining communication and scheduling. Screening and shortlisting involve establishing criteria for initial resume screening, conducting prescreening calls or assessments, shortlisting candidates based on qualifications and fit, and involving team members in the review process for diverse perspectives. The interview process is structured for a comprehensive evaluation, employing various formats like behavioral, technical, and panel interviews, with interviewers who have been trained in effective questioning and assessment to ensure consistency and fairness.

Candidate evaluation and decision making involves collecting and reviewing feedback from interviewers, comparing candidates against job requirements and company culture, involving critical decision makers in the final selection, and balancing objective data with intuitive assessment. Post-interview engagement and offer extension are also crucial, as are maintaining communication with top candidates, extending offers promptly, negotiating terms effectively, conducting reference checks and background verification, and ensuring a positive candidate experience throughout the recruitment journey.

Implementing an ATS for Efficiency

Implementing an ATS is a strategic move in modern recruitment, particularly for efficiently managing cybersecurity talent acquisition. Utilizing an ATS facilitates comprehensive tracking and management of candidates throughout the recruitment process. This system can significantly enhance the organization of applications, making it easier for recruiters to monitor the status of each candidate from the initial application to the final hiring stage. It enables a more structured approach to handling large volumes of applications, a common scenario in high-demand fields like cybersecurity.

An ATS also plays a crucial role in automating repetitive and time-consuming tasks in the recruitment process. This includes tasks such as filtering applications based on predefined criteria, sending automated responses to applicants, and managing the flow of communication. By automating these processes, recruiters can devote more time to strategic aspects of recruitment, such as candidate engagement and interview preparation. Additionally, an ATS helps organize and securely store candidate information. This is particularly important in cybersecurity recruitment, where handling sensitive data with utmost security is paramount. The system ensures that all candidate data is stored in a centralized, secure environment, simplifying data management and compliance with data protection regulations. Streamlining communication and scheduling within the ATS further enhances efficiency. The system can schedule interviews, send reminders, and inform all stakeholders about the recruitment process. This integrated communication approach ensures that candidates and hiring teams are on the same page, thus reducing misunderstandings and scheduling conflicts.

Screening and Shortlisting

In recruiting cybersecurity professionals, establishing criteria for initial resume screening is a fundamental step in screening and shortlisting. This involves clearly defining the essential qualifications, skills, and experiences required for the role. These criteria might include specific technical skills, certifications relevant to cybersecurity, years of experience in the field, and educational background. Setting these clear benchmarks aids recruiters in efficiently sorting through the influx of applications, ensuring that only those candidates who meet the fundamental requirements of the role are considered further.

The next phase includes conducting prescreening calls or assessments and involving key team members in the review process. Prescreening calls are helpful for gauging candidates' communication skills and understanding of the role, while assessments can evaluate technical competencies and problem-solving abilities. Shortlisting candidates based on these evaluations and their potential fit within the company ensures a more targeted selection. Additionally, involving various team members, especially those from the cybersecurity department, in the screening process allows for a more balanced assessment. Their insights can be crucial in determining the candidates' technical aptitude and cultural fit, leading to a more informed and collaborative decision-making process.

Interview Process and Techniques

Structuring interviews for a comprehensive evaluation is critical to selecting the right candidate. This involves planning interviews that assess technical skills and knowledge and explore candidates' problem-solving abilities, adaptability, and cultural fit within the company. A structured approach typically includes a combination of different interview formats. Behavioral interviews focus on understanding how candidates have handled past situations and challenges, giving insight into their soft skills and work ethic. Technical interviews assess the depth of their cybersecurity knowledge and practical skills, which are crucial in this field. Additionally, panel interviews involving multiple team members can provide varied perspectives on the candidate's suitability for the role.

Training interviewers on effective questioning and assessment techniques is crucial to ensure that interviews are informative and fair. Interviewers should be skilled in asking open-ended questions that encourage candidates to provide detailed responses and be aware of objectively evaluating answers. This training helps maintain a high standard of interviewing, thereby ensuring that all candidates are assessed based on their merits and fit for the role. Furthermore, ensuring consistency and fairness in the interview process is essential. All candidates should be evaluated against the same criteria, and steps should be taken to minimize unconscious biases. Consistency in the interview process helps make fair hiring decisions and upholds the integrity and reputation of the company as an equitable employer.

Candidate Evaluation and Decision Making

A systematic approach is essential in the critical stage of candidate evaluation and decision making, particularly cybersecurity recruitment. This begins with collecting and reviewing feedback from all interviewers who interacted with the candidates. Each interviewer's perspective is invaluable, offering insights into the candidate's skills, behavior, and potential fit within the organization. Consolidating this feedback provides a comprehensive view of each candidate, facilitating a more informed and balanced evaluation process. This step ensures that all relevant observations and assessments are considered before making a final decision.

The next phase involves carefully comparing candidates against the specific job requirements and the company's culture. This comparison is about matching technical skills and considering how well the candidate aligns with the company's values and work environment. Involving critical decision makers in this process—typically including hiring managers, HR personnel, and sometimes higher-level executives—ensures that the final selection is made collaboratively, reflecting the team's needs and the broader organizational goals. Balancing objective data from assessments and interviews with intuitive assessments of each candidate's potential contribution to the company is vital. This balanced approach helps in selecting a candidate who is technically proficient and an excellent cultural fit, ultimately contributing to the long-term success of the cybersecurity team and the organization.

Post-Interview Engagement and Offer

After the interview phase in the recruitment process, maintaining engagement with top candidates is crucial. This involves keeping open lines of communication post-interview, updating them on their status, and providing timelines for final decisions. This ongoing engagement is essential for keeping candidates interested and informed and building a positive perception of the company. It reflects the organization's respect for the candidates and their time, contributing to a positive overall candidate experience, regardless of the outcome.

When it comes to extending offers, promptness and effective negotiation are essential. Once a decision is made, extending an offer quickly demonstrates the company's eagerness and commitment to bringing the candidate on board. The negotiation phase should be handled professionally and empathetically, ensuring the terms meet the candidate's expectations and the company's capabilities. Alongside this, conducting thorough reference checks and background verification is crucial, especially in cybersecurity roles where trust and reliability are paramount. Throughout this phase, it is essential to maintain a positive experience for the candidate by ensuring that they feel valued and excited about the prospect of joining the organization. This approach helps secure the best talent and sets the stage for a successful and long-lasting professional relationship.

Cybersecurity Hiring Process Checklist
1. **Planning and Preparation**
    a. Define organizational needs
    b. Develop a recruitment plan
    c. Create job descriptions
    d. Set up a recruitment infrastructure
    e. Assess cybersecurity gaps
    f. Determine the scope of positions
    g. Align hiring with business objectives
    h. Consult with team leaders for role-specific requirements

2. **Developing a Recruitment Plan**
   a. Set clear timelines
   b. Allocate resources
   c. Decide on candidate sourcing channels
   d. Establish a cross-functional hiring team
   e. Draft accurate job descriptions
   f. Ensure legal and diversity compliance
   g. Implement an Applicant Tracking System (ATS)
   h. Prepare tools for candidate assessment
   i. Engage department heads
   j. Train interviewers
   k. Establish clear evaluation criteria

3. **Job Posting and Promotion**
   a. Craft compelling job advertisements
   b. Use SEO for better online visibility
   c. Select appropriate platforms for posting
   d. Regularly refresh postings
   e. Highlight employer branding (culture, values, achievements)
   f. Showcase career development opportunities
   g. Adapt strategies for remote hiring
   h. Address location-specific nuances
   i. Communicate responsively with applicants
   j. Acknowledge applications
   k. Maintain transparency and provide feedback

4. **Applicant Tracking and Management**
   a. Manage applicant tracking through an ATS
   b. Screen and shortlist candidates
   c. Structure interviews
   d. Ensure a fair and consistent interview process

5. **Final Decision Making**
   a. Collect feedback
   b. Compare candidates against job requirements
   c. Engage in post-interview processes
   d. Conduct reference checks
   e. Extend job offers
   f. Ensure a positive candidate experience throughout the hiring journey

6

EFFECTIVE INTERVIEW
STRATEGIES

An effective interview strategy in cybersecurity hiring includes creating a structured interview process, and it starts with designing a clear interview framework. This involves establishing objectives for each stage, developing standardized formats such as behavioral or technical interviews, and incorporating diverse team-member perspectives. Training interviewers in effective questioning techniques, educating them about unconscious biases, and aligning them with role requirements and company values are also crucial aspects. Candidate briefing and logistics, whether for remote or in-person interviews, must be prepared meticulously to ensure a conducive environment for candid discussions.

Practical assessments and traditional questions are integrated into the interview process to evaluate problem-solving and critical-thinking abilities. Continuous improvement is a key focus, with feedback from candidates being used to refine interview strategies. The questions asked during interviews cover technical proficiency, behavioral and situational responses, cultural fit, and communication skills. The evaluation of candidates involves balancing technical expertise and soft skills, using practical tasks to assess technical abilities, and observing interpersonal skills during interviews. Feedback from multiple interviewers and practical assessments is consolidated for unbiased evaluation, and decision making includes discussions within hiring committees, considering candidates' immediate needs and long-term potential, ensuring that selections align with team and organizational goals, and maintaining fairness and transparency throughout the process.

CREATING A STRUCTURED INTERVIEW PROCESS

Creating a structured interview process in cybersecurity hiring involves multiple vital steps. The interview framework is designed with clear objectives for each stage, incorporating standardized formats such as behavioral and technical interviews and determining the sequence and timing of various interview rounds with diverse team member perspectives. Interviewers are prepared through training in effective questioning techniques, education about unconscious biases, alignment on role requirements, and ensuring familiarity with candidates' profiles. Candidate briefing and logistics are meticulously handled, providing clear instructions, arranging logistics for both remote and in-person interviews, and creating a comfortable environment for open discussions. Practical assessments, such as job-related tasks or simulations, are incorporated to evaluate problem-solving and critical-thinking skills, balanced with traditional interview questions, and designed to respect candidates' time. Continuous improvement is emphasized through gathering candidate feedback, regularly reviewing and refining interview strategies, staying updated with best practices, and fostering a culture of continuous learning among interviewers.

Designing the Interview Framework

Designing a practical interview framework begins with establishing clear objectives for each stage. It is important to define what specific skills, experiences, and attributes are essential for the cybersecurity role and ensure that each interview stage is aligned with these requirements. The initial stages might focus on evaluating general technical knowledge and cultural fit, while subsequent rounds could probe deeper into specialized cybersecurity skills and problem-solving capabilities. This approach helps maintain a structured, goal-oriented interview process, which is crucial for fair and relevant assessments.

The balanced development of standardized interview formats, such as behavioral and technical interviews, is critical in assessing a candidate's full capabilities (see Figure 6.1). Behavioral interviews are instrumental in gauging soft skills and determining if the candidate is an excellent cultural fit, essential for team dynamics and long-term success. Technical interviews, on the other hand, focus specifically on the candidate's cybersecurity expertise and problem-solving skills. Balancing these formats provides a comprehensive view of the candidate's overall potential. Determining the sequence and timing of different interview rounds is crucial for streamlining the process. Finally, incorporating diverse perspectives by involving various team members in the interview process enhances the depth and breadth of the evaluation, allowing

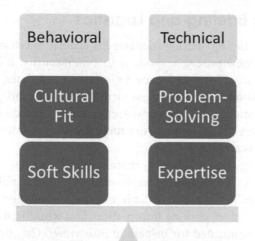

Figure 6.1 A balanced process.

for a more well-rounded assessment of each candidate's abilities and potential fit within the organization.

Preparing Interviewers

Training interviewers on effective questioning techniques is pivotal for successfully recruiting cyber talent. Interviewers should have the skills to craft and ask questions that accurately assess a candidate's cybersecurity technical expertise and problem-solving abilities. More than just querying technical knowledge, these techniques should encourage candidates to share experiences and thought processes, offering insights into their capabilities and potential fit within the organization. This approach gauges their current skills and their ability to grow and adapt to new challenges.

In addition to technical training, preparing interviewers involves educating them about unconscious biases and fair evaluation practices. This is crucial in creating an equitable recruitment process, ensuring that candidates are evaluated based on their merits rather than preconceived notions. Interviewers should also be aligned with the role's specific requirements and the company's core values, ensuring consistency in assessing candidates. Furthermore, interviewers must review candidates' profiles and resumes in advance, allowing for more meaningful and tailored interactions during the interview. This level of preparation demonstrates respect for the candidate's time and contributes to a more engaging and productive interview experience.

Candidate Briefing and Logistics

The candidate briefing and logistics stage is crucial in setting the stage for a successful interview process, especially in cybersecurity. It begins with providing clear instructions and expectations to candidates, which includes detailed information on the interview format, duration, and the types of questions they might expect. This transparency helps candidates prepare effectively and reduces anxiety, leading to a more productive interview where their true capabilities can shine.

Arranging logistics is another critical aspect, whether for remote or in-person interviews. For remote interviews, ensure that candidates can access the necessary technology and a stable internet connection. Details such as the interview location, parking information, and who to ask for upon arrival should be communicated for in-person interviews. Creating a comfortable and conducive environment for candid discussions is also essential. This means setting up a space that is quiet and free from interruptions, where candidates feel at ease to express themselves openly. Providing candidates with comprehensive information about the company and the specific role they are applying for is vital. This helps them understand the context of their potential job and enables them to ask more informed questions, making for a more engaging and insightful dialogue.

Incorporating Practical Assessments

Incorporating practical assessments into the interview process is an effective way to gauge a candidate's real-world skills. It is vital to design job-related tasks or simulations that closely mirror the challenges they would face in the role. These tasks should be crafted to test technical skills along with problem-solving and critical-thinking abilities, which are crucial in cybersecurity roles. Such practical assessments provide a deeper insight into how candidates approach and resolve complex issues and are often more telling than responses to traditional interview questions.

Balancing these practical assessments with traditional interview questions is essential in order to gain a well-rounded understanding of the candidate. While practical tasks assess hands-on abilities, traditional questions can probe into past experiences, theoretical knowledge, and personal attributes. This combination ensures a comprehensive evaluation of both hard and soft skills. Additionally, it is vital to ensure that the tasks are relevant to the job and respectful of the candidates' time. Overly lengthy or irrelevant tasks can be discouraging and may not accurately reflect the candidate's suitability for the role. Instead, tasks should be concise, focused, and reflective of job responsibilities, offering candidates a realistic preview of what the job entails while respecting their time and effort.

Feedback and Continuous Improvement

Feedback and continuous improvement are vital components in refining the interview process, especially in the dynamic field of cybersecurity. Gathering feedback from candidates on their interview experience is an essential step. This feedback can provide valuable insights into the effectiveness and fairness of the interview process, including the clarity of communication, the relevance of the questions asked, and the overall candidate experience. Such insights help identify areas that need improvement and ensure that the process remains candidate-friendly and efficient.

Regularly reviewing and refining interview strategies is another critical aspect. This involves analyzing the effectiveness of different interview stages, from initial screenings to practical assessments, and making necessary adjustments. It is essential to stay updated with the latest best practices in recruitment interviews and then adapt to new trends and technologies to enhance the interview process. This might include incorporating new interviewing tools, updating questionnaires, or revising practical assessments to better align with evolving job requirements in cybersecurity.

Encouraging a culture of continuous learning among interviewers can be achieved through regular training sessions, workshops, and sharing best practices within the team. It is essential that interviewers are skilled in assessing candidates and that they are aware of the latest developments in the cybersecurity field, which can inform more relevant and insightful interviews. By fostering a learning environment, interviewers can continually improve their techniques, ensuring that the organization remains at the forefront of effective and innovative hiring practices.

QUESTIONS TO ASK

In the interview process for cybersecurity positions, a range of questions are crucial for assessing a candidate's suitability. Questions on technical proficiency and knowledge focus on specific cybersecurity skills, problem-solving approaches, past projects, and awareness of emerging trends and technologies. Behavioral and situational questions evaluate adaptability, teamwork, leadership qualities, stress management, and work ethic—often by exploring past experiences to predict future performance. Cultural fit and alignment are assessed through inquiries about candidates' values, professional goals, compatibility with company culture, ethical considerations, and long-term career plans.

Critical thinking and creativity are gauged by posing complex problems, encouraging innovative thinking, and understanding candidates' approaches to learning and decision making in uncertain situations. Communication and collaboration skills are also vital; these are assessed by evaluating the clarity and effectiveness of communication, teamwork abilities, conflict resolution skills, and the ability to explain technical concepts to nontechnical audiences. Discussing candidates' experiences in team-based projects and leadership roles provides further insights into their collaborative and communication skills. These diverse questions collectively help fully understand each candidate's technical and interpersonal capabilities.

Technical Proficiency and Knowledge

Technical proficiency and knowledge are critical areas to focus on when interviewing candidates for cybersecurity roles. To assess specific cybersecurity skills and knowledge, interviewers should prepare questions that directly target the core competencies required for the role. This could include inquiries about their experience with particular security tools, understanding of network architectures, or knowledge of encryption methods. The questions should be tailored to gauge the depth of their technical expertise and their practical application in various scenarios.

Scenario-based queries are particularly effective in evaluating a candidate's problem-solving approaches. These questions place candidates in hypothetical situations related to cybersecurity challenges, asking them to explain how they would respond to or resolve these issues. This approach, as shown in Figure 6.2, offers insight into their critical-thinking and decision-making skills, along with the ability to apply their technical knowledge in real-world situations. Additionally, discussing past projects and experiences in detail can provide valuable context to their skills and approach to work. Candidates should be encouraged to share specific examples of their past work, including challenges they faced and how they overcame them.

An understanding of emerging trends and technologies in cybersecurity is also essential. Candidates should be well-versed in the latest developments in the field, such as advancements in threat detection, new types of cyber threats, or evolving best practices in information security. This shows their commitment to staying current in their field and indicates their potential to contribute to the organization's ongoing efforts to safeguard against evolving cybersecurity threats. Interviewers should engage candidates in discussions

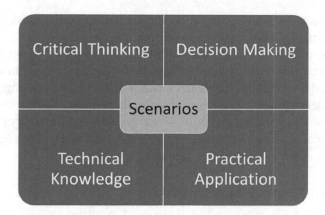

Figure 6.2   The advantages of scenario-based questions.

about these trends and assess their ability to adapt and learn new technologies and methods in the ever-changing cybersecurity landscape.

Behavioral and Situational Questions

Candidates should demonstrate their ability to adapt to changing environments and technologies, which is essential in a constantly evolving field. Questions should be designed to reveal how they have adapted to new tools, methodologies, or team dynamics in the past. Teamwork is another critical aspect; candidates should be able to articulate how they have effectively collaborated in teams, handled conflicts, and contributed to collective goals. Leadership qualities can be explored by asking how they have led projects or guided team members, showcasing their ability to take the initiative and drive the results.

Understanding how candidates handle stress and challenges is equally important. Cybersecurity roles often involve high-pressure situations and tight deadlines. Candidates should be asked about their experiences in handling stressful scenarios, their approach to problem solving under pressure, and strategies for maintaining composure and efficiency during challenging times. This gives insight into their resilience and capacity to maintain performance in demanding environments.

Exploring past experiences to predict future performance is a valuable strategy. By discussing specific examples from their previous roles, candidates can demonstrate their competencies and how they've applied their skills in real-world situations. These discussions can show how they might perform in similar situations. Delving into successes and failures is essential, as the latter can be particularly revealing regarding learning and growth.

Finally, questions that reveal candidates' motivation and work ethic are fundamental. This can include asking why they are interested in cybersecurity, what drives them in their career, and how they approach ongoing learning and development. Their responses indicate their passion for the field, commitment to personal and professional growth, and suitability for the role. It is essential to assess whether their motivation and work ethic align with the company's culture and the role's demands.

Cultural Fit and Alignment

Cultural fit and alignment are essential factors in the hiring process, especially in roles as collaborative and dynamic as those in cybersecurity. Inquiring about candidates' values and professional goals is a crucial first step. This involves asking questions about what they prioritize in their work environment and career. Understanding a candidate's core values, such as their approach to teamwork, attitude toward continuous learning, and perspective on work-life balance, can reveal how well they might integrate into the company's culture.

Another critical aspect is assessing compatibility with the company's culture and team dynamics. This involves evaluating whether the candidate's work style, communication methods, and problem-solving approaches align with those of the current team and the broader organizational ethos. Compatibility with the company culture is crucial for ensuring a cohesive work environment and can significantly impact a candidate's ability to work effectively within the team.

Discussing scenarios to understand candidates' ethical considerations is particularly important in cybersecurity roles, where integrity and ethical judgment are paramount. Presenting hypothetical situations involving ethical dilemmas or decisions can provide insight into how candidates might navigate complex moral issues. Their responses can reveal their ethical standards and decision-making processes when the right course of action is not immediately evident.

Evaluating long-term aspirations and career plans is also beneficial. Understanding a candidate's career trajectory and where they see themselves in the future can help determine if there's a mutual fit. It is essential to assess whether their long-term goals align with the opportunities and career paths available within the organization. This helps identify candidates who are likely to be satisfied and motivated in the role but also aids in building a stable and committed workforce.

Critical Thinking and Creativity

Critical thinking and creativity are indispensable skills in the cybersecurity field, where professionals often face complex and unprecedented challenges. Interviewers should pose complex problems that are relevant to the role in order to assess a candidate's analytical skills. These problems should test the candidate's ability to analyze information, identify critical issues, and apply logical reasoning to develop effective solutions. This approach evaluates their technical expertise and their ability to think critically under pressure.

Encouraging innovative thinking and creative solutions is equally important. Candidates should be prompted to share instances of thinking outside the box or implementing unconventional strategies to solve cybersecurity problems. This can involve asking them to describe a situation where traditional solutions were inadequate and how they devised a novel approach. Their responses can provide insights into their creativity, flexibility, and readiness to innovate in response to new challenges.

Understanding a candidate's approach to learning and development is crucial in a constantly evolving field. Candidates should be questioned about how they stay updated with the latest cybersecurity trends and technologies, their process for learning new skills, and how they apply this knowledge in practical scenarios. This assesses their commitment to professional growth and their ability to continuously adapt their skills and knowledge to the ever-changing cybersecurity landscape.

Cybersecurity professionals often have to make quick decisions when information is incomplete or ambiguous. Interviewers should explore how candidates have handled such situations, focusing on their ability to weigh different options, assess risks, and make informed decisions. This evaluation helps understand how they might perform in similar circumstances, ensuring they can navigate the complexities and uncertainties inherent in cybersecurity roles.

Communication and Collaboration

Assessing clarity and effectiveness in communication is essential in cybersecurity, where conveying complex information accurately and succinctly is crucial. Candidates should be evaluated on their ability to articulate thoughts clearly and effectively in verbal and written forms. This can be assessed through direct questions, scenario-based discussions, and practical exercises that require them to explain complex cybersecurity concepts or report on technical issues. Effective communication is not just about transmitting information but also about ensuring that it is understood by the audience, which is particularly important in cross-functional teams.

Understanding team collaboration and conflict resolution skills is another vital aspect. Cybersecurity is often a collaborative field, requiring professionals to work closely with various teams and departments. Candidates should be asked about their experiences working in team environments, focusing on how they contribute to team efforts, handle disagreements, and resolve conflicts. This can provide insights into their interpersonal skills, their ability to work in a team setting, and their approach to maintaining a harmonious and productive work environment.

Evaluating a candidate's ability to explain technical concepts to nontechnical audiences is increasingly important in the interconnected world of cybersecurity. Candidates should demonstrate their skill in breaking down complex technical issues into understandable terms for stakeholders who may not have a technical background. Additionally, discussing their experiences in team-based projects and leadership roles can shed light on their collaborative nature and leadership potential. This includes understanding their role in the team, the impact of their contributions, and how they have navigated the challenges of leading or being part of a diverse group. This holistic evaluation of communication and collaboration skills ensures the selection of technically proficient candidates who are adept at working effectively within a team and broader organizational context.

EVALUATING CANDIDATES' TECHNICAL AND SOFT SKILLS

Evaluating candidates' technical and soft skills in cybersecurity hiring involves carefully balancing different skill sets. This includes weighing technical expertise against soft skills, identifying essential core skills for the role, recognizing the value of diverse perspectives and abilities, and adapting evaluation criteria to the position's specific requirements. Technical skills are assessed through practical tasks or tests, discussions about industry certifications, evaluation of up-to-date knowledge in cybersecurity practices, and experience with specific tools and technologies.

Soft skills evaluation is equally important, focusing on communication and interpersonal skills, assessing problem solving and adaptability, evaluating teamwork and collaboration, and understanding candidates' self-awareness and emotional intelligence. The process also involves integrating feedback from multiple sources, including input from all interviewers and assessors, using standardized rating scales for unbiased evaluation, considering feedback from practical assessments, and balancing subjective impressions with objective data. Making informed decisions is a crucial final step that involves discussions in hiring committee meetings, considering candidates' immediate needs and long-term potential, aligning selections with team and organizational goals, and ensuring fairness and transparency throughout the decision-making process. This comprehensive approach ensures a holistic evaluation of candidates by considering their technical prowess and ability to thrive within the organizational culture.

Balancing Skill Sets

Balancing skill sets is critical to the hiring process, especially for cybersecurity roles. Weighing technical expertise against soft skills is a delicate but crucial task. While technical skills are undeniably necessary, soft skills are equally vital. Employers must assess both of these aspects to ensure that they hire well-rounded individuals. This balance is essential not only for the immediate requirements of the role but also for long-term success and adaptability within the team and organization.

Identifying core skills essential for the role is the next step. This requires a clear understanding of the job's responsibilities and challenges. For a cybersecurity role, this might include specific technical skills like knowledge of certain security protocols or systems, alongside soft skills like analytical thinking or resilience under pressure. It is essential to have a defined set of criteria that aligns with the organization's immediate and strategic needs.

Recognizing the value of diverse perspectives and abilities in a team is crucial. Diversity in skills and backgrounds can lead to more innovative solutions and a more resilient team. Therefore, evaluation criteria should not be rigid but, instead, adaptable to the position's specific requirements. This might mean prioritizing certain skills over others based on the team's current composition and the organization's future direction. Adaptability in evaluation criteria ensures that the hiring process remains dynamic and responsive to the evolving needs of the cybersecurity field.

Technical Skills Assessment

Technical skills assessment is a fundamental part of hiring for cybersecurity positions. Using practical tasks or tests is an effective way to evaluate a candidate's technical abilities. These tasks should mimic real-world challenges the candidate might face in the role, thereby testing their theoretical knowledge and practical problem-solving skills. This can include hands-on tasks like debugging a piece of code, configuring a network, or responding to a simulated security breach. Such practical evaluations clearly show a candidate's proficiency and performance under realistic conditions.

Discussing industry certifications and ongoing education is important in assessing a candidate's technical skills. Certifications like Certified Information Systems Security Professional, Certified Information Security Manager, or Computer Technology Industry Association Security+ can demonstrate a candidate's commitment to their professional development and mastery of specific cybersecurity areas. Moreover, discussing their ongoing education efforts, such as attending workshops, webinars, or pursuing advanced degrees, can provide insight into their dedication to staying current in a rapidly evolving field.

Assessing up-to-date knowledge in cybersecurity practices involves evaluating how well-versed the candidates are in the latest cybersecurity trends, threats, and technologies. Staying current is essential in this field due to the constant emergence of new threats and the evolution of technology. Finally, evaluating experience with specific tools and technologies that are relevant to the role is essential. This can include familiarity with particular security software, intrusion detection systems, or encryption technologies. Understanding the depth of their experience with these tools can help gauge their readiness to tackle the specific technical challenges they would face in the position.

Soft Skills Evaluation

Observing communication and interpersonal skills during the interview process is vital. This involves listening to what candidates say and noting how they say it. Their ability to articulate thoughts clearly, explain complex ideas, and engage effectively with interviewers provides insight into their potential for effective communication within a team.

Assessing problem solving and adaptability in real time is crucial. This can be achieved through situational questions or tasks that mimic real-world challenges, requiring candidates to think independently. Such assessments show how they might handle unexpected situations or rapidly evolving scenarios that are common in cybersecurity. How candidates approach these problems, adjust their strategies, and find solutions while under pressure reveals their adaptability and problem-solving prowess.

Evaluating teamwork and collaboration during group assessments is another essential component. Group exercises or collaborative tasks can demonstrate how candidates interact with others, contribute to group efforts, and handle conflicts or differences of opinion. These interactions indicate their ability to work well in team settings, a critical skill in most cybersecurity roles where collaboration is often crucial to success.

Understanding candidates' self-awareness and emotional intelligence includes their ability to recognize their strengths and weaknesses, understand their impact on others, and manage their emotions effectively. Candidates with high emotional intelligence are typically better at handling stress, empathizing with team members, and maintaining positive workplace relationships. These traits are invaluable in creating a harmonious and productive work environment.

Integrating Feedback from Multiple Sources

Integrating feedback from multiple sources is critical in making informed hiring decisions, particularly in roles as complex as those in cybersecurity. Consolidating input from all interviewers and assessors ensures a comprehensive view of each candidate. This involves gathering observations and evaluations from everyone who interacted with the candidate, including those who conducted technical interviews, soft skills assessments, and practical exercises. By comparing notes and insights from these various sources, hiring teams can form a more complete and enhanced picture of each candidate's abilities and fit for the role.

Utilizing standardized rating scales for unbiased evaluation is crucial in this process. These scales help quantify the subjective judgments of interviewers, making it easier to compare candidates objectively. Such scales can cover various aspects of the candidate's performance—from technical and problem-solving abilities to communication and teamwork skills. Standardizing how candidates are rated across different criteria minimizes the risk of bias, and the evaluation process becomes more equitable and consistent.

Considering feedback from practical assessments and exercises is also vital. These assessments often provide the most direct evidence of a candidate's abilities and how they might perform in real-world scenarios. It is important to weigh this practical demonstration of skills alongside the impressions and evaluations gathered during interviews.

While objective metrics and standardized ratings are essential for fairness and consistency, subjective impressions can provide valuable insights into a candidate's personality, work ethic, and cultural fit. The challenge lies in striking the right balance between these two types of information, ensuring that hiring decisions are based on a thorough and holistic understanding of each candidate's strengths and potential areas for growth.

Making Informed Decisions

Making informed decisions often begins with discussing candidate profiles in hiring committee meetings. These meetings provide a platform for various stakeholders who are involved in the hiring process to share their insights and evaluations. It is a collaborative effort where each member's perspective on the candidate's skills, experiences, and potential fit within the organization is considered. Such discussions help build a consensus and ensure that different viewpoints are considered before making a final decision.

Considering both the immediate needs and the long-term potential of each candidate is essential. While it is crucial to fill current gaps in skills or expertise, it is also vital to think about how a candidate might grow and contribute to the company in the long run. This involves assessing their potential for professional development, their adaptability to future technological advancements, and their capacity to take on larger or more complex organizational roles.

Aligning candidate selection with team and organizational goals is another critical aspect. This means ensuring that the chosen candidate not only fills the current requirements of the role but also complements the existing team dynamics and contributes to the organization's broader objectives. It is about finding a candidate to help drive the company's strategic vision while thriving in the specific team environment.

Ensuring fairness and transparency in the decision-making process is fundamental. This involves clear communication about the criteria used for selection and the reasons for the final decision, as well as maintaining an unbiased approach throughout the process. Transparency in decision making not only upholds the integrity of the hiring process but also contributes to a positive perception of the company among candidates and employees. By adhering to these principles, organizations can make well-informed, equitable decisions that benefit the company and its workforce.

7

ASSESSING TECHNICAL COMPETENCY

Assessing technical competency in cybersecurity involves designing tailored technical assessments and challenges and utilizing various tools and platforms for thorough evaluation. The process begins with understanding role-specific competencies, identifying the critical technical skills that are required for the role, aligning assessment content with job responsibilities, and ensuring the relevance and practicality of tasks. Creating realistic challenges involves designing simulations and real-world scenarios that reflect current cybersecurity threats, allowing candidates to showcase their problem-solving abilities and creativity.

Balancing the time and complexity of candidate assessments is crucial, as well as setting realistic time frames for completion, avoiding overly complex challenges, and respecting each candidate's time and effort. Ethical considerations are paramount, ensuring confidentiality, data privacy, clear communication of guidelines, and providing equal opportunities for all candidates. Feedback and evaluation criteria include establishing clear criteria for evaluating tasks, providing constructive feedback, using standardized scoring systems, and updating criteria based on industry developments.

Selecting appropriate tools and platforms for technical evaluation is another crucial aspect, as are reviewing the various tools that are available, evaluating their features, and ensuring a positive user experience. Online coding and problem-solving platforms are used for customized tasks that are specific to cybersecurity, while simulation and virtual environment tools create scenarios for practical skills demonstration. Incorporating interactive and collaborative elements, such as collaborative tools for group assessments, allows for observation of teamwork and communication in technical tasks. Finally, analytics and reporting are leveraged for detailed performance insights, tracking progress, identifying strengths and areas for improvement, and utilizing data for fair and informed decision making. This comprehensive approach ensures a thorough and ethical assessment of technical competencies in cybersecurity candidates.

DESIGNING TECHNICAL ASSESSMENTS AND CHALLENGES

Designing technical assessments and challenges for cybersecurity roles involves a detailed understanding of role-specific competencies, including identifying essential technical skills, aligning assessment content with job responsibilities, and ensuring relevance and practicality. The complexity of tasks is carefully balanced with the position level to provide realistic challenges. Simulations and real-world scenarios are created to reflect current cybersecurity threats and trends, allowing candidates to demonstrate their problem-solving abilities and creativity, along with providing a variety of tasks to assess different technical skills.

Time and complexity are balanced by setting realistic assessment time frames and avoiding overly complex challenges that may not reflect the job demands, thereby ensuring that tasks are challenging yet achievable (see Figure 7.1). Ethical considerations are integral to the process, such as maintaining

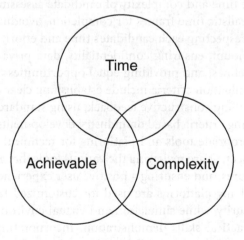

Figure 7.1 Developing technical assessments.

confidentiality and data privacy, avoiding tasks that could lead to unethical behavior, clearly communicating guidelines and expectations, and ensuring equal opportunities for all candidates.

Clear criteria should be established for evaluating technical tasks, providing constructive feedback post-assessment, using standardized scoring systems for unbiased evaluation, and continuously updating these criteria to stay aligned with industry developments. This comprehensive approach ensures a fair, effective, and ethical assessment of each candidate's technical abilities.

Understanding Role-Specific Competencies

Understanding role-specific competencies is essential for effective recruitment, particularly in specialized fields like cybersecurity. The first step involves identifying the critical technical skills required for the role. This requires a thorough analysis of the role's responsibilities and its challenges. For cybersecurity positions, this might include skills in network security, threat analysis, encryption technologies, or experience with specific security tools. Identifying these skills ensures that the recruitment process is targeted and relevant.

The evaluation methods, whether through interviews, practical tests, or scenario-based questions, should directly relate to the role's day-to-day tasks. This ensures that the assessments are theoretically sound and practical, providing a realistic gauge of the candidate's ability to perform in the role. For example, a candidate for a cybersecurity analyst role might be assessed on their ability to detect and respond to security breaches or their proficiency in using specific cybersecurity software.

Ensuring relevance and practicality in the context of the role is critical. The assessment tasks and questions should be designed to reflect real-world situations and challenges that the candidate will likely encounter in the position. This approach helps evaluate how well they can apply their knowledge and skills in practical scenarios.

Finally, balancing the complexity of tasks with the position level is essential. For entry-level positions, the focus might be more on foundational knowledge and the potential for learning. In contrast, for more advanced roles, the assessments might involve complex problem-solving or leadership skills. This balance ensures that candidates are not overwhelmed or under-challenged by the assessment, thus providing a fair and accurate evaluation of their suitability for the role.

Creating Realistic and Practical Challenges

Creating realistic and practical challenges involves designing simulations and real-world scenarios that closely mimic the situations that candidates face on the job. These simulations should be as realistic as possible, encompassing typical tasks, common challenges, and scenarios that require quick thinking and technical acumen. By placing candidates in these simulated environments, employers can clearly understand how they might perform in real-life situations, thereby assessing their practical skills beyond theoretical knowledge.

Incorporating current cybersecurity threats and trends into these scenarios is vital to ensure the relevance of the assessment. The field of cybersecurity is constantly evolving, with new threats emerging regularly. By including recent trends and current threats in the simulations, candidates can demonstrate their up-to-date knowledge and ability to apply it practically. This approach also tests their ability to stay informed and adapt to the rapidly changing cybersecurity landscape.

Providing a range of tasks to assess various technical skills allows for a comprehensive evaluation of the candidate's abilities. These tasks should be diverse enough to cover different aspects of the role, such as threat detection, system security analysis, or incident response. This variety assesses the breadth of their technical skills and allows candidates to demonstrate their problem-solving and creative-thinking abilities. By observing how candidates approach and solve different problems, employers can gain insights into their analytical skills, flexibility, and innovation potential.

Balancing Time and Complexity

Balancing time and complexity in assessments creates a fair and effective recruitment process. Setting realistic time frames for the completion of assessments is the first step. It is essential to allocate enough time for candidates to demonstrate their skills and thought processes without rushing, but also not so much time that the task becomes unrepresentative of the real-world pressures of the job. The time frame should reflect the actual demands they would face in the role, providing a balance between thoroughness and efficiency.

Avoiding overly complex challenges that may not reflect the realities of the job is also essential. While it is crucial to test each candidate's ability to handle challenging situations, the tasks should be grounded in what will likely be encountered in the position. Overcomplicating the assessment can lead to unnecessary stress for candidates and may not accurately gauge their suitability for the job. The focus should be on creating complex scenarios in order to test their skills but still be realistic and relevant to the role.

Ensuring that the tasks are challenging yet achievable is vital to a fair assessment process. The challenges should stretch the candidates' abilities and encourage them to use their skills and knowledge to their fullest extent. However, they should also be designed in a way that is achievable and fair, considering the level of the position being applied for. This approach ensures that candidates are tested on relevant skills and knowledge without being overwhelmed or discouraged. Finally, respecting candidates' time and effort in recruitment is important. This not only involves setting appropriate lengths for assessments but also valuing the effort candidates put into preparing and completing these tasks. A respectful and considerate approach to each candidate's time reflects positively on the organization and contributes to a positive candidate experience.

Ethical Considerations in Technical Testing

Ethical considerations play a vital role in technical testing, especially in cybersecurity, where handling sensitive information is a daily occurrence. Ensuring confidentiality and data privacy in assessments involves safeguarding any personal or sensitive information that candidates may come across during the testing process. It is crucial to design assessments so they do not expose confidential data or compromise security protocols. The integrity of the testing process must be maintained to uphold the candidates' trust and adhere to legal and ethical standards.

Avoiding tasks that could lead to unethical hacking or data misuse is also essential. The challenges and scenarios presented to candidates should be carefully constructed to prevent any activities that border on unethical practices, such as unauthorized access or exploitation of systems and data. This is particularly important in cybersecurity roles, where ethical boundaries must be clearly defined and respected. It is vital to ensure that the tasks align with ethical hacking guidelines and professional standards of conduct.

Candidates should be fully informed about the nature of the tasks, the rules governing the execution of those tasks, and the ethical standards they are expected to uphold. This transparency helps to set a clear framework for what is acceptable and what is not, reducing the likelihood of misunderstandings or unethical conduct during the assessment.

Providing equal opportunities for all candidates is crucial to ensure a fair and unbiased testing process. This means creating an assessment environment that does not favor specific candidates due to their background or other factors unrelated to their skills and abilities. The focus should be on creating a level playing field where all candidates have an equal chance to showcase their skills and are evaluated based on their merit and suitability for the role. This approach not only upholds ethical standards in recruitment but also enhances the diversity and quality of the talent pool.

Feedback and Evaluation Criteria

Establish clear criteria to evaluate technical tasks. These criteria should be well-defined, transparent, and directly related to the job requirements. They should cover various aspects of the tasks, such as accuracy, creativity in problem solving, efficiency, and adherence to best practices. With these criteria in place, assessors can ensure that each candidate is evaluated fairly and consistently based on the same standards. Table 7.1 covers various aspects of a candidate's performance in a cybersecurity role, providing balanced feedback that recognizes strengths and highlights areas for improvement. Remember, constructive feedback aims to encourage development and growth, so it should be delivered in a supportive and positive manner.

Providing constructive feedback to candidates *post-assessment* should highlight areas of strength and offer insights into areas for improvement. Constructive feedback helps candidates understand how they performed concerning the set criteria and can be a valuable learning experience, regardless of the outcome of their application. It reflects well on the organization's commitment to candidate development and maintains a positive relationship with potential future talent.

Using standardized scoring systems for unbiased evaluation is essential in maintaining fairness throughout the assessment process. Such systems help consistently quantify performance, thereby reducing the influence of subjective biases. Standardized scores enable a more objective comparison between candidates, ensuring that decisions are based on merit and aligned with the criteria.

Updating the criteria based on industry developments is vital, especially in fast-evolving fields like cybersecurity. As new technologies emerge and industry best practices evolve, the evaluation criteria should be reviewed and updated accordingly. This ensures that the assessment process remains relevant and aligned with current industry standards, thus attracting and identifying candidates who are equipped to handle contemporary challenges. Keeping the evaluation criteria up-to-date enhances the effectiveness of the hiring process and positions the organization as a forward-thinking and adaptive employer.

Table 7.1 Useful feedback for candidates.

Area of Evaluation	Constructive Feedback Statement	Questions for Reflection
Technical Skills	Your ability to identify vulnerabilities was strong, but there was some difficulty in implementing effective countermeasures.	How do you plan to enhance your skills in implementing cybersecurity solutions?
Problem Solving	You demonstrated good analytical skills, but there were instances where quicker decision making could have been beneficial.	Can you think of alternative approaches to the problems you faced during the assessment?
Communication Skills	Your technical communication is clear, but simplifying complex concepts for nontechnical stakeholders could be improved.	How might you explain a complex cybersecurity issue to someone without a technical background?
Team Collaboration	While you work well independently, greater engagement with the team could lead to more comprehensive cybersecurity strategies.	What strategies might you use to improve collaboration with your team in future projects?
Adaptability	You showed adaptability in dynamic situations, but there were moments of hesitation when faced with unexpected challenges.	What steps could you take to feel more prepared for unexpected cybersecurity challenges?
Attention to Detail	Your attention to detail in some areas was commendable, yet in others, especially in documentation, there was room for improvement.	What methods could you employ to ensure consistency in your attention to detail across all tasks?
Ethical Understanding	You have a strong ethical foundation, but applying these principles in practical scenarios can be further developed.	How do you balance ethical considerations with practical cybersecurity needs in real-world situations?
Continuous Learning	Your eagerness to learn is evident, but applying new knowledge to practical situations could be more consistent.	What areas of cybersecurity are you most interested in pursuing for further learning and development?

TOOLS AND PLATFORMS FOR TECHNICAL EVALUATION

In cybersecurity recruitment, selecting appropriate tools and platforms for technical evaluation is important. This involves reviewing various tools that are available for technical assessments, evaluating their features and capabilities, considering the user experience for candidates and recruiters, and ensuring compatibility with company systems and requirements. Online coding and problem-solving platforms are utilized for conducting coding tests and algorithm challenges, with tasks customized to the cybersecurity domain, enabling real-time performance monitoring and practical remote assessments.

Simulation and virtual environment tools are crucial in creating virtual settings for network and system security tasks, simulating cybersecurity incidents, and allowing candidates to demonstrate their practical skills in a controlled environment. These simulations assess a candidate's abilities to navigate and resolve complex security situations. Interactive and collaborative elements are integrated into the assessment process through collaborative tools for group assessments, observing teamwork and communication skills during technical tasks, and allowing for interaction with the hiring team. Scenarios that require critical thinking and team coordination are provided to evaluate a candidate's skills even further.

Use analytics to gain detailed performance insights, track candidate progress, and identify areas of strength and improvement. Data is utilized for fair and informed decision making, ensuring that feedback that is provided to the candidates aligns with the assessment data and observations. This structured approach to using tools and platforms ensures a comprehensive and fair evaluation of each candidate's technical competencies in cybersecurity.

Selecting Appropriate Tools and Platforms

Selecting appropriate tools and platforms for technical assessments is a critical step in the recruitment process, particularly in fields that require specialized skills like cybersecurity. The first stage involves a comprehensive review of the various tools and platforms available for conducting these assessments. This review should encompass various options, from coding challenge platforms to simulation environments that are tailored for cybersecurity scenarios. Each tool should be evaluated for suitability in assessing the specific skills required for the role, ensuring that it aligns with the job's technical demands and the organization's overall recruitment strategy.

Assess the robustness of the testing environment, the types of tasks it can simulate, and its ability to provide accurate and insightful evaluations of a candidate's skills. Factors like security, scalability, and the ability to customize assessments according to specific job requirements are also important considerations. Moreover, the platform's ability to integrate with other human resources (HR) tools and systems for a seamless recruitment process is essential for efficient candidate tracking, data management, and reporting.

For candidates, the platform should offer a straightforward, intuitive interface and a fair testing environment that accurately reflects the skills and knowledge that are required for the role. For recruiters and hiring managers, the platform should offer ease of use in setting up and administering assessments, along with analyzing and interpreting the results. Ensuring compatibility with the company's existing systems and requirements will facilitate a smooth and efficient recruitment process. The chosen platform should be technically robust, feature-rich, user-friendly, and aligned with the organization's technological infrastructure and hiring objectives.

Online Coding and Problem-Solving Platforms

Online coding and problem-solving platforms have become increasingly important tools in recruiting technical roles. Utilizing these platforms for coding tests and algorithm challenges offers a practical and efficient way to assess a candidate's technical skills. These platforms typically provide a wide range of coding challenges and scenarios that test various aspects of a candidate's programming abilities and problem-solving approach. The challenges range from basic coding exercises to complex algorithmic problems, offering a comprehensive assessment of a candidate's technical proficiency.

Customizing tasks and problems that are specific to cybersecurity is an essential aspect of using these platforms effectively. This involves tailoring the challenges to reflect real-world cybersecurity scenarios, such as creating secure code, identifying vulnerabilities, or solving encryption-related problems. By customizing the tasks, employers can gain insights into how candidates might handle specific cybersecurity challenges, thus assessing their skills in a context that is directly relevant to the role. This customization ensures that the assessment is not only a test of generic coding abilities but also a reflection of the skills required in cybersecurity.

Monitoring performance in real time and facilitating remote assessments effectively are critical benefits of these platforms. Many offer features that allow recruiters and technical assessors to observe candidates' problem-solving processes as they happen, providing deeper insights into their approach and methodology. This real-time monitoring can reveal how candidates handle pressure, think critically, and adapt to challenging problems. Furthermore, these platforms make it easier to conduct assessments remotely, breaking down geographical barriers and broadening the talent pool. They offer a standardized and scalable way to evaluate candidates from anywhere, ensuring a consistent and fair assessment process that is accessible and convenient for both candidates and recruiters.

Simulation and Virtual Environment Tools

Simulation and virtual environment tools are increasingly utilized in the recruitment process, offering a dynamic and practical approach to candidate assessment. Creating virtual environments for network and system security tasks allows candidates to engage in hands-on activities that closely mimic real-world scenarios. These environments can simulate a range of situations, from securing a network to identifying and mitigating vulnerabilities in a system. This approach offers a more accurate assessment of a candidate's practical skills and ability to apply theoretical knowledge in real-world contexts.

Simulating cybersecurity incidents and response scenarios is another significant application of these tools. They can replicate various types of cyber threats and attacks, such as phishing, ransomware, or distributed denial-of-service attacks, and require candidates to respond as they would in an actual situation. This type of simulation tests not only their technical skills but also their ability to work under pressure and make quick, informed decisions. It provides insights into how they would handle emergencies, manage crisis communication, and implement recovery procedures.

Allowing candidates to demonstrate their practical skills in a controlled setting is critical to assessing their real-world capabilities. These virtual environments provide a safe space for candidates to showcase their ability to navigate and resolve complex security situations without the risk of real-world repercussions. This setup benefits both candidates and employers; candidates can prove their skills in a realistic setting, while employers can evaluate their competence more tangibly and meaningfully. These simulations are critical in determining a candidate's readiness to handle the specific challenges and responsibilities of a cybersecurity role while ensuring that the hiring decisions are based on comprehensive and practical assessments.

Integrating Interactive and Collaborative Elements

Integrating interactive and collaborative elements into the recruitment process is increasingly important, particularly for roles in the cybersecurity sector where teamwork and communication are critical. Using collaborative tools for group assessments is an effective way to evaluate these skills. These tools can facilitate group activities where candidates work together to solve problems, complete projects, or respond to simulated scenarios. This group dynamic allows assessors to observe a candidate's abilities to communicate, collaborate, and contribute effectively within a team setting.

Observing teamwork and communication during technical tasks offers valuable insights into how candidates interact with others under technical and potentially stressful conditions. It is crucial to see how they share information, divide tasks, negotiate solutions, and manage conflicts. These interactions provide a realistic view of their potential fit within an existing team and their ability to contribute to collaborative efforts in a professional environment.

Another beneficial approach is allowing for interaction with the hiring team during assessments. This interaction can be Q&A sessions, discussions, or collaborative problem-solving exercises. It allows candidates to demonstrate their communication and teamwork skills and provides a glimpse into how they would interact with potential colleagues and superiors. Moreover, it allows the hiring team to assess the candidate's interpersonal skills and ability to integrate into the team's culture.

Providing scenarios that require critical thinking and team coordination should challenge candidates to work together to solve complex problems, requiring a combination of technical skills, critical thinking, and effective communication. Such tasks can reveal how candidates approach problem solving in a team context, their willingness to listen to others' ideas, their ability to lead or follow as required, and their compatibility with collaborative work environments. By integrating these interactive and collaborative elements into the assessment process, employers can make more informed hiring decisions, thereby ensuring that new hires are technically proficient and influential team players.

Analytics and Reporting for Evaluation

Leveraging analytics for detailed performance insights allows hiring teams to understand each candidate's abilities better. Advanced analytics tools can break down a candidate's assessment performance into metrics such as speed, accuracy, and problem-solving efficiency. These insights are invaluable in objectively assessing a candidate's technical skills and problem-solving abilities. Moreover, analytics can highlight patterns and trends in a candidate's responses, providing a comprehensive view of a candidate's strengths and weaknesses.

Tracking progress and identifying critical areas of strength and improvement is another significant benefit of using analytics. By analyzing a candidate's performance throughout different assessments or tasks, recruiters can identify areas where a candidate excels and where further development may be necessary. This information is not only helpful in making hiring decisions but also for providing targeted feedback to candidates. It helps create a transparent and constructive dialogue about each candidate's capabilities and potential areas for growth, which can benefit the candidate's professional development.

Utilizing data for fair and informed decision making is crucial in the recruitment process. Data-driven evaluations help mitigate biases and ensure that decisions are based on objective criteria. By relying on analytics and standardized reporting, hiring teams can make decisions that are justifiable and grounded in evidence. Additionally, ensuring that feedback to candidates aligns with the assessment data and observations is essential. Feedback should be consistent with the analytics and reflect what was observed during the assessments. This consistency reinforces the feedback's credibility and the overall integrity of the evaluation process. By integrating analytics and reporting effectively, organizations can enhance the fairness, accuracy, and efficiency of their recruitment evaluations, which will ultimately lead to better hiring outcomes.

8

BUILDING A CYBERSECURITY INTERNSHIP PROGRAM

Building a cybersecurity internship program brings multifaceted benefits and establishes a structured platform for nurturing future talent. Such programs provide practical experience to interns, complementing their academic learning and creating a talent pipeline for future hiring, thereby enhancing the industry's overall skill level and preparedness. The program facilitates mutual learning and development, offering fresh perspectives to the organization while enabling current employees to develop mentorship and leadership skills. It strengthens industry relations through connections with educational institutions and enhances the company's reputation within the cybersecurity community.

Cost-effective resource utilization is another significant benefit since interns provide the additional workforce for projects without long-term commitments, which also helps reduce recruitment costs. The program also reflects the company's commitment to corporate social responsibility by contributing to closing the skills gap in cybersecurity and supporting diversity and inclusion in tech.

Structuring the internship involves defining clear objectives that are aligned with organizational goals, creating meaningful projects and roles that offer genuine learning opportunities, and ensuring the integration of interns into teams. Regular monitoring, feedback, and end-of-internship evaluations are crucial for the program's success and for the professional growth of the interns. Mentorship and guidance are integral to selecting and training interns, establishing structured mentor-intern relationships, focusing on personal and professional development, and building a supportive environment. The program also aims to provide long-term career guidance, offer advice on career paths, assist with networking, and aid in portfolio and resume development. This comprehensive approach, illustrated in Figure 8.1, ensures that the

Figure 8.1   Structuring balanced and meaningful internships.

internship program benefits both the interns and the organization, fostering a robust future workforce in cybersecurity.

BENEFITS AND IMPORTANCE

A cybersecurity internship program offers substantial benefits and importance, primarily fostering future talent by nurturing the next generation of professionals and providing practical experience to complement academic learning—ultimately creating a talent pipeline for future organizational needs while enhancing the industry's skill level. The program facilitates mutual learning and development by injecting fresh perspectives and innovative ideas into the organization while allowing current employees to develop mentorship and leadership skills through knowledge exchange with interns and to adapt to new technologies and methods introduced by younger generations. It also strengthens industry relations by building connections with educational institutions and by enhancing the company's reputation in the cybersecurity community. Cost-effective resource utilization is another advantage because it provides an additional workforce for projects and a means to assess potential employees in a real-world context, which may reduce recruitment costs. The program underlines the company's commitment to corporate social responsibility by contributing to closing the skills gap in cybersecurity, supporting diversity and inclusion in tech, and engaging in community outreach and educational programs.

Fostering Future Talent

In the rapidly evolving field of cybersecurity, fostering the next generation of professionals is crucial for meeting future challenges and maintaining a robust security posture. This involves nurturing emerging talent by providing opportunities that complement their academic learning with practical, real-world experience. Initiatives such as internships, mentorship programs, and collaborative projects with educational institutions can offer valuable hands-on experience to aspiring cybersecurity professionals. These opportunities not only help students and recent graduates apply their theoretical knowledge in practical settings but they also allow them to understand the nuances and complexities of working in cybersecurity.

Moreover, creating a talent pipeline for future hiring needs is essential for organizations to ensure a continuous influx of skilled professionals. This can be achieved by establishing relationships with universities, participating in career fairs, and offering cybersecurity-related scholarships or research funding. These efforts not only aid in identifying and attracting early talent but also enhance the industry's overall skill level and preparedness. By investing in the development of future talent, organizations play a pivotal role in shaping the cybersecurity landscape, ensuring that the industry remains dynamic, innovative, and capable of addressing emerging threats and challenges.

Mutual Learning and Development

Mutual learning and development are crucial to a dynamic work environment, especially in fields like cybersecurity, where continuous evolution is the norm. Young professionals, including interns and recent graduates, often bring fresh perspectives and innovative ideas to the organization. Their insights, drawn from recent academic experiences or familiarity with cutting-edge technologies, can inspire new approaches and solutions to cybersecurity challenges. This infusion of fresh ideas not only stimulates innovation within the organization but keeps it abreast of the latest trends and methodologies in the field.

Moreover, emerging talent provides an excellent opportunity for current employees to develop their mentorship and leadership skills. By guiding and supporting less experienced colleagues, seasoned professionals can hone their leadership abilities, improve their communication skills, and gain a renewed understanding of their field through teaching. Encouraging a knowledge exchange between interns, new staff, and full-time employees fosters a collaborative learning environment. This exchange can take many forms, such as joint projects, team meetings, or informal mentoring sessions, and is beneficial for all parties involved. It allows experienced staff to share their practical knowledge and insights while newer team members can introduce fresh perspectives and ideas.

Additionally, adapting to new technologies and methods brought in by younger generations is vital for keeping the organization current and competitive. Young professionals often have a natural proficiency with new tools and platforms, and their knowledge can help streamline processes and introduce more efficient working methods. Embracing these new technologies and methodologies enhances the organization's capabilities and demonstrates a commitment to staying at the forefront of the cybersecurity field. This adaptability is critical to fostering a culture of continuous learning and innovation within the organization.

Strengthening Industry Relations

Strengthening industry relations fosters a robust network that benefits the company and the wider industry. Building connections with educational institutions and communities is fundamental to this strategy. By forming partnerships with universities, technical colleges, and online learning communities, organizations can tap into emerging talent and contribute to the educational process. These relationships offer mutual benefits—students gain practical insights and opportunities while companies access a pool of potential recruits with the latest knowledge and skills.

Enhancing the company's reputation within the cybersecurity community can be achieved by actively participating in industry conferences, seminars, and online forums and contributing to thought leadership through research publications and speaking engagements. A strong industry presence elevates the company's profile and positions it as a key player and influencer in cybersecurity. Collaborating on projects that mutually benefit academia and industry is another practical approach. Joint research projects, internships, and collaborative workshops can bridge the gap between theoretical knowledge and practical application, enriching the learning experience for students and providing valuable insights for the industry.

Furthermore, contributing to the broader cybersecurity ecosystem is essential. This can involve initiatives like sponsoring cybersecurity competitions, offering training programs for professionals, or engaging in community outreach programs to raise awareness about cybersecurity threats and best practices. Such contributions not only enhance the industry's overall skill level and preparedness but also demonstrate the organization's commitment to advancing the field and addressing the growing challenges in cybersecurity. This holistic approach to strengthening industry relations is crucial for the ongoing development and resilience of the cybersecurity sector.

Cost-Effective Resource Utilization

Cost-effective resource utilization is a strategic approach in the cybersecurity industry that is particularly beneficial in managing workforce needs and recruitment costs. One of the key advantages of this approach is gaining an additional workforce for projects without the necessity of long-term commitments. Temporary or contract-based roles, including interns or freelancers, can be invaluable for specific projects or peak work periods. This flexible staffing model allows companies to scale their workforce up or down as needed, providing agility and efficiency while managing labor costs effectively.

Internship programs or temporary positions also offer a unique opportunity to assess potential employees in a real-world context. Rather than relying solely on interviews and resumes, companies can evaluate candidates based on their performance and contributions in a work setting. This approach can lead to more informed hiring decisions by providing a clearer picture of a candidate's skills, work ethic, and compatibility with the company's culture.

Additionally, utilizing interns or contract workers can significantly reduce recruitment costs. Companies can build a proven talent pool to hire for permanent positions, minimizing the need for extensive external recruitment efforts. This internal talent pipeline often includes candidates who are already familiar with the company's operations and culture, thereby reducing the time and resources needed for onboarding and training.

Interns, in particular, can be a valuable resource for research and development initiatives. They often bring fresh perspectives and up-to-date academic knowledge, which can be particularly useful in innovative projects or exploring new technological frontiers. By involving interns in research and development, companies can accelerate their innovation efforts while providing meaningful educational experiences for the interns.

Corporate Social Responsibility

Corporate social responsibility (CSR) in the context of cybersecurity goes beyond traditional business practices by encompassing a commitment to education and professional development while also addressing broader industry challenges. Demonstrating a commitment to education and professional development is essential for companies in the tech industry. This can be achieved by investing in training programs, offering scholarships, and supporting continuous employee learning opportunities. Such initiatives not only enhance the workforce's skill set but also signal the company's dedication to the growth and advancement of its employees, thus fostering a culture of knowledge and innovation.

Contributing to closing the skills gap in cybersecurity is another critical aspect of CSR. Cybersecurity is rapidly evolving, and the demand for skilled professionals often outpaces the supply. Companies can play a pivotal role in equipping individuals with the necessary skills by partnering with educational institutions to develop relevant curricula, offering internships, and facilitating workshops or boot camps. These efforts help build a more competent and prepared workforce, which is important for tackling the complex cybersecurity challenges of the modern world.

Supporting diversity and inclusion in the tech industry is also vital to CSR. This involves creating an inclusive work environment, promoting diverse hiring practices, and supporting initiatives that encourage underrepresented groups to pursue careers in tech and cybersecurity. Embracing diversity enriches the workplace and leads to more innovative and comprehensive solutions in cybersecurity since diverse teams bring various perspectives and ideas.

Engaging in community outreach and educational programs reflects a company's commitment to societal well-being. This can include organizing awareness campaigns on cybersecurity threats, offering training for small businesses or vulnerable groups, and participating in community events. These activities help raise public awareness about cybersecurity, promote safe online practices, and position the company as a responsible and community-oriented organization. Through these CSR efforts, companies in the cybersecurity industry can make a significant impact, not just within their organizations but also in the broader community and industry in which they operate. A table of possible activities is shown in Table 8.1.

Table 8.1   Possible activities.

Activity Type	Description	Expected Impact
Awareness Campaigns	Organize campaigns to inform the public about common cybersecurity threats, such as phishing, malware, etc.	Increases public knowledge and vigilance against cyber threats.
Training for Small Businesses	Offer specialized cybersecurity training sessions for small business owners to protect their digital assets.	Empowers small businesses with knowledge to defend against cyberattacks.
Workshops for Vulnerable Groups	Conduct workshops for groups, such as seniors or students, teaching them about online safety and privacy.	Enhances the digital literacy and safety of vulnerable community members.
Participation in Community Events	Actively participate in local community events to promote cybersecurity awareness.	Fosters community engagement and positions the company as a community partner.
Educational Programs in Schools	Partner with schools to provide educational programs on safe online practices and cyber ethics.	Prepares the younger generation for the challenges of the digital world.
Public Webinars on Cybersecurity	Host free webinars on various cybersecurity topics and make them accessible to the general public.	Broadens the reach of cybersecurity education to a wider audience.
Collaboration with Nonprofits	Collaborate with nonprofit organizations to extend cybersecurity support to underprivileged communities.	Aids in bridging the digital divide and enhancing cybersecurity for all.
Sponsorship of Cybersecurity Events	Sponsor and participate in events like cybersecurity conferences or hackathons.	Contributes to the growth and development of the cybersecurity community.

STRUCTURING THE INTERNSHIP

Structuring a cybersecurity internship program involves several key steps, starting with defining clear objectives and outcomes that align with organizational goals, setting achievable goals for interns, and determining the program's scope and duration, along with metrics for success and evaluation. Creating meaningful projects and roles is essential to ensuring that they offer real value and learning opportunities, are relevant to both the company's needs and the interns' career goals, and balance challenging tasks and appropriate support. Integration into the team is facilitated through effective onboarding, encouraging interaction with various departments, and fostering a sense of belonging and contribution. Regular monitoring and feedback are crucial, with check-ins and progress reviews, constructive feedback and guidance, and the flexibility to adjust projects and roles based on intern performance and interests. At the end of the internship, thorough evaluations are conducted to assess the possibility of full-time roles or future opportunities. These evaluations offer career advice and guidance for professional development and will serve to maintain connections with former interns for ongoing networking and collaboration.

Defining Objectives and Outcomes

When establishing an internship program, particularly in a specialized field like cybersecurity, aligning the program with the organization's broader goals is crucial. This alignment ensures that the program offers valuable learning experiences for interns and contributes meaningfully to the company's objectives—such as advancing specific projects, exploring new technologies, or enhancing the organization's cybersecurity posture. Defining clear and achievable objectives for interns is also essential. These objectives should be tailored to provide interns with real-world experience and skills development while contributing to the organization's needs. Setting specific goals helps interns understand what is expected of them and what they can aspire to achieve during their tenure.

The program should be structured to allow sufficient time for interns to engage deeply with their projects and integrate into the team. Still, it should also be concise enough to maintain focus and momentum. Establishing metrics for success and evaluation methods is critical for assessing the effectiveness of the internship program. These metrics might include project completion, skills acquired, contributions to team objectives, and feedback from supervisors and peers. Regular evaluation against these metrics provides valuable insights into how well the program meets its objectives, both for the interns' professional development and the organization's benefit. This structured approach to defining objectives and outcomes ensures that the internship program is mutually beneficial and aligned with the organization's strategic goals.

Creating Meaningful Projects and Roles

It is essential to design projects that offer real value and substantial learning opportunities. The projects that are assigned to interns should contribute to the company's objectives while also enhancing the interns' understanding of the cybersecurity landscape. This involves creating roles that are tailored to be relevant to both the company's current needs and the intern's career aspirations. By aligning projects with the latest trends and challenges in cybersecurity, interns can gain hands-on experience that complements their academic knowledge, making their time both educational and impactful.

Furthermore, it is essential to balance challenging task assignments while also providing appropriate support. Interns should be encouraged to take on responsibilities that stretch their capabilities, thereby fostering growth and confidence. However, this should be coupled with adequate guidance and support from experienced team members to ensure a productive learning environment. Additionally, providing opportunities for interns to contribute to significant projects reinforces the value of their role within the company. This involvement enhances their learning experience and allows them to make tangible contributions, fostering a sense of accomplishment and professional development. By carefully crafting these roles and projects, companies can create a mutually beneficial environment where interns can actively contribute to essential initiatives while developing their skills and professional network.

Integration into the Team

Successfully integrating interns into the team begins with a comprehensive onboarding experience introducing interns to the company's culture, practices, and expectations. This initial phase is crucial for helping interns acclimate to the professional environment and understand the organization's ethos and work ethic. An effective onboarding process covers everything from company policies and security protocols to team dynamics and the company's strategic goals.

Once onboarded, integrating interns into existing teams and projects is the next critical step. This involves assigning them to specific projects where they can work alongside experienced team members, providing a real-world context to apply their theoretical knowledge. Encouraging interaction and collaboration with various departments within the company broadens their experience and understanding of cybersecurity work. This cross-departmental collaboration can be enriching, exposing interns to diverse perspectives and approaches within the field.

Fostering a sense of belonging and contribution makes interns feel valued and motivated. Inclusion in team meetings, brainstorming sessions, and social events can help interns feel like a part of the team, enhancing their engagement and commitment to their projects. Recognizing their contributions, whether through feedback, acknowledgment in team settings, or opportunities to present their work, reinforces their sense of belonging and the value they bring to the organization.

Monitoring and Feedback

An integral component of a successful internship program is the implementation of regular check-ins and progress reviews. These periodic assessments allow for monitoring the interns' progress, ensuring they are on track with their projects and are effectively integrating into the team. Regular check-ins provide a structured opportunity for interns to discuss their experiences, raise any concerns, and seek guidance on their tasks. This ongoing dialogue is crucial for keeping the interns engaged and aligned with the company's goals while allowing supervisors to closely observe their development and contributions.

Feedback should be specific, actionable, and aimed at helping interns improve their skills and understanding of the cybersecurity domain. It is also essential to adjust projects and roles based on each intern's performance and evolving interests. This flexibility ensures that the internship remains dynamic and responsive to the intern's learning curve and emerging preferences. Additionally, soliciting feedback from interns about their experiences is essential for the continuous improvement of the program. Their insights into what works well and what could be enhanced are invaluable for refining the structure, content, and management of future internship cycles. This two-way feedback process benefits the current interns and contributes to the long-term success and relevance of the internship program.

End-of-Internship Evaluation and Transition

The end-of-internship phase is crucial in an internship program, especially in a specialized field like cybersecurity. Conducting thorough evaluations after the internship provides valuable insights into the interns' performance, growth, and overall contribution to the company. This evaluation should encompass technical skills and project accomplishments and aspects like teamwork, problem-solving abilities, and adaptability. It is an opportunity to assess the extent to which the internship has been mutually beneficial and to recognize the achievements of the interns.

Upon completing the internship, considering options for full-time roles or identifying future opportunities within the company can be a natural next step for outstanding performers. Interns with exceptional skills and a strong fit with the company culture can be valuable assets as full-time employees. Even if immediate hiring isn't feasible, keeping the door open for future opportunities benefits both parties. Offering career advice and guidance is also essential to the transition process. Providing feedback on professional development, advising on career paths within cybersecurity, and helping interns understand the industry landscape can significantly impact their future career choices and success.

Maintaining connections with former interns is vital to building a solid professional network. Encouraging them to stay in touch through alumni networks, professional social media connections, or company events fosters ongoing relationships. These connections can lead to future collaboration, networking opportunities, and even potential rehiring as the former interns advance in their careers. By investing in these relationships, companies not only support the interns' professional growth but also enrich their talent network, which can be a valuable resource for future projects and collaborations.

MENTORSHIP AND GUIDANCE

In a cybersecurity internship program, mentorship and guidance play a pivotal role, starting with selecting and training mentors with the right skills and temperament for practical guidance. These mentors are provided with the necessary training and resources, and expectations and responsibilities are established to foster a culture of mentorship within the organization. Structured mentor-intern relationships are formed based on matching skills, interests, and goals, with regular meetings and communication channels facilitating hands-on experience and insights. The program emphasizes personal and professional development by focusing on technical and soft skills, encouraging interns to set learning and career objectives, and assisting in creating professional development plans. Build a supportive environment where interns feel welcomed, included, and valued as part of the team, with access to necessary resources, tools, and learning materials. Additionally, long-term career guidance should be offered, including advice on career paths, assistance with networking and professional connections, guidance in portfolio and resume development, and providing references and recommendations for future opportunities. This comprehensive mentorship approach ensures that interns receive valuable learning experiences, thus contributing to their professional growth in the cybersecurity field.

Selecting and Training Mentors

The selection and training of mentors are critical components of any successful mentorship program, particularly in technical and specialized fields like cybersecurity. Identifying employees who possess not only the requisite technical skills and knowledge but also the right temperament for mentorship is essential. Ideal mentors are those who demonstrate strong communication skills, patience, and a genuine interest in nurturing others' growth. They should be individuals who are respected in their roles and have a deep understanding of the company's culture and values.

Once suitable mentors are identified, it is crucial to provide them with the necessary training and resources to guide their mentees effectively. This training might include workshops on coaching techniques, communication skills, and ways to provide constructive feedback. It is also beneficial to equip mentors with resources that can help them address their mentees' specific career development needs, such as training materials, professional development plans, and access to networking opportunities. Establishing clear expectations and responsibilities for mentors is another crucial aspect. This includes defining the scope of their mentorship role, the frequency of meetings with mentees, and the goals to be achieved through the mentorship relationship.

Encouraging a culture of mentorship within the organization is vital for the program's sustainability. This involves promoting mentorship as a valued activity within the company, recognizing and rewarding effective mentorship, and creating opportunities for mentors to share their experiences and learn from each other. By fostering a culture where mentorship is viewed as integral to professional development and organizational growth, companies can enhance knowledge-sharing employee engagement and, ultimately, build a more skilled and cohesive workforce.

Structured Mentor-Intern Relationships

Pair interns with mentors based on careful consideration of skills, interests, and professional goals. This tailored approach ensures the mentorship is relevant and beneficial to both parties. The mentors, with their depth of experience and knowledge in specific areas of cybersecurity, can provide guidance that resonates with the intern's aspirations and learning objectives. By aligning these elements, the mentor-intern relationship becomes a powerful tool for personal and professional development, allowing for the transfer of valuable skills and knowledge.

Facilitating regular meetings and open communication channels between mentors and interns is essential for nurturing this relationship. Scheduled in-person or virtual interactions allow interns to seek advice, discuss challenges, and gain insights from their mentors' experiences. These interactions should be more than just check-ins; they should be avenues for meaningful dialogue and hands-on learning experiences. Encouraging mentors to share theoretical knowledge, practical insights, and real-world applications enhances the learning value of the mentorship. Monitoring the effectiveness of these relationships is also essential. Regular feedback from interns and mentors can help identify areas where the relationship could be improved, ensuring the mentorship remains a mutually rewarding and productive experience. This continuous evaluation helps fine-tune the mentorship program, making it an invaluable component of the intern's professional journey and growth within the organization.

Personal and Professional Development

In cybersecurity, where the landscape is constantly evolving, interns' personal and professional development is crucial to their success. Focusing on both technical and soft skills development is essential. Technical skills are the bedrock of proficiency in cybersecurity roles, involving an understanding of systems, networks, coding, and security protocols. However, soft skills like problem solving, communication, teamwork, and adaptability cannot be overstated. These skills enable interns to work effectively in teams, communicate complex ideas clearly, and adapt to the rapidly changing cyber environment. A well-rounded development approach prepares interns for immediate tasks and long-term career challenges.

Encouraging interns to set personal learning and career objectives is important in their professional journey. By identifying their goals and areas of interest within cybersecurity, interns can take ownership of their growth and development. Assisting them in creating a professional development plan that aligns with these objectives helps provide a clear roadmap for their learning journey. This plan can include specific skills to acquire, certifications to pursue, and milestones to achieve. Additionally, providing resources for continued learning and growth is crucial. This could include access to online courses, workshops, seminars, and industry conferences. These resources enable interns to stay updated with the latest trends and technologies in cybersecurity, fostering a culture of continuous learning and keeping them engaged and motivated in their professional development.

Building a Supportive Environment

Creating a supportive environment begins with establishing a welcoming and inclusive atmosphere for interns. Such an environment encourages interns to freely express their ideas, ask questions, and fully engage in their learning experience. It is essential for them to feel comfortable and accepted, regardless of their experience level. A workplace culture that celebrates diversity, fosters inclusion, and promotes open communication sets the foundation for a positive and enriching internship experience.

Encouraging existing team members to support and actively engage with interns is also crucial. When team members are open to sharing their knowledge, offering guidance, and involving interns in various projects, it accelerates the interns' learning process and integration into the team. Another vital aspect is providing interns with access to necessary resources, tools, and learning materials. This includes the technical tools required for their work and resources that aid their broader professional development, such as access to internal training sessions, workshops, or industry journals. Acknowledging their contributions, celebrating their successes, and including them in team activities and discussions can enhance their sense of belonging and motivation. This supportive approach not only enriches the interns' experience but also contributes positively to the overall dynamics and productivity of the team.

Long-Term Career Guidance

Offering advice on various career paths and potential opportunities within the industry is invaluable for interns as they navigate their future. Experienced professionals within the organization can share insights about different roles in cybersecurity, the skills required for each, and the potential career trajectories. This guidance helps interns make informed decisions about their professional journey and align their learning with future career goals.

Assisting interns with networking and building professional connections is also crucial. Introducing them to industry contacts, encouraging them to attend relevant events, and facilitating interactions with other professionals in the field can open doors to future opportunities. Networking is often a key component of career success, particularly in a field as dynamic and interconnected as cybersecurity.

Another essential element of career guidance is guiding interns in developing their portfolios and resumes. This involves helping them articulate their experiences, projects, and skills in a way that effectively showcases their capabilities to future employers. Guidance on how to present their internship experience, technical projects, and any research work can significantly enhance their employability.

Finally, providing references and recommendations for interns as they progress in their careers is a significant way to support their professional growth. A positive reference from the internship can be a powerful asset as interns apply for jobs or further educational opportunities. These recommendations can attest to the intern's skills, work ethic, and contributions and can be instrumental in helping them secure future opportunities. By investing in these aspects of long-term career guidance, organizations not only aid in the professional development of interns but also contribute to the cultivation of skilled professionals in the cybersecurity industry.

9

DIVERSITY AND INCLUSION IN CYBERSECURITY HIRING

Diverse teams are shown to improve problem solving and decision making while addressing cybersecurity challenges through a multifaceted approach. Reflecting global and customer diversity aligns team composition with their customer bases and enhances product and service relevance. Diversity also boosts a company's reputation and attractiveness, thereby attracting top talent and building employee and customer loyalty while ensuring compliance with legal and ethical standards in workplace diversity.

Inclusive hiring strategies include implementing bias-free recruitment processes, blind recruitment, and diverse hiring panels to minimize unconscious bias. Expanding talent sourcing channels involves engaging with diverse talent pools and partnering with organizations that promote diversity in tech. Crafting inclusive job descriptions and promoting a company culture of diversity and inclusion in employer branding is also crucial. Diversity training and awareness for hiring teams and management, setting clear goals and metrics for diversity and inclusion, and holding leadership accountable are essential components of the strategy.

Building a supportive environment fosters an inclusive culture where all employees feel valued, encourages open dialogue, and celebrates diversity. Supporting career development for all includes equal access to training and advancement opportunities, promoting diversity in leadership, and establishing employee resource groups for underrepresented employees to provide networking and advocacy platforms. Inclusive policies and practices, such as accommodations and fair compensation, are vital, along with continuous learning and improvement through employee feedback, staying informed about best practices, and regularly refining strategies and initiatives. This comprehensive approach to diversity and inclusion is crucial for building a robust and innovative cybersecurity workforce.

IMPORTANCE OF DIVERSITY

The importance of diversity in cybersecurity is multifaceted—enhancing innovation and creativity by bringing together diverse perspectives that lead to innovative solutions and by fostering creativity through a mix of backgrounds and experiences, thereby driving technological advancement. Diversity ensures compliance with legal and ethical standards, addressing legal requirements regarding workplace diversity, upholding ethical standards and social responsibilities, and mitigating risks of discrimination and bias in hiring practices. Emphasizing diversity is a moral and ethical imperative and a strategic advantage in cybersecurity.

Enhancing Innovation and Creativity

Innovative solutions often stem from a variety of viewpoints. Different backgrounds bring unique approaches to problem solving, which is particularly valuable in cybersecurity, where challenges are constantly evolving. This diversity of thought can lead to breakthroughs in developing secure systems and novel approaches to protecting digital assets.

Fostering creativity through various backgrounds and experiences is essential for a vibrant and dynamic work environment. When individuals with different professional experiences, cultural backgrounds, and educational paths collaborate, they bring a rich tapestry of ideas and perspectives. This variety enriches the brainstorming process and enhances the team's ability to think outside the box and approach problems from multiple angles.

Emphasizing diversity as a driver of technological advancement is critical to staying at the forefront of innovation. In the technology sector, particularly cybersecurity, the rapid pace of change requires constant innovation to stay ahead of threats. A diverse team is better equipped to anticipate various scenarios and develop more comprehensive solutions. By valuing and promoting diversity, organizations create a more inclusive and dynamic workplace and position themselves to lead in technological advancement and innovation.

Improving Problem Solving and Decision Making

Including diverse perspectives in a team leads to a richer pool of ideas and approaches when tackling problems. This diversity can come from different educational backgrounds, professional experiences, cultural insights, and even varied approaches to problem solving. In cybersecurity, where challenges are multifaceted and ever-evolving, drawing on various viewpoints and experiences is invaluable. It allows teams to anticipate different scenarios and think more creatively about solutions.

Leveraging varied insights for decision making leads to more comprehensive and well-rounded outcomes. When team members with different viewpoints collaborate, they challenge each other's assumptions and broaden the collective understanding of the issues at hand. This process leads to a more thorough analysis and consideration of different angles, resulting in decisions that are more robust and considerate of various implications. Such thoroughness is essential in cybersecurity, where decisions often have significant and far-reaching consequences.

Addressing cybersecurity challenges with a multifaceted approach is particularly effective. Cybersecurity issues are rarely one-dimensional; they often involve technical, ethical, legal, and practical considerations. A team that can collectively address these dimensions by bringing expertise from different areas is better equipped to develop effective strategies. This comprehensive approach not only enhances the immediate problem-solving process but also contributes to developing more sustainable and forward-thinking solutions.

Reflecting Global and Customer Diversity

In today's interconnected world, where cybersecurity concerns transcend borders, aligning team diversity with a global customer base is vital. A workforce that mirrors the diversity of the global market is better equipped to understand and respond to the varying needs and perspectives of customers from different regions and cultures. This alignment is crucial in cybersecurity, where threats and challenges can be unique to specific locales or cultures. A diverse team brings a deeper understanding of these varied contexts, leading to more effective and culturally sensitive solutions.

Understanding diverse customer needs and security concerns is integral to providing effective cybersecurity solutions. Each customer or user group may have unique concerns and requirements based on their geographical location, regulatory environment, or specific threats they face. A team with a broad range of experiences and cultural insights is more adept at recognizing and addressing these nuances. This understanding is critical for developing cybersecurity strategies and solutions that are technically sound, relevant, and accessible to a diverse user base.

Enhancing product and service relevance across different demographics is another critical benefit of reflecting global and customer diversity within cybersecurity teams. With inputs from a diverse workforce, products and services can be tailored to cater to a broader range of needs and preferences, making them more inclusive and effective. This relevance is significant in cybersecurity, where one-size-fits-all solutions are often insufficient. Cybersecurity teams can provide more robust protection and support by ensuring that products and services are sensitive to diverse requirements, thereby reinforcing customer trust and satisfaction across varied demographics.

Boosting Company Reputation and Attractiveness

In cybersecurity's competitive landscape, the role of diversity in enhancing a company's image cannot be understated. Embracing and celebrating diversity reflects a progressive and modern corporate ethos and resonates with broader societal values of inclusivity and equality. A company known for its diverse workforce and inclusive culture often stands out as a more attractive and responsible entity in the market. This positive reputation is crucial in the cybersecurity sector, where trust and reliability are paramount. Showcasing a commitment to diversity and inclusion can significantly enhance the company's public image, depicting it as an employer that values varied perspectives and fosters a welcoming environment for all employees.

Furthermore, a demonstrable commitment to inclusion attracts top talent. Skilled professionals, especially in the diverse and evolving field of cybersecurity, are often drawn to companies that prioritize a diverse and inclusive workplace. Prospective employees are more likely to join an organization where they feel represented and valued, irrespective of their background. By actively promoting its dedication to diversity and inclusion, a company can attract a wider pool of candidates, enriching its talent pool with various skills, experiences, and viewpoints.

Building trust and loyalty among employees and customers is another significant outcome of a diversity-focused approach. Employees who work in an environment that respects and values their unique backgrounds are likelier to feel satisfied and be loyal to their employer. This loyalty translates into higher employee retention rates, better team dynamics, and a more positive workplace atmosphere. Similarly, customers who see a company reflecting diversity and inclusivity are likelier to trust and feel connected to the brand. In the cybersecurity industry, where customer relationships are often long-term and based on trust, company reputation is crucial in maintaining and growing a loyal customer base.

Mitigating Risks of Discrimination and Bias in Hiring Practices

In cybersecurity, as in any field, compliance with legal and ethical standards concerning workplace diversity is not just a regulatory requirement but a moral imperative. Addressing legal requirements involves adhering to laws and regulations that promote workplace diversity and prevent discrimination. This includes equal employment opportunity laws and affirmative action policies, among others. Companies must ensure that their hiring practices, promotion criteria, and workplace policies comply with these legal standards. This compliance is essential to avoid legal repercussions and foster a fair and equitable work environment.

Upholding ethical standards and social responsibilities goes beyond mere compliance with the law. It involves actively fostering an inclusive and diverse workplace where every employee feels valued and respected. Ethical recruitment and team management practices demonstrate a company's commitment to fairness and equality. This commitment is crucial in cybersecurity, where diverse perspectives and experiences can significantly enhance problem solving and innovation.

Mitigating risks of discrimination and bias in hiring practices involves implementing fair and transparent recruitment processes, using standardized criteria for evaluating candidates, and training hiring managers and recruiters about unconscious biases. Regular audits of recruitment and employment practices can help identify and rectify any inadvertent biases or discriminatory practices. By actively working to eliminate discrimination and bias, companies comply with legal and ethical standards and enhance their reputation as fair and responsible employers. This commitment to diversity and inclusivity is essential for building a skilled, innovative, and loyal workforce in the cybersecurity industry.

STRATEGIES FOR INCLUSIVE HIRING

Strategies for inclusive hiring in cybersecurity focus on creating bias-free recruitment processes, which include implementing strategies to minimize unconscious bias, utilizing blind recruitment, and employing diverse hiring panels with standardized interview questions and assessment criteria (see Figure 9.1). Expanding talent sourcing channels means engaging with diverse talent pools, partnering with organizations that promote diversity in tech, and leveraging social media for broader outreach. Crafting inclusive job descriptions and branding involves creating job postings that appeal to a broad range of candidates and promoting a company culture of diversity and inclusion, highlighted in employer branding.

Diversity training and awareness are essential—consisting of education for hiring teams and management on the value of diversity, training in inclusive practices, and fostering an understanding of different perspectives. Finally, setting clear goals and metrics for diversity and inclusion, regularly reviewing and reporting on diversity initiatives, and holding leadership accountable for outcomes are crucial to ensuring the effectiveness and continual improvement of inclusive hiring practices. Collectively, these strategies contribute to a more diverse, inclusive, and equitable hiring process in the cybersecurity industry.

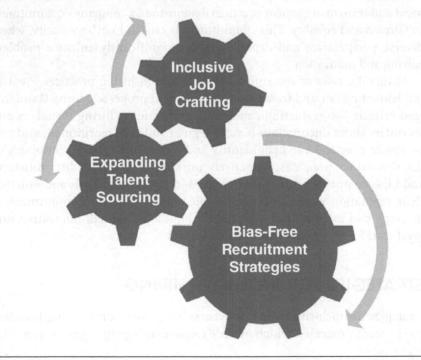

Figure 9.1   Strategies for inclusive hiring.

Bias-Free Recruitment Processes

In pursuing a more equitable and effective workforce, particularly in the specialized field of cybersecurity, implementing bias-free recruitment processes is critical. One key strategy is to actively minimize unconscious bias, which can inadvertently influence hiring decisions. This involves training recruiters and hiring managers to recognize and counteract their implicit biases, ensuring that candidate evaluations are based on merit and qualifications rather than subjective perceptions. Awareness programs and workshops on unconscious bias can significantly sensitize the recruitment team to these issues.

Blind recruitment methods and diverse hiring panels are practical tools in this endeavor. Blind recruitment involves anonymizing resumes and applications to remove identifying information that could lead to biased assessments, such as names, gender, age, or educational background. This focus on skills and experiences helps create a level playing field for all candidates. Additionally, assembling diverse hiring panels ensures a range of perspectives in the evaluation process, reducing the likelihood of collective biases impacting hiring decisions. A diverse panel can offer varied insights and assessments, leading to more objective and fair candidate evaluations.

Standardizing interview questions and assessment criteria is another vital component of bias-free recruitment. Organizations can ensure that all applicants are assessed equitably by having a consistent set of questions and a clear framework for evaluating candidates. This standardization not only helps in fair candidate comparison but also ensures that the selection process is focused on the specific skills and competencies that are required for the role. Such structured and unbiased processes are fundamental in cybersecurity recruitment, where the demand for highly specialized skills is often high, and the need for objective, merit-based hiring is paramount.

Talent-Sourcing Channels

Expanding talent-sourcing channels to engage with a broader range of candidates, as shown in Figure 9.2, is essential in cybersecurity. Actively reaching out to diverse talent pools and communities can significantly broaden the scope of recruitment efforts. This involves tapping into various groups and forums that cater to underrepresented demographics in the tech industry. Participating in job fairs, conferences, and seminars focused on diversity can also effectively connect with potential candidates from varied backgrounds.

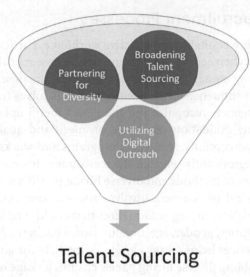

Talent Sourcing

Figure 9.2   Talent sourcing.

Partnering with organizations and institutions that are dedicated to promoting diversity in technology is another strategic approach. These partnerships can provide access to a pool of skilled candidates who might otherwise be overlooked in traditional recruitment channels. Collaborations include sponsoring events, setting up scholarship programs, or engaging in joint training initiatives. Such efforts aid in sourcing diverse talent and demonstrate the company's commitment to fostering inclusivity in the tech sector.

LinkedIn, Twitter (now X), and specialized tech community forums can be powerful tools for connecting with potential candidates globally. Social media campaigns and online networking events that are focused on diversity in cybersecurity can attract talent from different regions and backgrounds, providing a rich pool of candidates. These digital platforms offer the flexibility to reach out to candidates in various geographical locations and from diverse professional and personal backgrounds, enhancing the diversity and quality of the talent pool.

Inclusive Job Descriptions and Branding

Creating inclusive job descriptions involves using language that is welcoming to all, regardless of gender, ethnicity, age, or background. This includes avoiding jargon or terms that might unconsciously appeal to specific groups more than others. The focus should be outlining the skills and qualifications necessary for the job, ensuring that the criteria are strictly relevant to the role's requirements. By doing so, companies can encourage applications from a vast talent pool that encompasses varied experiences and perspectives.

Promoting a company culture of diversity and inclusion is equally crucial in employer branding. This goes beyond mere statements in job postings; it is about demonstrating the company's commitment to these values in its practices and policies. Showcasing real examples of diversity and inclusion in action within the company, such as employee stories or diversity-focused initiatives, can reinforce this message. This approach helps in creating an environment where prospective employees can foresee themselves being valued and supported.

Highlighting the company's diversity policies and initiatives in its employer branding is essential in order to attract candidates from diverse backgrounds. This might involve discussing programs or policies that support work-life balance, equal opportunities, antidiscrimination practices, and initiatives that foster an inclusive workplace. By transparently communicating these efforts in employer branding, companies can appeal to a broad spectrum of job seekers who are increasingly looking for workplaces that accept and celebrate diversity. This strategy enhances the company's attractiveness as an employer and contributes to building a more diverse and dynamic workforce.

Diversity Training and Awareness

Incorporating diversity training and awareness into the fabric of an organization, especially in a field as dynamic as cybersecurity, is vital for fostering an inclusive work environment. Educating hiring teams and management about the value of diversity is the first step in this process. This involves highlighting how diverse perspectives can drive innovation, enhance problem solving, and contribute to more robust cybersecurity solutions. Training should focus on the tangible benefits of a diverse workforce, including improved team performance, increased creativity, and a broader understanding of global and cultural nuances that are especially crucial in cybersecurity.

Providing training on inclusive practices and cultural competency includes educating staff on creating an inclusive environment, communicating respectfully with people from different backgrounds, and understanding the impact of cultural differences on work styles and interactions. Training should also cover implicit biases, how they can affect decision making, and strategies for mitigating them. Such training helps in building a workforce that is not only diverse but also inclusive, where every member feels valued and empowered to contribute fully.

Fostering an understanding of different perspectives and experiences among employees is crucial for creating a culture of empathy and respect. This understanding can be enhanced by encouraging open dialogue, sharing experiences, and facilitating workshops or team-building activities that celebrate diversity. These initiatives help break down barriers, reduce misconceptions, and build a more cohesive team. By prioritizing diversity training and awareness, organizations in the cybersecurity sector can create a more inclusive and effective workforce that is better equipped to face the diverse challenges of the digital world.

Metrics and Accountability

For any organization, but particularly cybersecurity, setting clear goals and metrics for diversity and inclusion are essential to track progress and ensure commitment. Establishing quantifiable targets for diversity in recruitment, retention, and promotion within the organization provides a clear benchmark for success. These metrics might include the percentage of employees from underrepresented groups, gender parity in different roles, or retention and promotion rates of diverse employees. Companies can objectively assess their progress and identify improvement areas by setting specific, measurable goals.

Regularly reviewing and reporting on the effectiveness of diversity initiatives is crucial for maintaining transparency and driving continuous improvement. This involves not just measuring quantitative aspects but also qualitatively assessing the inclusivity of the work environment. Surveys, feedback sessions, and reviews of company policies can provide insights into how employees perceive these initiatives and where gaps may exist. Regular reporting on these metrics, both internally and externally, holds the organization accountable and demonstrates a genuine commitment to fostering diversity and inclusion.

Holding leadership accountable for diversity and inclusion outcomes is critical to ensuring these initiatives are taken seriously and integrated into the company's core values. This accountability can be instilled through performance evaluations, tying diversity and inclusion metrics to leadership key performance indicators and making them a part of executive responsibilities. Leaders should be champions of diversity, setting an example and driving change within the organization. Their active involvement and accountability are instrumental in building an inclusive culture and achieving set diversity goals, ultimately leading to a more diverse, equitable, and influential organization in cybersecurity.

BUILDING A SUPPORTIVE ENVIRONMENT

Building a supportive environment in cybersecurity involves fostering an inclusive culture where all employees feel valued and included, thereby encouraging open dialogue and celebrating cultural and individual diversity. This includes supporting career development for all by ensuring equal access to training and mentorship, addressing barriers to career progression, and promoting diversity in leadership roles. Establishing employee resource groups and networks for underrepresented employees provides networking, support, and advocacy platforms while encouraging allyship and participation across the organization. Inclusive policies and practices are essential, involving reviewing and updating policies to support diversity and inclusion, implementing accommodations and flexible work arrangements, and ensuring fairness in compensation and benefits. Continuous learning and improvement are encouraged through soliciting employee feedback, staying informed about best practices in diversity and inclusion, and regularly evaluating and refining strategies and initiatives. This comprehensive approach ensures a workplace environment that is not only diverse but also supportive and conducive to the growth and success of all its members.

Fostering an Inclusive Culture

Creating an environment where all employees feel valued and included goes beyond mere policy implementation; it requires a deep-rooted commitment to nurturing a workplace that celebrates diversity in all its forms. This involves establishing a culture where every team member, regardless of their background or identity, feels that they belong and that their contributions are valued. Such an environment encourages individuals to bring their whole selves to work, boosting morale, creativity, and productivity.

Encouraging open dialogue and respect for different viewpoints is a cornerstone of this inclusive culture. This means creating spaces and opportunities for employees to share their experiences and perspectives and actively listening to and considering these viewpoints in decision making. Open dialogue fosters mutual respect and understanding, and it can lead to more innovative and effective solutions in the cybersecurity sector, where diverse perspectives can provide unique insights into challenges and threats.

Recognizing and celebrating cultural and individual diversity further enriches this inclusive environment. This can be achieved through cultural awareness events, diversity training sessions, and inclusive team-building activities. Celebrating diverse holidays, recognizing individual achievements, and supporting employee-led diversity groups are also effective ways to acknowledge and appreciate the company's rich tapestry of backgrounds and experiences. By actively celebrating diversity, companies enhance employee engagement and satisfaction and signal to current and potential employees that they are committed to fostering an inclusive and welcoming workplace.

Supporting Career Development for All

Supporting employee career development means equal access to training, mentorship, and advancement opportunities. This includes providing all employees with the resources to grow and advance in their careers, regardless of their background or identity. It involves offering various training programs, mentorship opportunities, and clear pathways for career progression that are accessible and applicable to everyone. Such initiatives help employees develop the necessary skills and knowledge to succeed and progress within the company.

Identifying and addressing barriers to career progression is also crucial in supporting equitable career development. This involves recognizing systemic issues or biases that might impede the advancement of specific groups within the organization. Regular assessments and feedback mechanisms can help identify these barriers, whether they relate to unconscious bias in promotions, lack of representation in leadership, or other structural inequalities. By actively working to dismantle these barriers, companies can create a more inclusive environment where every employee has the opportunity to reach their full potential.

Promoting diversity in leadership and decision-making roles is critical to achieving a truly inclusive workplace. Employees at all levels need to see themselves represented in these roles. Diversity in leadership provides varied perspectives that can enhance decision making and problem solving and sets a powerful example for the rest of the organization. It demonstrates the company's commitment to diversity and inclusion and inspires employees from diverse backgrounds to aspire to these positions. Companies can promote diversity in leadership by implementing inclusive recruitment and promotion practices, offering leadership training to underrepresented groups, and actively seeking diverse candidates for high-level roles.

Employee Resource Groups and Networks

Employee resource groups (ERGs) and networks play a pivotal role in fostering an inclusive workplace. Establishing groups specifically for underrepresented employees gives them a sense of community and belonging within the organization. These groups can offer a safe space for members to share their experiences, discuss challenges that are specific to their identity or background, and support each other personally and professionally. Such groups are support networks and platforms for empowerment and growth.

ERGs can organize events, workshops, and meetings that offer opportunities for professional development, networking, and mentorship. They can also serve as powerful advocacy groups within the organization, voicing the concerns and needs of their members and working with management to address them. This can lead to positive changes in company policies and practices, making the workplace more inclusive and equitable.

Encouraging allyship and participation across the organization in these groups is essential for building a genuinely inclusive environment. This means inviting employees from different backgrounds, including those not part of underrepresented groups, to participate in ERG events and initiatives. Such involvement fosters a deeper understanding and appreciation of different perspectives and challenges faced by colleagues. It also promotes a culture of allyship, where employees support each other's growth and success. By encouraging widespread participation in ERGs, organizations can enhance understanding and cooperation among all employees, creating a more unified and supportive workplace.

Inclusive Policies and Practices

Developing inclusive policies and practices is a fundamental step for any organization that is committed to diversity and inclusion. Regularly reviewing and updating company policies to support diversity and inclusion is crucial. This process involves assessing current policies through the lens of inclusivity to ensure that they cater to the needs of a diverse workforce. It includes examining recruitment practices, antidiscrimination policies, harassment prevention, and any other policies that impact the daily experiences of employees.

Updating these policies to reflect the organization's commitment to inclusivity can create a more welcoming and supportive environment for all employees.

Another critical aspect of fostering an inclusive workplace is implementing accommodations and flexible work arrangements. Recognizing that employees have different needs and circumstances is essential. This can include offering flexible working hours, remote work options, or special accommodations for employees with disabilities. Such practices demonstrate the organization's recognition and support of its employees' varied lifestyles and responsibilities outside of work, which can significantly enhance employee satisfaction and productivity.

Ensuring fairness in compensation, benefits, and recognition practices is essential for maintaining a sense of equity and respect within the workplace. Regular audits of compensation and benefits can help identify and rectify any possible disparities. This includes ensuring that employees in similar roles and qualifications are compensated equally, regardless of their background or identity. Additionally, recognition programs that somewhat acknowledge the contributions and achievements of all employees, regardless of their level or role within the organization, are crucial. Fair and transparent practices in these areas contribute to a positive work environment and reinforce the organization's commitment to diversity and inclusion.

Continuous Learning and Improvement

Fostering an environment of continuous learning and improvement in diversity and inclusion, as expanded in Table 9.1, is critical to long-term success. This involves actively soliciting feedback and ideas from employees at all levels. Encouraging open and honest communication allows employees to share their experiences, suggestions, and concerns regarding the workplace's inclusivity efforts. This feedback can be gathered through surveys, focus groups, or regular meetings. By listening to employees, organizations can gain valuable insights into the effectiveness of their diversity and inclusion strategies and identify areas that need more attention or a different approach.

Staying informed about best practices in diversity and inclusion is crucial for ensuring that the organization's efforts are up-to-date and effective. This can be achieved by attending conferences, participating in workshops, and engaging with thought leaders in diversity and inclusion. Keeping abreast of the latest research, trends, and successful case studies allows organizations to benchmark their efforts against industry standards and adopt new and innovative strategies. This continuous learning approach is fundamental in the fast-paced world of cybersecurity, where the workforce's needs and dynamics can rapidly change.

Table 9.1 Continuous learning and improvement.

Strategy	Action Steps	Expected Outcomes
Continuous Learning and Improvement	1. Solicit feedback through surveys, focus groups, or regular meetings. 2. Attend conferences, workshops, and engage with diversity thought leaders. 3. Regularly evaluate and refine strategies using quantitative and qualitative metrics.	1. Gain insights into the effectiveness of diversity strategies. 2. Stay informed about industry best practices and innovations. 3. Ensure ongoing relevance and impact of diversity efforts.
Open Communication	1. Encourage open dialogue about inclusivity experiences. 2. Provide platforms for honest sharing of suggestions and concerns.	1. Foster an inclusive workplace environment. 2. Better understand employee needs and concerns.
Industry Benchmarking	1. Keep abreast of latest research and successful case studies. 2. Compare efforts with industry standards.	1. Adopt innovative diversity strategies. 2. Stay competitive in diversity and inclusion practices.
Regular Assessment	1. Measure diversity metrics periodically. 2. Assess impact on company culture and employee satisfaction.	1. Identify successful strategies and areas for improvement. 2. Enhance company culture and employee retention.

Regularly evaluating and refining strategies and initiatives related to diversity and inclusion ensures these efforts remain relevant and impactful. This means measuring the quantitative aspects, such as diversity metrics, and assessing the qualitative impact on the company culture and employee satisfaction. Regular assessments help identify what is working well and what needs adjustment. Viewing diversity and inclusion as an ongoing journey that requires constant effort and adaptation is crucial. By committing to this continuous evaluation and improvement process, organizations can foster a truly inclusive culture, enhancing their ability to attract, retain, and nurture a diverse and talented workforce.

10

ONBOARDING AND TRAINING

Best practices for onboarding, as shown in Figure 10.1, include engaging with new hires before their start date, providing essential information about the company and role, setting clear expectations, and facilitating administrative requirements in advance. A structured onboarding program introduces new hires to the company culture, values, and goals and provides a clear road-map for their initial period—balancing information delivery with hands-on experience. Integration into the team is facilitated through introductions, team-building activities, assigning a buddy or mentor, and fostering a welcoming environment. Role-specific orientation is tailored to cybersecurity roles, aligning expectations with business objectives.

Figure 10.1 Onboarding best practices.

Training programs involve developing a curriculum tailored to cybersecurity, which includes incorporating technical, soft skills, and policy training, and aligning with industry standards. Blended learning approaches combine various methods such as online courses, in-person workshops, and simulations for practical experience. Mentorship and coaching offer personalized guidance, while continuous skill development encourages lifelong learning, attending industry events, and pursuing certifications.

Performance monitoring includes setting clear objectives that are aligned with organizational goals, conducting regular reviews, offering constructive feedback, and discussing career advancement opportunities. A structured feedback system promotes open communication, and performance issues are addressed with fairness and consistency. This comprehensive approach ensures that employees in cybersecurity are well onboarded and continuously trained, and their performance is effectively monitored, thereby contributing to their personal growth and the organization's success.

BEST PRACTICES FOR SUCCESSFUL ONBOARDING

Best practices for successful onboarding in cybersecurity involve strategic steps to ensure that new hires are well-integrated and prepared for their roles. Pre-onboarding communication is vital, engaging with new hires before their official start date, providing essential information about the company and role, setting expectations, and addressing any preliminary queries while facilitating paperwork and administrative tasks in advance.

A structured onboarding program is developed to provide a comprehensive introduction to the company culture, values, and goals alongside a clear roadmap for the initial weeks and months, balancing information delivery with hands-on experience. Integration into the team is facilitated through introductions, team-building activities, assigning mentors or buddies for guidance, encouraging participation in team meetings and projects, and fostering a welcoming environment.

Role-specific orientation tailors the onboarding process to the specific needs of the cybersecurity role, including detailed overviews of tools, systems, and processes, aligning role expectations with business objectives, and offering insights into ongoing and upcoming projects. Continuous support and resources are provided, maintaining open communication channels, addressing concerns and questions promptly, and encouraging feedback to improve the onboarding process continually. This approach ensures that new hires are effectively integrated, supported, and equipped to succeed in their cybersecurity roles.

Pre-Onboarding Communication

Effective pre-onboarding communication is crucial in setting the stage for a new employee's journey, especially in specialized fields like cybersecurity. Engaging with new hires before their official start date helps build a connection and ease any apprehensions they may have. This engagement can include welcome messages, emails introducing them to the team, or even informal virtual meet-and-greets. Such interactions signal to the new hire that they are valued, and the company eagerly anticipates their arrival.

Providing essential information about the company and the specific role is another crucial aspect of pre-onboarding communication. This information can range from the company's history and culture to details about the team they will join and an overview of their roles and responsibilities. Clear and concise information helps new hires better understand what to expect and how they fit into the larger picture of the organization. Setting expectations and addressing any preliminary queries is also essential. This might involve discussing the first week's schedule, the onboarding process, or answering any questions the new hire might have about their role or the company in general. Such clarity can alleviate first-day nerves and set a positive tone for their upcoming start.

Completing necessary forms, setting up email and IT systems, and handling other logistical aspects before the new hire's first day can significantly streamline their onboarding experience. By taking care of these administrative details beforehand, the new employee can focus more on acclimating to their new role and environment from day one rather than being bogged down with paperwork. Effective pre-onboarding communication thus not only enhances the new hire's initial experience but reflects the organization's efficiency and commitment to a smooth integration process.

Structured Onboarding Program

A structured onboarding program should encompass all aspects of a new employee's introduction to the company, including administrative processes, training sessions, and team introductions. This plan should make the transition as smooth as possible, helping new hires understand their role, the company's operations, and how they fit into the larger organizational structure.

A well-thought-out onboarding program provides essential information and helps build a solid foundation for the new employee's future success in the company.

Introducing new hires to the company culture, values, and goals is critical to the onboarding process. This introduction can include presentations, meetings with key team members, and interactive sessions that convey the company's mission, work ethics, and core values. Understanding the company culture helps new hires to adapt and thrive in their new environment. Providing a clear roadmap for the first weeks and months helps new employees understand what is expected of them and what they can expect regarding training, project involvement, and performance evaluations. This roadmap should outline critical milestones and objectives, offering a sense of direction and purpose right from the start.

Ensuring a balance between information delivery and hands-on experience is crucial for an effective onboarding process. While it is essential to provide new hires with necessary information about the company and their role, engaging them in practical, job-related activities early on is equally important. Hands-on experience allows new employees to apply what they have learned, integrate more quickly into the team, and better understand their role in the organization's context. This balanced approach ensures that the onboarding process is not overwhelming and provides a more engaging and effective transition into the company.

Integration into the Team

Successful integration into the team is a critical component of the onboarding process, especially in fields that require close collaboration, like cybersecurity. Facilitating introductions and organizing team-building activities can be significant in this integration. Introductions to team members and key personnel in the company help new hires establish initial connections and understand their team dynamics. Team-building activities, whether formal workshops or informal social events, can further aid in breaking the ice and fostering a sense of camaraderie among team members.

Assigning a buddy or mentor to new hires is an effective strategy for providing personalized guidance and support. This buddy or mentor, typically an experienced team member, can act as a go-to person for any queries or concerns the new hire might have. They can assist in navigating the company's processes, understanding project specifics, and acclimating to the company culture. This one-on-one support system can significantly ease the transition period for new employees.

Encouraging active participation in team meetings and projects from the outset is also vital to integration. Involving new hires in discussions, brainstorming sessions, and projects allows them to contribute their ideas and skills early on. This involvement not only helps them to understand their role within the team more clearly but also provides an opportunity for other team members to appreciate the new hire's capabilities and perspective.

A welcoming and inclusive team environment is fundamental to making new hires feel comfortable and valued. This includes ensuring that the team is open to and respectful of diverse viewpoints and backgrounds and that new members feel as though their contributions are acknowledged and appreciated. A positive and inclusive team atmosphere encourages new hires to engage more fully, share their ideas, and integrate more seamlessly into the team. Organizations can create a supportive environment by prioritizing these aspects of team integration, thereby enabling new employees to thrive and effectively contribute to the team from the beginning.

Role-Specific Orientation

Tailoring the onboarding process to the cybersecurity role ensures that the new employee receives relevant and targeted information. This approach goes beyond general company policies and culture to focus on the specific skills, knowledge, and responsibilities associated with their role. It involves a deep dive into the technical aspects of the job, ensuring that the new hire is well-prepared to take on their specific duties.

Providing a detailed overview of the tools, systems, and processes used in the role is essential to this orientation. For a cybersecurity professional, this might include training on security software, threat detection systems, protocols for handling security breaches, and standard operating procedures. Familiarizing them with the specific tools and systems they will be using boosts their confidence and enhances their efficiency and effectiveness from the start.

Aligning role expectations with the organization's business objectives helps new hires understand how their role fits the larger picture and contributes to the company's overall goals. It gives them a sense of purpose and clarity about the impact of their work. Furthermore, offering insights into ongoing and upcoming projects can help new employees understand the team's current priorities and challenges. This knowledge allows them to hit the ground running and immediately contribute to essential projects. Overall, a role-specific orientation that is tailored to the unique aspects of a cybersecurity position sets the foundation for a successful and productive tenure in the organization.

Continuous Support and Resources

Continuous support and access to necessary resources are vital for their successful acclimation and growth within the organization. Maintaining open channels of communication is fundamental in this support system. This means ensuring that new employees feel comfortable contacting their supervisors, human resources, or mentors with any questions or concerns they might have. Regular check-ins can also be a part of this, where managers or mentors proactively engage with new hires to discuss their progress, address any challenges they face, and provide guidance.

Access to the necessary resources and support enables new hires to perform their roles effectively. This includes the technical tools and software required for their cybersecurity tasks and comprehensive resources for professional development, such as training materials, online courses, and opportunities to attend workshops or conferences. Easy access to these resources empowers new employees to continuously develop their skills and stay abreast of the latest trends and technologies in cybersecurity.

Addressing concerns and questions promptly is critical to building trust and ensuring that new hires feel valued and supported. Responsive support in resolving any issues or queries they may have demonstrates the organization's commitment to its success and well-being. This responsiveness is essential in the early stages of employment when new hires are still learning to navigate and understand the nuances of their role and the company.

Encouraging feedback from new hires about their onboarding experience is also beneficial for continuous process improvement. Feedback can provide insights into what aspects of the onboarding were most helpful, what could be improved, and how to support future new hires better. This continuous loop of feedback and improvement enhances the onboarding process and fosters a culture of open communication and continuous development within the organization.

TRAINING PROGRAMS AND CONTINUOUS LEARNING

Training programs and continuous learning in cybersecurity include developing a structured training curriculum tailored to specific roles, incorporating technical skills, soft skills, and policy training, and aligning with industry standards and certifications. Training must be kept relevant, up-to-date, and practical. Blended learning approaches may be a combination of online courses, in-person workshops, and simulations, thereby leveraging e-learning platforms for flexibility and encouraging self-paced learning alongside structured learning sessions.

Mentorship and coaching are integral—pairing employees with mentors for personalized guidance, providing opportunities for coaching and career advice, and facilitating knowledge sharing and skill transfer. This approach fosters collaborative learning and peer mentorship. Continuous skill development is emphasized by promoting a lifelong learning culture, offering resources for advanced learning and specialization, encouraging attendance at industry events, and supporting the pursuit of further certifications and education.

Measuring training effectiveness is crucial; this involves establishing metrics to evaluate outcomes, gathering feedback for continuous improvement, assessing the application of skills and their impact on job performance, and adapting training to meet evolving cybersecurity trends and needs. This comprehensive training and learning approach ensures that employees in cybersecurity are continuously progressing, staying abreast of the latest industry developments, and contributing effectively to their roles and the broader cybersecurity field.

Developing a Training Curriculum

A structured training program should encompass a comprehensive approach, addressing the technical aspects of cybersecurity and incorporating soft skill development and policy training. This holistic approach ensures that employees are proficient in technical skills like threat analysis, encryption, and network security and that they are equipped with soft skills, such as critical thinking, problem solving, and effective communication, which are all vital in the collaborative and dynamic environment of cybersecurity.

A mix of technical and soft skills and policy training helps create well-rounded professionals. Technical training should cover the latest cybersecurity tools, technologies, and methodologies. Soft skill training focuses on developing interpersonal skills, teamwork, and adaptability. On the other hand, policy training is essential for ensuring that employees are well-versed in regulatory standards, ethical considerations, and compliance requirements that are related to cybersecurity.

Aligning the training with industry standards and certifications ensures that the training program is not only comprehensive but also relevant to the current demands of the cybersecurity industry. Training that prepares employees for recognized certifications can enhance their credibility and proficiency, keeping them at the forefront of the field. Furthermore, these certifications often serve as benchmarks for skill and knowledge levels in the industry.

Ensuring that the training is relevant, up-to-date, and practical is critical for applying learned skills. Cybersecurity is rapidly evolving, and training programs should reflect the latest threats, technologies, and best practices. Practical, hands-on training exercises, simulations, and real-world case studies are essential for applying theoretical knowledge. This approach helps employees better understand and retain information, thereby enhancing their ability to apply their skills in real-world scenarios.

Table 10.1 expands on the concept of developing a training curriculum for cybersecurity roles. It categorizes the training into different aspects, outlines their components, states the objective for each, and suggests methodologies. This format provides a structured approach to ensure a comprehensive and effective training program that is both relevant and practical.

Table 10.1 Example training development format.

Training Aspect	Components	Objective	Methodology
Technical Skills	1. Threat analysis 2. Encryption techniques 3. Network security	Equip with essential cybersecurity skills	Use of latest tools, technologies, and techniques
Soft Skills	1. Critical thinking 2. Problem solving 3. Effective communication	Enhance interpersonal and teamwork abilities	Focus on interpersonal skill development and adaptability
Policy Training	1. Regulatory standards 2. Ethical considerations 3. Compliance requirements	Ensure awareness of legal and ethical aspects	Training in regulatory, ethical, and compliance standards
Industry Alignment	—	Align with current industry demands and standards	Training for recognized certifications and industry benchmarks
Relevance and Practicability	—	Ensure applicability in real-world scenarios	Incorporate latest threats, technologies, best practices, hands-on exercises, simulations, and case studies

Blended Learning Approaches

In cybersecurity, where the landscape is rapidly changing and diverse skill sets are required, adopting blended learning approaches can significantly enhance the effectiveness of training programs. Blending various training methods, such as online courses, in-person sessions, and interactive workshops, caters to different learning styles and needs. This combination allows for a more comprehensive learning experience. In-person sessions can facilitate direct interaction and personalized feedback, while online courses offer the convenience of learning at one's own pace and time. Workshops and group activities can foster collaboration and problem-solving skills, which are crucial in cybersecurity.

Leveraging e-learning platforms is particularly beneficial for providing flexibility and accessibility in training. E-learning platforms enable employees to access various courses and materials online, which makes fitting training into their schedules easier. This flexibility is essential in cybersecurity where professionals must stay abreast of the latest developments and technologies continuously. E-learning platforms can offer various formats, such as videos, interactive modules, and forums for discussion, thus making learning more engaging and effective.

Encouraging self-paced learning alongside structured sessions allows employees to take ownership of their learning journey. Self-paced learning enables them to explore topics in depth at their chosen speed and according to their interests, which can lead to a deeper understanding and retention of knowledge. At the same time, structured sessions ensure a comprehensive coverage of essential topics and that all learners are on the same page regarding key concepts and skills.

Utilizing simulations and real-world scenarios for hands-on experience is crucial in cybersecurity training. Simulations and practical exercises replicate real-life cybersecurity challenges and scenarios, allowing learners to apply their knowledge in a controlled environment. This hands-on experience is invaluable because it helps learners understand how to respond to cybersecurity threats and incidents. Such practical training can significantly enhance the readiness and confidence of cybersecurity professionals in dealing with real-world challenges.

Mentorship and Coaching

Pairing employees with experienced mentors offers personalized guidance that significantly enhances learning. With their wealth of knowledge and experience in the field, mentors can provide insights, advice, and support that is tailored to their mentees' specific needs and goals. This one-on-one interaction accelerates the learning curve and helps navigate career paths and workplace challenges more effectively.

Providing opportunities for coaching and career advice is crucial for employees' professional development in cybersecurity. Coaching sessions can focus on specific skill enhancements, overcoming professional challenges, or general career guidance. These sessions offer a platform for employees to discuss their aspirations, receive feedback, and develop strategies for achieving their career objectives. Coaches can help employees set realistic goals, identify improvement areas, and develop the necessary skills to advance in their cybersecurity careers.

Facilitating knowledge sharing and skill transfer within the organization is another crucial aspect of mentorship and coaching. Experienced professionals can share their insights and experiences with less experienced colleagues, fostering a culture of continuous learning and skill development. This knowledge transfer benefits the mentees and strengthens the cybersecurity team's overall skill set.

Encouraging collaborative learning and peer mentorship is essential for building a supportive and dynamic learning environment. Peer mentorship, where employees mentor each other, can be particularly effective in a rapidly changing field like cybersecurity. It allows employees to learn from their peers who may have expertise in different areas or have had more recent training in certain aspects of the field. Collaborative learning activities, such as group projects or study groups, also promote a sense of teamwork and shared purpose. These interactions facilitate the exchange of knowledge and skills and build a sense of community and support among team members.

Continuous Skill Development

Encouraging employees to continually seek new knowledge and stay curious about emerging trends and techniques in cybersecurity fosters an environment where continuous improvement is the norm. This culture of ongoing learning keeps the team current with the latest developments and drives innovation and a proactive approach to cybersecurity challenges.

Offering advanced learning and specialization resources is essential in order to support continuous skill development. This can include access to specialized online courses, internal training programs, and resources for self-study. By providing these resources, organizations empower their employees to delve deeper into specific areas of cybersecurity, such as network security, ethical hacking, or cryptography. Specialization in these areas can significantly enhance the team's capabilities and adaptability in addressing diverse cybersecurity challenges.

Encouraging attendance at conferences, webinars, and industry events is another critical strategy for continuous learning. These events offer opportunities for employees to learn from thought leaders in the field, stay abreast of industry trends, and network with peers. Participation in such events can bring fresh perspectives and ideas back to the organization and spark innovative approaches to cybersecurity. It also keeps the team connected with the broader cybersecurity community, essential for collaborative learning and staying informed about global cybersecurity issues.

Pursuing certifications and further education is vital for professional growth and skill enhancement. Certifications in cybersecurity are often recognized benchmarks of expertise and are highly valued in the industry. Supporting employees in obtaining these certifications through funding, providing study leave, or offering exam preparation resources demonstrates the organization's commitment to their professional development. Additionally, supporting further education, such as advanced degrees in cybersecurity or related fields, can significantly benefit the employee and the organization by bringing advanced knowledge and skills to the team. This support for formal education and certification not only enhances the capabilities of the cybersecurity team but also contributes to employee satisfaction and retention.

Measuring Training Effectiveness

Measuring the effectiveness of training programs is essential to ensure that they meet the needs of employees and the organization. Establishing clear metrics to evaluate training outcomes is the first step in this process. These metrics can include quantitative measures, such as completion rates, test scores, and certification achievements, and qualitative measures like participant satisfaction and self-reported confidence in applying new skills. By analyzing these metrics, organizations can gauge the immediate impact of their training programs and identify improvement areas.

Gathering feedback from participants is a critical component of this evaluation process. Soliciting feedback after training sessions through surveys or discussions provides insights into how the training was received, what was most beneficial, and what could be enhanced. This feedback is invaluable for continuously improving training programs to align with employees' needs and learning preferences. It ensures that the training remains relevant, engaging, and effective in equipping employees with the necessary skills.

Assessing the application of newly acquired skills and their impact on job performance is crucial in understanding the real-world effectiveness of training. This assessment can be conducted through performance reviews, observing improvements in work processes, or measuring changes in cybersecurity metrics within the organization. Understanding how training translates into practical application provides a clear picture of its return on investment and helps with developing future training initiatives.

Adapting training programs to align with evolving cybersecurity trends and organizational needs is vital in a constantly changing industry. This involves staying informed about the latest cybersecurity threats, technologies, and best practices and integrating this knowledge into training curriculums. Regular updates and revisions to training content ensure that the workforce is skilled and prepared to tackle current and emerging cybersecurity challenges. By continuously measuring and refining their training programs, organizations can maintain a highly skilled cybersecurity workforce that is capable of protecting against and responding to the ever-evolving digital threats.

PERFORMANCE MONITORING AND FEEDBACK

Performance monitoring and feedback in cybersecurity are crucial to fostering employee growth and aligning individual goals with organizational objectives. Clear performance objectives are set, measurable and realistic indicators are established, expectations are clarified, and goals are regularly reviewed and updated. Ongoing performance reviews involve regular check-ins, offering constructive feedback and recognition, discussing challenges, and encouraging self-assessment.

A structured feedback system is implemented to facilitate open and honest communication, thereby providing a safe space for expressing concerns and utilizing feedback for personal and professional development. Career pathing and advancement discussions focus on identifying opportunities within the organization, guiding skill enhancement for career progression, and aligning individual strengths with organizational needs.

Addressing performance issues involves early identification and intervention, implementing improvement plans as needed, offering additional training or support, and handling such issues fairly and consistently. This comprehensive performance monitoring and feedback approach ensures a supportive environment that promotes continuous learning and career advancement. It addresses challenges effectively, contributing to both individual and organizational success in cybersecurity.

Setting Clear Performance Objectives

Setting clear performance objectives is fundamental to effective workforce management. Aligning individual goals with organizational objectives ensures that each employee's efforts contribute to the broader mission and goals of the organization—defining how individual roles and responsibilities feed into the company's larger strategy and success. By creating this connection, employees can see the impact of their work, thus fostering a sense of purpose and engagement.

Establishing measurable and realistic performance indicators is another critical step. These indicators should be quantifiable, allowing for an objective assessment of performance. Depending on the role, they might include specific targets, project milestones, or quality standards. Importantly, these performance indicators should be achievable and set in a way that challenges employees but also considers the available resources and support. This balance ensures that employees are motivated to strive for excellence while feeling that their goals are attainable.

Providing clarity on expectations and success criteria is essential for employees to understand their requirements. Clear communication regarding these expectations helps remove ambiguity and enables employees to focus their efforts more effectively. Regularly reviewing and updating performance goals is also essential. The cybersecurity field is fast-evolving, so the objectives and requirements of roles can change. Regular reviews allow for adjustments in performance goals to reflect new priorities, challenges, or changes in the business environment. This flexibility ensures that performance objectives remain relevant and aligned with the current needs and strategy of the organization.

Ongoing Performance Reviews

Ongoing performance reviews mean conducting regular check-ins and progress assessments often. These weekly, monthly, or quarterly check-ins allow managers and employees to discuss progress, address immediate issues, and realign goals. Regular assessments help monitor progress against set objectives, allowing for timely interventions if needed. This approach keeps employees engaged and focused on their performance and development.

Offering constructive feedback and recognition during these reviews is vital. Feedback should be specific, actionable, and balanced, highlighting areas of strength and opportunities for improvement. Recognizing achievements and progress boosts morale and reinforces positive behaviors and outcomes. When delivered effectively, constructive feedback can motivate employees to continue developing their skills and contribute more effectively to the organization.

Discussing challenges and supporting improvement is another essential aspect of ongoing performance reviews. Managers should encourage employees to discuss obstacles and collaboratively develop strategies to overcome them openly. This support might include additional training, mentorship, or adjustments in workload or responsibilities. Encouraging self-assessment and reflection is also beneficial. Employees who regularly reflect on their performance and set personal goals are often more engaged and proactive in their development. This self-reflection can be facilitated through guided questions or self-assessment tools, helping employees think critically about their strengths, weaknesses, and areas for growth. By incorporating these elements into ongoing performance reviews, organizations can foster a culture of continuous improvement and development, which is essential in cybersecurity.

Feedback Mechanisms

Implementing a structured feedback system ensures that feedback is not sporadic or informal but a regular and integral part of the work environment. This system might include scheduled one-on-one meetings, performance reviews, or anonymous feedback channels. It should be designed to capture a wide range of feedback, from day-to-day observations to more comprehensive work performance and behavior evaluations.

Encouraging open and honest communication is vital to the success of any feedback mechanism. Employees should feel comfortable sharing their thoughts and opinions without fear of negative repercussions. This environment of openness fosters trust and encourages a more candid exchange of feedback, which is essential for personal and professional growth. Managers play a critical role in this by modeling transparency in their communications and being receptive to the feedback they receive.

Employees should have access to platforms to express their ideas, concerns, and suggestions freely. This could be through regular team meetings, suggestion boxes, or one-on-one sessions with supervisors. Ensuring that these channels are accessible and genuinely considered by management encourages employees to contribute their insights, leading to a more inclusive and dynamic workplace.

Utilizing feedback for personal and professional development is the ultimate goal of these mechanisms. Feedback should be seen not just as a tool for assessment but as a vital resource for growth and improvement. Employees should be encouraged to actively use the feedback to develop their skills, address areas of weakness, and enhance their strengths. Likewise, managers should use the feedback to refine their leadership approach and to better support their team's development. Organizations can foster a culture of continuous improvement, adaptability, and shared success by effectively leveraging feedback.

Career Pathing and Advancement

Discussing career aspirations and potential growth paths with employees is an important part of career pathing and advancement. These discussions help managers understand each employee's professional goals and aspirations. Managers can better support their career development by knowing what each team member aims to achieve. These conversations should be an ongoing dialogue, reflecting the evolving goals of the employee and changes within the organization.

Identifying opportunities for advancement within the organization is crucial for motivating employees and retaining top talent. Managers should help employees understand the various career paths available and what each path entails. This might involve outlining potential roles they could grow into, additional responsibilities they could take on, or new projects they could lead. By clearly mapping out these opportunities, employees can see a future within the company and understand what they need to do to progress.

Providing guidance on skill enhancement for career progression is equally essential. This involves identifying the skills and competencies that employees need to develop in order to advance in their chosen paths. Managers should help employees identify these areas of development and provide resources and opportunities for learning. This could include training programs, mentorship, industry conference participation, or cross-functional project involvement.

Aligning individual strengths and interests with organizational needs is the final piece of the puzzle. This alignment ensures that employees are engaged and motivated, along with working in areas that interest them and play to their strengths. At the same time, it ensures that the organization is leveraging its talent effectively to meet its strategic goals. Finding this alignment requires a deep understanding of the employee's capabilities and interests and the organization's current and future needs. By effectively aligning these elements, organizations can foster a workforce that is not only highly skilled but also deeply committed and aligned with the company's long-term vision.

Addressing Performance Issues

Addressing performance issues effectively is crucial in maintaining a highly functioning workforce. Identifying and addressing performance gaps early is the first step in this process. Early identification allows for timely interventions, preventing minor issues from escalating into major problems. Regular performance reviews and monitoring can help in spotting these gaps. Once identified, addressing these issues directly with the employee is essential, discussing areas where improvement is needed and understanding any underlying causes.

Implementing performance improvement plans (PIPs) when necessary is a structured approach to help employees overcome their performance issues. A PIP is a formal document that outlines the specific areas that need improvement, sets clear and achievable goals, and provides a timeline for achieving these objectives. It should be a collaborative effort between the employee and manager, ensuring that the goals are realistic and that the employee is committed to the improvement process. Regular check-ins should be part of the PIP to monitor progress and provide ongoing support.

Offering additional training or support where needed is essential in helping employees improve. This could include formal training programs, mentorship, or additional resources and tools. The support offered should be tailored to the individual's needs and the specific skills or competencies they need to develop. The goal is to empower employees with the knowledge and skills they need to succeed in their roles.

Handling performance issues with fairness and consistency is vital to maintaining trust and morale within the team. Every employee should be held to the same standards, and the process for addressing performance issues should be transparent and consistent. This includes having clear policies and procedures for performance management and ensuring that all employees are treated with respect and dignity throughout the process. A fair and consistent approach helps resolve performance issues effectively and reinforces a culture of accountability and professionalism within the organization.

11

EMPLOYEE RETENTION AND CAREER DEVELOPMENT

Building a positive work culture involves fostering a collaborative and inclusive environment that promotes teamwork, diversity, and inclusivity, along with supporting cross-departmental collaborations (see Figure 11.1). Recognition and reward systems, transparency in decision making, regular feedback, and leadership and management skills development are essential. Ensuring work-life balance through flexible work arrangements and supporting personal challenges are also crucial.

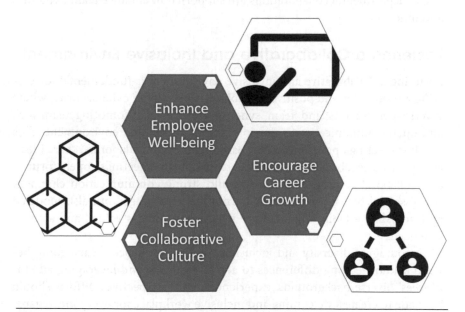

Figure 11.1   Employee retention and career development.

Career advancement opportunities include outlining clear career pathways, investing in professional development and training, encouraging internal mobility and promotion, and implementing mentorship and coaching programs. Regular performance reviews, aligning individual goals with company objectives, and addressing skill gaps are part of effective performance management.

Employee benefits and well-being are addressed through comprehensive benefits packages, mental health and well-being initiatives, creating a conducive work environment, and engaging in social activities. Continuous feedback and improvement on these initiatives will ensure that they remain relevant and beneficial to employees. This comprehensive approach contributes to a satisfied, engaged workforce that is crucial for retaining talent and fostering career growth in the cybersecurity field.

BUILDING A POSITIVE WORK CULTURE

Building a positive work culture in cybersecurity involves fostering a collaborative and inclusive environment. This includes promoting teamwork and open communication, encouraging diversity and inclusivity, and creating a workplace where everyone feels a sense of belonging and mutual respect. Cross-departmental collaborations are supported to enhance team dynamics and innovation.

Fostering a Collaborative and Inclusive Environment

Fostering a collaborative and inclusive environment is fundamental for creating a productive and positive workplace, especially in cybersecurity, where diverse perspectives and team synergy are crucial. Promoting teamwork and open communication is the cornerstone of such an environment. This involves creating opportunities for team members to collaborate, share ideas, and provide feedback. Encouraging regular team meetings, open forums, and collaborative projects can help build strong communication channels. It is essential that these practices are not just encouraged but also modeled by leadership, establishing a culture where teamwork is valued and actively practiced.

Encouraging diversity and inclusivity in the workplace means going beyond acknowledging differences to actively valuing and leveraging all employees' diverse backgrounds, experiences, and perspectives. Efforts should be made to create a welcoming and inclusive workplace for everyone, regardless of race, gender, age, or any other characteristic. This can involve diversity training, inclusive hiring practices, and policies that support a diverse workforce. A diverse and inclusive environment enriches the workplace culture and drives innovation and creativity.

Establishing a sense of belonging and mutual respect among employees is essential. Every team member should feel valued and recognized for their contributions. Creating an environment where employees feel safe, respected, and part of the broader organizational community is critical to fostering a sense of belonging. This can be achieved through team-building activities, recognition programs, and an open-door policy where employees feel comfortable sharing their thoughts and concerns.

Supporting cross-departmental collaborations and interactions is also beneficial. Encouraging teams to work with different departments can enhance understanding, break down silos, and lead to more innovative solutions. This cross-functional collaboration can be facilitated through joint projects, interdepartmental meetings, and informal networking events. Such interactions broaden the horizons of individual team members and strengthen the overall organizational structure, leading to a more cohesive and dynamic workplace.

Recognition and Reward Systems

Implementing effective recognition and reward systems is crucial in motivating employees and acknowledging their hard work, especially in demanding sectors like cybersecurity. Recognition programs for achievements and contributions play a significant role in this. These programs should be designed to acknowledge significant accomplishments and smaller, consistent efforts that contribute to the success of the team and the organization. Whether completing a challenging project, contributing innovative ideas, or consistently exhibiting a strong work ethic, recognizing these efforts can significantly boost morale and motivation.

Providing tangible rewards and incentives for performance is another critical element. These rewards could range from bonuses and raises to nonmonetary incentives like additional vacation days, flexible working arrangements, or professional development opportunities. Celebrating milestones and successes, both big and small, contribute to a positive workplace culture. This could be through company-wide announcements, award ceremonies, or team gatherings. Recognizing these achievements publicly not only honors the individual or team but also inspires others.

Tailoring recognition to individual preferences and motivations is essential for the effectiveness of these programs. Different employees may value different forms of recognition and rewards. Public acknowledgment might be highly motivating for some, while others might appreciate private recognition or specific rewards. These personal preferences can be understood through regular communication, surveys, or feedback mechanisms. By personalizing recognition and rewards, organizations can ensure that their efforts resonate more effectively with each employee, thereby enhancing the overall impact of these programs. This personalized approach demonstrates that the organization values and understands its employees, fostering a positive and engaging work environment.

Transparency and Open Communication

Transparency and open communication are fundamental to building trust and engagement in the workplace. Maintaining transparency in decision making and company developments involves openly sharing information about organizational changes, reasons behind certain decisions, and plans. When employees are kept informed and understand the context of decisions, they are more likely to feel valued and involved. This transparency helps create a culture where employees feel more connected to the organization's mission and goals.

Encouraging employee feedback and suggestions is vital for fostering a sense of involvement and ownership. Employees should feel comfortable sharing their ideas and opinions, knowing their input is welcomed and valued. This can be facilitated through regular feedback channels, suggestion boxes, or town hall meetings. Providing regular updates on company performance and goals is also essential. This could be newsletters, meetings, or reports informing everyone about the organization's progress and future directions. Regular communication about the company's performance helps employees understand how their work contributes to the organization's overall success.

Facilitating open forums for discussion and input is another important aspect. These forums can be structured meetings, informal gatherings, or digital platforms where employees can discuss various topics, ask questions, and share their perspectives. Open forums encourage a culture of openness and inclusivity where diverse viewpoints are heard and considered. They also provide leadership with valuable insights into employee sentiment and can uncover areas for improvement within the organization. By prioritizing transparency and open communication, organizations can foster a more collaborative, inclusive, and high-trust workplace environment, which is especially important in fields that rely heavily on teamwork and innovation.

Leadership and Management Development

Leadership and management development are critical for building strong teams and ensuring organizational success—particularly in cybersecurity, where the pace of change and the stakes are high. Training leaders and managers in influential people management is the foundation of this development. This training should cover various aspects, including motivating teams, managing conflicts, communicating effectively, and fostering an inclusive work environment. By equipping leaders with these skills, organizations can ensure that their teams are managed effectively and that employees feel supported and valued.

Encouraging leadership styles that promote trust and empowerment is also essential. Leaders should be encouraged to adopt styles that involve listening to team members, valuing their contributions, and empowering them to take the initiative and make decisions. This approach boosts morale and fosters a sense of ownership and accountability among team members. It creates a positive and productive work environment where employees feel trusted and supported.

Providing opportunities for leadership roles and responsibilities allows for the growth and development of potential organizational leaders. This can include leading projects, heading committees, or taking on mentorship roles. These opportunities help employees develop their leadership skills in a practical setting and prepare them for future managerial positions. Fostering a culture of mentorship and support further enhances this development. Experienced leaders and managers should be encouraged to mentor less experienced colleagues by sharing their knowledge and providing guidance. This mentorship not only aids in the professional development of the mentees but also strengthens the organization's leadership pipeline. Organizations can build a strong foundation of practical and inspiring leaders by focusing on leadership and management development through training, empowerment, opportunities, and mentorship.

Work-Life Balance and Flexibility

Work-life balance and flexibility are increasingly recognized as critical factors in employee satisfaction and productivity. Offering adjustable work arrangements and remote work options is an effective way to support this balance. These arrangements can include flexible hours, work-from-home, or compressed workweeks. Such policies allow employees to manage their work and personal responsibilities better, thereby reducing stress and improving job satisfaction.

Encouraging a healthy balance between professional and personal life is essential. Employers should promote a culture where taking time off and disconnecting from work is accepted and encouraged. This could involve setting clear expectations about work hours, discouraging after-hours communication, and encouraging employees to take their full vacation time. Such practices help maintain a healthy work environment and prevent burnout, which is particularly important in high-stress fields.

Employers should be mindful of employees' workloads and ensure they are manageable. Regular check-ins can help identify if employees are overburdened and allow for adjustments before burnout occurs. Additionally, supporting personal challenges and family commitments is essential for building a supportive and understanding workplace. This support could include offering additional leave for family emergencies, resources for mental health and well-being, or childcare support. Organizations can create a more engaged, productive, and satisfied workforce by prioritizing work-life balance and flexibility, leading to better overall performance and retention.

Table 11.1 expands on the concept of work-life balance and flexibility, particularly in the cybersecurity sector. It details the features and benefits of each aspect and offers implementation strategies to help organizations create

Table 11.1 Work-life balance and flexibility.

Aspect	Features	Benefits	Implementation Strategies
Flexible Work Arrangements	1. Flexible hours 2. Work-from-home 3. Compressed workweeks	Reduces stress Improves job satisfaction	Tailor arrangements to individual needs Provide necessary tools for remote work
Healthy Work-Life Balance	1. Encourage time off 2. Discourage after-hours communication 3. Full vacation utilization	Prevents burnout Maintains a healthy work environment	Set clear work-hour policies Promote a culture of disconnection from work
Boundary Respect and Burnout Reduction	1. Manageable workloads 2. Regular check-ins 3. Adjustments to prevent burnout	Reduces overtime Enhances employee well-being	Monitor workloads Offer support for personal challenges
Support for Personal Challenges	1. Additional leave for emergencies 2. Mental health resources 3. Childcare support	Builds a supportive workplace Fosters understanding and engagement	Implement flexible leave policies Provide resources for mental health and family care

a more engaged, productive, and satisfied workforce. This approach aims to enhance employee satisfaction and productivity, leading to better overall performance and retention.

CAREER ADVANCEMENT OPPORTUNITIES

Career advancement opportunities in cybersecurity are vital for employee growth and satisfaction. Clear career pathways must be outlined that provide visibility into advancement opportunities and criteria, offer guidance for career progression, and align individual aspirations with organizational needs. Professional development and training should be emphasized, as well as investing in continuous learning programs, supporting certifications and further education, encouraging participation in industry events, and providing resources for skill enhancement.

Clear Career Pathways

Clear career pathways are essential in motivating employees and aiding their professional development, especially in specialized fields such as cybersecurity. Outlining potential career paths within the organization is a fundamental first step. This involves clearly defining the various roles and opportunities within the organization and how one can progress from one level to the next. A well-defined career ladder or roadmap helps employees understand the potential growth trajectories and what they need to achieve to advance in their careers.

Providing visibility into advancement opportunities and criteria is crucial. Employees should have access to information about what is required to move up within the organization, including the necessary skills, experiences, and performance standards. This transparency helps set clear expectations and allows employees to work toward specific goals. This information must be easily accessible and regularly updated to reflect organizational structure or requirements changes.

Offering guidance and planning for career progression can include career counseling, mentorship programs, or development plans tailored to each employee's career goals. These resources help employees plan their careers and take proactive steps toward professional growth. Aligning individual aspirations with organizational needs is essential in this process. This alignment ensures that while employees work toward their personal career goals, they contribute to the organization's objectives. Companies can foster a motivated and forward-thinking workforce by providing clear career pathways, visibility into advancement opportunities, guidance for career progression, and aligning individual and organizational goals.

Professional Development and Training

Organizations should provide and support ongoing training opportunities to help employees keep up with the latest industry developments, technologies, and best practices. This can include in-house training sessions, online courses, and skill development programs. A culture that values and encourages continuous learning helps maintain a knowledgeable and skilled workforce and boosts employee motivation and engagement.

Supporting certifications, workshops, and further education plays a significant role in professional development. Many roles in specialized fields require specific certifications or ongoing education to maintain expertise. Employers can support this by subsidizing certification costs, providing study leave, or reimbursing education expenses. This support demonstrates a commitment to employees' professional growth and helps attract and retain top talent.

Encouraging participation in industry conferences and events is another important aspect. These events offer valuable opportunities for learning, networking, and staying abreast of industry trends and innovations. Participation can also provide fresh perspectives and ideas to be brought back to the organization. In addition, providing resources for skill enhancement and specialization is crucial. This might involve access to specialized training programs, subscriptions to industry publications, or opportunities to work on challenging projects that foster skill development. By prioritizing professional development and training, organizations can ensure that their workforce remains highly skilled and adaptable and, thus, ready to meet the challenges and opportunities of their field.

Internal Mobility and Promotion

Internal mobility and promotion are crucial for retaining talent and fostering a culture of growth and opportunity within an organization, particularly in specialized fields like cybersecurity. Encouraging internal applications for open positions is a crucial strategy. This approach provides existing employees with opportunities for advancement and helps the organization retain valuable institutional knowledge and expertise. When employees see clear pathways for advancement within the company, they are more likely to be engaged and motivated.

Facilitating job rotations and cross-functional experiences is another effective way to enhance internal mobility. These initiatives allow employees to develop a broader skill set and better understand different aspects of the organization. Such experiences can be invaluable in building a more versatile and adaptable workforce. They also help employees explore various career paths within the company, aiding in informed career decisions.

Supporting both upward and lateral moves within the company is essential. While upward mobility is often the focus, lateral moves can provide valuable learning experiences and help employees find the role that best fits their skills and interests. Recognizing and promoting talent from within rewards hard work and dedication and sends a positive message to the workforce about the company's commitment to employee development and recognition. By implementing policies and practices that support internal mobility and promotion, organizations can create a dynamic and motivating work environment where employees feel valued and see a future for themselves.

Mentorship and Coaching Programs

Mentorship and coaching programs are invaluable tools for employee development. Pairing employees with mentors for career guidance is a foundational element of these programs. Mentors, often experienced professionals within the organization or industry, can provide invaluable insights, advice, and support. They can help guide mentees through career challenges, offer perspectives on professional growth, and assist in setting and achieving career goals. This mentor-mentee relationship is not only beneficial for the professional development of the mentee but can also be a rewarding experience for the mentor.

Unlike mentorship, which tends to be more guidance and advice-based, coaching focuses on developing specific skills and competencies. Coaches work with employees to identify areas for improvement, set development goals, and create actionable plans to achieve these goals. These sessions can be tailored to the individual's needs, focusing on leadership skills, technical expertise, or soft skills development.

Fostering relationships with industry experts and leaders can give employees broader perspectives and insights into the industry. This can be facilitated through guest lectures, networking events, or partnerships with industry associations. Such interactions allow employees to learn from the experiences and knowledge of leaders in their field, which can be particularly inspiring and informative.

Enabling knowledge-sharing and networking opportunities is also crucial. This can be achieved through internal forums, discussion groups, or company-wide events where employees can share their experiences, learn from each other, and build professional networks. These opportunities support learning and development and help build a collaborative and engaged organizational culture. By implementing effective mentorship and coaching programs, organizations can support their employees' professional growth, encourage knowledge sharing, and foster a culture of continuous learning and development.

Performance Management and Feedback

Performance management and feedback are integral to employee development and organizational success, particularly in cybersecurity, where the landscape is constantly evolving. Conducting regular performance reviews should not only assess past performance but also guide future development. Regular, structured feedback sessions allow for open dialogue between employees and managers, fostering a culture of continuous improvement. These sessions are opportunities to discuss achievements, challenges, and areas for growth, ensuring that employees understand how their work aligns with the organization's expectations and goals.

Aligning individual goals with company objectives is essential for ensuring that employees' efforts contribute to the organization's broader mission. This alignment helps employees understand the impact of their work and see how their contributions fit into the larger picture. Setting goals that are challenging and rewarding for the individual and advance the company's objectives creates a sense of shared purpose and direction.

Providing constructive feedback and actionable development plans is critical to effective performance management. Feedback should be specific, balanced, and focused on helping employees grow and improve. It should be coupled with precise, achievable development plans that outline steps for improvement and growth. These plans can include additional training, mentoring, or stretch assignments that challenge and develop the employee's skills.

Managers should be adept at identifying areas where employees could improve or where they have untapped potential. Addressing these gaps through targeted development initiatives not only enhances the workforce's capabilities but also helps retain talent by demonstrating the organization's investment in their growth. Organizations can create a robust performance management system that drives employee development and organizational success by focusing on regular performance reviews, goal alignment, constructive feedback, and addressing skill gaps.

EMPLOYEE BENEFITS AND WELL-BEING

Employee benefits and well-being are crucial for a satisfied and productive workforce in cybersecurity. Comprehensive benefits packages offer competitive salaries, bonus structures, health, dental, and vision insurance, retirement plans, and benefits tailored to individual employee needs and preferences. Mental health and well-being initiatives should also be emphasized, as well as implementing programs that are focused on mental health and stress management, providing access to counseling, and organizing wellness activities.

Comprehensive Benefits Packages

Comprehensive benefits packages are important in attracting and retaining top talent. Offering competitive salaries and bonus structures is the foundation of these packages. Competitive pay attracts high-quality candidates and shows existing employees that they are valued and fairly compensated for their skills and contributions. Bonus structures that are tied to performance, company success, or other metrics can further motivate employees and align their goals with the organization's goals.

Providing health, dental, and vision insurance is essential for employee well-being. Comprehensive health benefits are often a top priority for employees because they offer security for themselves and their families. These benefits can include various healthcare services, from preventative care and routine checkups to more extensive medical procedures. Offering a robust health insurance package can significantly enhance the overall attractiveness of the benefits package.

Retirement plans like 401(k)s—often with employer matching contributions—help employees plan for their future and demonstrate the company's commitment to their long-term financial well-being. Financial wellness programs, such as financial planning services or education on investment and saving strategies, can further support employees in achieving their financial goals.

Offering benefits tailored to employee needs and preferences ensures that the benefits package is comprehensive and relevant. This can involve conducting surveys to understand what employees value most—offering flexible benefits options or including unique benefits like childcare support, wellness programs, or remote work opportunities. Tailoring benefits to the diverse needs of the workforce shows a commitment to addressing employees' specific needs and preferences, thereby enhancing job satisfaction and loyalty. By offering a well-rounded benefits package that includes competitive pay, health insurance, retirement plans, and tailored benefits, organizations can create a supportive and attractive work environment that appeals to current and prospective employees.

Mental Health and Well-Being Initiatives

Mental health and well-being initiatives are increasingly important in the workplace, particularly in high-stress fields like cybersecurity. Implementing mental health and stress management programs is critical to supporting the overall well-being of employees. These programs can include workshops, seminars, or training sessions that provide employees with strategies to manage stress, build resilience, and maintain mental health. Such initiatives help reduce work-related stress and contribute to a more positive and productive work environment.

Providing access to counseling and support services can offer employees confidential and professional help to deal with personal or work-related issues. Access can be provided through employee assistance programs, which may include counseling sessions, mental health resources, and referral services. Offering these resources demonstrates an organization's commitment to the holistic well-being of its employees.

Encouraging a culture that prioritizes mental well-being is essential for these initiatives to be effective. This involves creating an environment where mental health is openly discussed, destigmatized, and treated as importantly as physical health. Leadership plays a critical role in setting the tone, sharing their experiences or support for mental health initiatives, and ensuring that policies and practices around workloads, work-life balance, and employee support are conducive to mental well-being.

Organizing wellness activities and initiatives is another way to support mental health in the workplace. These include mindfulness sessions, fitness classes, health and wellness challenges, or relaxation and meditation workshops. Such activities provide a break from the daily work routine and promote healthy habits that can contribute to better mental health. By integrating a range of mental health and well-being initiatives into the workplace, organizations can help ensure that their employees are successful in their roles and happy and healthy in their personal lives.

Work Environment and Facilities

Creating an optimal work environment and providing the proper facilities are critical factors in promoting employee productivity and satisfaction. Creating a comfortable and safe physical work environment is the first step. This involves ensuring that the workplace is physically safe and conducive to focused and efficient work. This can mean providing well-lit, clean, and adequately ventilated workspaces and ensuring that all safety protocols and guidelines are in place and adhered to.

Providing tools and resources for efficient and comfortable work is crucial. Employees should have access to the necessary technology and equipment to perform their jobs effectively. This includes high-quality computers, reliable software, fast internet connections, and other relevant tools. Additionally, providing resources like standing desks, ergonomic chairs, or dual monitor setups can significantly enhance comfort and productivity.

Workstations should be designed with ergonomics in mind to prevent strain or injury. This includes proper chair and desk height, keyboard and mouse placement, and monitor positioning. Environmental considerations, such as adequate lighting, temperature control, and noise management, also significantly create a comfortable work environment.

Facilitating relaxation and social interaction spaces is vital to maintaining a balanced work environment. This could involve creating designated lounge areas, break rooms, or outdoor spaces where employees can relax and interact with colleagues. These areas can help reduce stress, promote mental well-being, and encourage a sense of community within the workplace. By focusing on these aspects of the work environment and facilities, organizations can create a workspace that not only meets the functional needs of employees but also supports their overall well-being and job satisfaction.

Employee Engagement and Social Activities

Employee engagement and social activities are pivotal in building a cohesive and vibrant workplace culture. Organize team-building events and social gatherings to help foster this engagement. These events range from casual team lunches and after-work outings to more structured team-building exercises and company-wide retreats. Such activities allow employees to interact more flexibly, build relationships, and strengthen team dynamics.

Encouraging participation in community and volunteer activities is another aspect of enhancing employee engagement. Involvement in community service or corporate social responsibility initiatives can be advantageous and help employees develop a sense of purpose and connection to the broader community. Companies can facilitate this by organizing group volunteer days, supporting causes important to their employees, or providing time off for individual volunteer efforts.

Facilitating interest groups and clubs within the company can also significantly contribute to employee engagement. These groups or clubs could be based on various interests or hobbies, such as sports, arts, technology, or reading. They offer employees a chance to connect with colleagues with similar interests, fostering a sense of camaraderie and belonging. Such groups can also serve as informal networks for support and knowledge sharing.

Promoting a sense of community and belonging is crucial in making the workplace more than just a workplace. This involves creating an environment where employees feel valued, connected, and part of a larger community. It is about nurturing a workplace culture where diversity is celebrated, achievements are recognized, and everyone feels they are a vital part of the team and company. Organizations can build a more connected, motivated, and productive workforce by investing in employee engagement and social activities.

Feedback and Continuous Improvement

Feedback and continuous improvement are essential to maintaining a dynamic and responsive work environment. Regularly soliciting feedback on benefits and well-being initiatives can be done through surveys, suggestion boxes, or regular meetings where employees can openly discuss their views on current programs and policies. Encouraging honest feedback helps organizations understand what works well and what areas need improvement. It also shows employees that their opinions are valued and considered in decision making.

Adapting and evolving programs based on employee input is critical to ensuring that these initiatives remain relevant and practical. Employers should be willing to change benefits, well-being initiatives, and workplace policies based on the feedback received. This adaptive approach demonstrates a commitment to meeting the evolving needs of the workforce and can lead to more effective and appreciated programs.

Staying informed about industry trends and best practices is also essential. This involves keeping abreast of the latest employee benefits, well-being programs, and workplace culture developments. Attending industry conferences, participating in professional networks, and conducting benchmarking studies can provide valuable insights. Organizations can innovate and improve their programs by understanding what other companies are doing and what is considered best practice in the industry.

Continuously striving to enhance employee satisfaction and engagement is the ultimate goal of these efforts. This means not settling for the status quo but always looking for ways to make the workplace more supportive, engaging, and fulfilling for employees. By focusing on regular feedback, adaptability, staying informed, and a commitment to continuous improvement, organizations can foster a workplace environment that attracts top talent and retains and motivates them effectively.

12

FUTURE TRENDS IN CYBERSECURITY HIRING

The future of the hiring process within cybersecurity will revolve around a number of factors (see Figure 12.1), not the least of which is anticipating the arrival of new cyber threats. Regulatory changes in data protection and privacy laws will impact hiring practices, and the persistent skills gap and talent shortage will necessitate innovative strategies and exploration of alternative talent pools. Remote work opens access to a global talent pool, but also

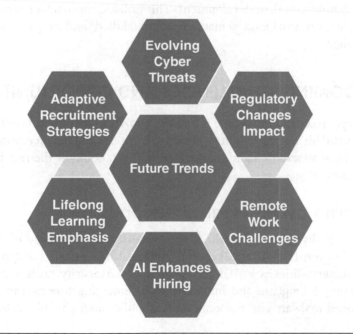

Figure 12.1 Future trends in cybersecurity hiring.

presents challenges in managing remote cybersecurity workforces. Additionally, the increasing importance of interdisciplinary skills for roles that merge cybersecurity with other domains will require broader hiring criteria.

The role of artificial intelligence (AI) and automation in cybersecurity hiring is significant. AI can enhance talent acquisition through efficient resume screening and predictive analytics, while automation of cybersecurity tasks will shift skill demands. Anticipating AI-driven cyber threats necessitates integrating AI skills into cybersecurity roles. Ethical considerations of AI in hiring that ensure fairness and balance efficiency with human judgment are crucial. The future of AI in cybersecurity training involves personalized learning experiences and keeping training content relevant.

Continuous adaptation and learning will continue to be important, with lifelong learning and upskilling being vital in cybersecurity. Keeping pace with technological advancements, like quantum computing and the Internet of Things (IoT), requires integrating new technology skills into hiring and training programs. Adaptive recruitment strategies must respond to the job market and technology trends for future-proofing cybersecurity talent by anticipating future skill requirements and focusing on foundational skills. Collaboration and knowledge sharing within the cybersecurity community and building partnerships with industry, academia, and government are essential for talent development. This holistic approach ensures that the cybersecurity workforce remains resilient, skilled, and prepared for future challenges.

UPCOMING CHALLENGES AND OPPORTUNITIES

The cybersecurity landscape is rapidly evolving, thereby presenting challenges and hiring opportunities. New cyber threats and the increasing sophistication of attacks demand an updated understanding of the required skills and knowledge.

Evolving Cyber-Threat Landscape

In the rapidly changing world of cybersecurity, staying ahead of the evolving cyber-threat landscape is crucial. Anticipating new types of cyber threats and vulnerabilities is a vital part of this. Cybersecurity professionals must constantly be vigilant and informed about emerging threats, ranging from advanced malware and ransomware to sophisticated phishing schemes and state-sponsored cyberattacks. This proactive approach involves keeping abreast of the latest developments in the field and engaging in predictive analysis to foresee potential future vulnerabilities and threats. Cybersecurity teams can develop more effective defense strategies and preventive measures by understanding and anticipating these evolving risks.

As technology advances, so do the techniques and tools used by cybercriminals. Cybersecurity professionals must therefore continuously update and enhance their skills to counteract these advanced threats. This preparation involves not just technical training but also developing a deep understanding of the strategies and tactics used by attackers. Staying updated with the latest cybersecurity technologies, such as AI and machine learning (ML), and understanding how these can be leveraged for defense is also essential.

Understanding the implications of these evolving threats for skills and knowledge requirements helps maintain an effective cybersecurity workforce. As the nature of threats changes, so do the skills needed to combat them. This means that ongoing education and training are vital. Cybersecurity professionals must be versatile and adaptable, with a solid foundation in core cybersecurity principles and the agility to learn and apply new techniques and tools as required. Organizations must recognize and address these changing skill requirements, thereby ensuring that their teams are always equipped to handle the latest cybersecurity challenges.

Impact of Regulatory Changes

In cybersecurity, the impact of regulatory changes, particularly those related to data protection and privacy laws, is profound and far-reaching. Keeping abreast of these changes on a global scale is essential for organizations to ensure compliance and protect against legal risks. This involves monitoring and understanding the developments in regulations such as the General Data Protection Regulation in the European Union, the California Consumer Privacy Act, and other emerging data protection laws worldwide. These laws have significant implications for how organizations collect, store, process, and secure personal data, making it crucial for cybersecurity professionals to understand and implement compliant practices.

Adapting hiring practices to comply with new regulations is another important aspect. This includes ensuring that the recruitment process, from collecting candidates' data to storing and handling their information, adheres to the latest data protection regulations. Organizations must constantly update their human resources policies and procedures to reflect these regulatory changes by incorporating necessary safeguards and consent protocols as part of their recruitment and onboarding processes.

Understanding the impact of regulatory changes on cybersecurity roles is crucial for aligning the skills and responsibilities of the cybersecurity team with compliance requirements. As regulations evolve, so do the demands placed on cybersecurity professionals. They must safeguard against technical threats and ensure that their organization's data handling and security practices comply with legal standards. This means that cybersecurity roles increasingly intersect with legal and regulatory compliance, requiring a broad understanding of the technical and legal aspects surrounding data protection. Continuous training and awareness programs for cybersecurity teams regarding these regulatory changes are imperative in order to maintain an organization's compliance and data security posture.

Skills Gap and Talent Shortage

The cybersecurity industry is facing the significant challenge of a skills gap and talent shortage, making finding qualified professionals increasingly difficult. This gap is mainly due to the rapid pace of technological advancements and the evolving nature of cyber threats, which outstrip the rate at which skilled professionals enter the field. Organizations must recognize and proactively address this challenge to ensure that their cybersecurity teams can effectively protect against these threats.

Developing strategies to mitigate the impact of skill shortages can involve investing in training and development programs to enhance the skills of existing employees. Upskilling current staff helps fill immediate skills gaps and contributes to employee retention by providing career growth opportunities. Additionally, implementing internship and graduate programs can help cultivate the next generation of cybersecurity professionals. These programs can bridge the gap between academic learning and industry needs, providing fresh talent with the practical skills and experience that is required in cybersecurity.

Exploring alternative talent pools and nontraditional hiring paths is another effective strategy to address the talent shortage. This includes looking beyond candidates with traditional cybersecurity backgrounds and considering professionals with transferable skills from other industries or disciplines. People with backgrounds in mathematics, physics, or even liberal arts can bring valuable perspectives and skills to cybersecurity roles. Moreover, leveraging diverse talent pools, including underrepresented groups in technology, can also help alleviate the shortage. This approach broadens the available talent pool and contributes to a more diverse and innovative workforce. By adopting a more inclusive and flexible approach to hiring, organizations can tap into a broader range of talent and effectively address the skills gap in cybersecurity.

Remote Work and Global Talent Access

The advent of remote work has opened up opportunities for organizations, especially in cybersecurity, to access a global talent pool. Leveraging remote work allows companies to tap into a broader range of skills and expertise that may not be available locally. By extending their search for talent beyond geographical boundaries, organizations can find highly specialized cybersecurity professionals who bring unique perspectives and capabilities to the team.

However, accessing global talent comes with managing a remote cybersecurity workforce. This includes ensuring effective communication, maintaining team cohesion, and managing different time zones. Additionally, cybersecurity teams often deal with sensitive information and require robust security measures, which can be more complex to implement in a remote work environment. Organizations must develop strategies to manage these challenges effectively, such as implementing secure remote access technologies, fostering a strong culture of cybersecurity awareness among remote employees, and establishing clear communication protocols.

Adapting hiring strategies to support remote team integration is also essential. This involves assessing technical skills and considering each candidate's ability to work effectively in a remote setting. Self-motivation, excellent communication skills, and the ability to work independently are crucial for remote workers. The onboarding process for remote employees should also be adapted to ensure that they feel connected and integrated with the team. This can include virtual meet-and-greets, remote training sessions, and regular check-ins. By adapting their hiring and management strategies, organizations can effectively leverage remote work to access global talent and build a robust and diverse cybersecurity workforce.

Interdisciplinary Skills and Roles

Cybersecurity challenges are no longer confined to isolated technical domains; they intersect with various fields such as data analysis, regulatory compliance, ML, and psychology. This intersection creates a demand for professionals with a strong foundation in cybersecurity principles and skills in these related areas. For example, understanding behavioral psychology can be crucial in combating social engineering attacks, while knowledge of data analytics can enhance threat detection and response strategies.

Therefore, preparing for roles that merge cybersecurity with other domains is becoming essential. Organizations must anticipate the need for roles that, for example, combine cybersecurity expertise with legal knowledge to navigate data privacy laws or business acumen to align security strategies with organizational goals. This shift requires reevaluating the skill sets considered valuable in cybersecurity professionals. It may create new, hybrid roles that bridge gaps between traditional cybersecurity tasks and these emerging interdisciplinary areas.

Rather than focusing solely on conventional cybersecurity qualifications, organizations should consider candidates with diverse backgrounds and experiences that can contribute to a more holistic approach to cybersecurity. This might include individuals with expertise in risk management, regulatory compliance, or behavioral science. By valuing interdisciplinary skills and incorporating them into hiring criteria, organizations can build a more versatile and practical cybersecurity team that is capable of addressing complex and multifaceted security challenges in an increasingly interconnected world.

THE ROLE OF AUTOMATION AND AI

The role of automation and AI in cybersecurity is increasingly influential. AI is utilized for efficient resume screening and candidate matching, along with leveraging predictive analytics for talent sourcing and retention, thereby significantly improving recruitment process efficiency. Automation impacts cybersecurity roles, requiring preparation for shifts in skill demands and balancing the human element in automated processes. Anticipating AI-driven cyber threats is becoming crucial, thus creating a necessity for AI-savvy professionals and for integrating AI awareness into cybersecurity roles to stay ahead of advancements in the field. Ethical considerations are also critical in AI-assisted hiring—addressing potential biases and ensuring fairness and ethical use in candidate evaluation and selection. Additionally, the future of AI in cybersecurity training involves implementing AI for personalized learning experiences, keeping training content relevant and up-to-date, and exploring AI-driven simulations for practical learning. These AI and automation advancements are reshaping the landscape of cybersecurity talent acquisition, task automation, and ongoing professional development.

AI in Cybersecurity Talent Acquisition

Integrating AI in cybersecurity talent acquisition is revolutionizing the recruitment process, making it more efficient and effective. Utilizing AI for resume screening and candidate matching is one of the primary applications in this domain. AI algorithms can quickly parse extensive resumes to identify candidates who match the job requirements. This speeds up the screening process and enhances its accuracy, reducing the likelihood of human bias and error. AI can identify patterns and qualifications that might be missed in manual reviews, ensuring that top candidates are shortlisted for consideration.

Leveraging predictive analytics is another significant application of AI in talent sourcing and retention. Predictive analytics can analyze trends and patterns from existing data to forecast future outcomes. In talent acquisition, this means predicting the success of candidates in specific roles, identifying potential retention issues, and even foreseeing future talent needs based on company growth and industry trends. This proactive approach can help organizations stay ahead in the highly competitive cybersecurity talent market, ensuring they have the right talent at the right time.

Assessing the impact of AI on the recruitment process efficiency is crucial for organizations that adopt this technology. AI can streamline many aspects of recruitment, from initial candidate sourcing to the final stages of the hiring process. However, it is essential to continuously evaluate the effectiveness of AI tools in improving these processes. This assessment can include measuring changes in the time to hire, the quality of the hire, and candidate satisfaction with the recruitment process. By continuously monitoring and refining the use of AI in talent acquisition, organizations can ensure they are leveraging these technologies to their fullest potential, ultimately enhancing their ability to attract and retain top cybersecurity talent.

Table 12.1 outlines the integration of AI in cybersecurity talent acquisition, detailing its various applications, functions, benefits, and assessment metrics. It highlights how AI is revolutionizing the recruitment process, making it more efficient and effective, and emphasizes the importance of continuously evaluating the effectiveness of these AI tools.

Table 12.1   The application of AI in hiring.

AI Application	Function	Benefits	Assessment Metrics
AI for Resume Screening and Candidate Matching	Parses extensive resumes quickly Identifies candidates matching job requirements	Speeds up screening process Reduces human bias and error Enhances accuracy in shortlisting	Measure changes in time to screen, accuracy of match, reduction in bias
Leveraging Predictive Analytics	Analyzes trends for future predictions Forecasts candidate success and retention issues Identifies future talent needs	Predicts candidate success in roles Proactively addresses talent needs Stays ahead in competitive market	Evaluate forecasting accuracy, impact on talent retention, alignment with company growth
Assessing Impact on Recruitment Process Efficiency	Streamlines recruitment from sourcing to hiring	Improves overall recruitment efficiency Enhances candidate satisfaction	Track changes in time to hire, quality of hire, candidate satisfaction

Automation of Cybersecurity Tasks

The automation of cybersecurity tasks is reshaping the landscape of cyber-security roles and the skills required in this field. Understanding the implications of automation is crucial for both cybersecurity professionals and organizations. Automation technologies, such as ML algorithms and AI, are increasingly used to handle routine tasks like monitoring network traffic, identifying potential threats, and enforcing security protocols. This shift can significantly reduce the workload on cybersecurity teams, allowing them to focus on more complex and strategic tasks that cannot be automated.

Preparing for shifts in skill demands due to automated systems is an essential response to this trend. As routine tasks become automated, the demand for skills in managing, monitoring, and optimizing these automated systems increases. Cybersecurity professionals must develop skills in overseeing these automated processes, analyzing the data they produce, and making strategic decisions based on this analysis. Additionally, there will be a growing need for skills in developing and maintaining these automation systems, including programming, data science, and ML expertise.

Balancing the human element with automated processes is also a key consideration. While automation can handle many routine tasks, human insight is critical, especially for interpreting complex threat patterns, making context-based decisions, and strategizing cybersecurity measures. The human element is also crucial in incident response, where nuanced understanding and decision making are required. Cybersecurity professionals must therefore be adept at working alongside automated systems, leveraging their capabilities while also applying their human judgment and expertise where necessary. This balance is essential for ensuring that cybersecurity measures are efficient and effective, leveraging the strengths of automated systems and human professionals.

AI and Cybersecurity Threats

Integrating AI into cybersecurity is a double-edged sword, presenting opportunities and challenges. Anticipating AI-driven cyber threats is becoming increasingly crucial as malicious actors leverage AI to carry out sophisticated cyberattacks. This escalation calls for a new breed of AI-savvy cybersecurity professionals who are adept in traditional cybersecurity practices and understanding and countering AI-driven threats. These professionals need to know how AI can be used in cyberattacks, such as through automated malware creation and AI-driven phishing attacks, and by exploiting ML systems.

In response, it is vital to integrate AI awareness and skills into cybersecurity roles. Cybersecurity training and education programs must evolve to include AI-related content, equipping professionals with the necessary knowledge and skills to defend against AI-powered threats. This includes understanding the basics of AI and ML, the potential vulnerabilities of AI systems, and the strategies for defending against AI-exploited attacks. It is about defending against AI threats and leveraging AI to enhance cybersecurity defenses. AI can be a powerful tool for detecting unusual patterns, predicting potential threats, and automating response protocols.

The field of AI is rapidly evolving, and keeping up with the latest developments is essential for cybersecurity professionals. This involves continuous learning and staying informed about the latest AI research, tools, and techniques as they pertain to cybersecurity. Organizations must also foster a culture of innovation and adaptability, allowing their cybersecurity teams to experiment with and adopt new AI technologies. By staying ahead of the curve in AI advancements, cybersecurity professionals can better defend against AI-driven threats and harness AI to improve their cybersecurity strategies and defenses.

Ethical Considerations of AI in Hiring

AI in recruitment brings forth significant ethical considerations, particularly around bias and fairness. AI-powered recruitment tools promise efficiency and objectivity, such as resume screening algorithms and predictive analytics for candidate assessment. However, they also pose risks of perpetuating biases. These biases can stem from the data used to train AI systems, often reflecting historical hiring patterns that may be skewed against certain groups. Addressing these biases is crucial to ensure fairness in the recruitment process. This involves carefully examining and continually auditing the AI algorithms for inherent biases and making necessary adjustments to promote equitable candidate evaluation.

Ensuring the ethical use of AI in candidate evaluation and selection is a crucial responsibility for organizations. This means being transparent about using AI in the hiring process and ensuring that AI tools are used to augment, not replace human decision making. Ethical considerations include safeguarding candidates' privacy and ensuring their data is used responsibly and securely. Organizations need to establish clear guidelines and principles on the ethical use of AI in hiring, which should align with broader organizational values and ethical standards.

While AI can significantly streamline the recruitment process and analyze candidate data more efficiently than humans, it lacks human recruiters' nuanced understanding and empathy. Human judgment is crucial in interpreting the context, understanding the unique aspects of each candidate's profile, and making final hiring decisions. Therefore, the most effective approach is a hybrid model where AI enhances and supports human decision making rather than replaces it. This balance ensures that the recruitment process is efficient and data-driven but also fair, ethical, and human-centric.

Future of AI in Cybersecurity Training

Integrating AI in cybersecurity training represents a transformative shift in how training programs are developed and delivered. Implementing AI in training programs can significantly enhance personalized learning experiences. AI algorithms can analyze an individual's learning style, progress, and areas of strength and weakness, tailoring the training content to suit their specific needs. This personalized approach ensures that learners are engaged with the most relevant material, enhancing their learning efficiency and effectiveness. Such customization is particularly beneficial in the diverse and complex field of cybersecurity, where professionals may have varying levels of expertise and specializations.

Utilizing AI to keep training content up-to-date and relevant is another critical application. Cybersecurity evolves very quickly, with new threats and technologies emerging constantly. AI can assist in analyzing current trends, threats, and technological advancements in real-time and updating the training content accordingly. This ensures that cybersecurity professionals are learning about the latest threats and the most current defensive strategies. AI can also help curate content from various sources, providing learners with a comprehensive and current view of the cybersecurity landscape.

Exploring AI-driven simulations and scenarios for hands-on learning is an exciting development in cybersecurity training. AI can generate realistic cyber-threat scenarios and simulations, providing learners practical, hands-on experience in a controlled environment. These simulations can mimic real-world cyberattacks, allowing trainees to apply their knowledge and test their skills in responding to these threats. This active, experiential learning is invaluable in preparing cybersecurity professionals for the challenges they will face in their roles. Additionally, AI-driven simulations can adapt to the learner's responses, increasing complexity and adapting to their skill level, providing a continuously challenging and educational experience. The future of AI in cybersecurity training looks toward more personalized and up-to-date learning experiences and more engaging and practical hands-on training.

CONTINUOUS ADAPTATION AND LEARNING

Emphasizing the importance of lifelong learning, ongoing skill development, certification, and adapting hiring practices to prioritize candidates with learning agility is essential. Keeping pace with technological advancements involves staying informed about emerging technologies like quantum computing and the IoT, and integrating these new technology skills into hiring and training programs. Developing adaptive recruitment strategies that are flexible and responsive to job market and technology trends is crucial, as is fostering a culture that embraces change and innovation. Future-proofing cybersecurity talent requires anticipating future skill requirements, focusing on foundational skills that adapt to technological changes, and maintaining a balance between specialization and broad cybersecurity knowledge. Collaboration and knowledge sharing within the cybersecurity community are vital, encouraging the sharing of best practices for talent development and building partnerships between industry, academia, and government. These approaches ensure that the cybersecurity workforce remains resilient, skilled, and prepared for future challenges.

Lifelong Learning and Upskilling

In the rapidly evolving field of cybersecurity, emphasizing the importance of continuous learning is crucial for both individuals and organizations. Cybersecurity is a discipline where new threats and technologies emerge constantly, making continuous education and skill updating essential. This commitment to lifelong learning ensures that cybersecurity professionals remain knowledgeable and effective in facing new challenges. Encouraging employees to engage in ongoing learning keeps their skills sharp and motivates them by demonstrating the organization's investment in their professional growth.

Ongoing skill development and certification are critical components of this lifelong learning approach. Cybersecurity professionals should be encouraged to pursue advanced training, certifications, and even higher education opportunities that align with the field's evolving needs. These certifications and courses provide up-to-date knowledge and skills, along with validating a professional's expertise and dedication to the field. Organizations can support this development by offering access to training programs, covering certification costs, or providing time off for educational pursuits.

Adapting hiring practices to prioritize learning agility is also important. When recruiting new talent, organizations should look beyond current technical skills and consider candidates' ability and willingness to learn new technologies and methodologies. This includes assessing candidates' self-directed learning, curiosity, and adaptability track records. Hiring for learning agility ensures that the cybersecurity team remains versatile and can quickly adapt to new challenges. By prioritizing lifelong learning and upskilling, cybersecurity teams can stay ahead in a constantly changing and evolving field.

Keeping Pace with Technological Advancements

Cybersecurity professionals must be vigilant and proactive in understanding how advancements such as AI, ML, the IoT, and quantum computing can influence security landscapes. This continuous learning about new technologies is essential for defending against sophisticated cyber threats that leverage these technologies and for harnessing their potential to enhance security measures. Staying updated requires regular engagement with industry news, participation in professional forums, and continuous research.

Integrating new technology skills into hiring and training programs is vital for building a capable, future-ready cybersecurity team. As new technologies emerge, the skills required to manage and secure these technologies also evolve. Organizations therefore need to adapt their hiring criteria and training programs to include proficiency in these new areas. This could involve updating job descriptions to reflect new skill requirements, incorporating contemporary technologies into training modules, and offering specialized training courses focusing on these emerging areas.

Preparing for the impact of advanced technologies like quantum computing and the IoT is particularly crucial. Quantum computing, for example, poses a significant challenge to traditional cryptographic methods, and cybersecurity professionals need to be prepared for the paradigm shifts it will bring. Similarly, the proliferation of IoT devices expands the attack surface dramatically, requiring new approaches to securing many interconnected devices. Preparing for these technologies involves understanding their implications and developing strategies and tools to mitigate the associated risks. Organizations should invest in research and development, participate in industry collaborations, and seek expertise in these cutting-edge areas to ensure their cybersecurity practices remain effective and resilient against rapid technological change.

Adaptive Recruitment Strategies

In the dynamic landscape of cybersecurity, developing flexible and adaptable hiring strategies is essential for organizations to attract top talent. The rapid pace of change in technology and cybersecurity threats means that the skills and competencies required today may evolve tomorrow. Hence, recruitment strategies need to be agile, with an ability to quickly respond to changing needs. This might involve regularly updating job descriptions to reflect emerging skills, adopting a more skill-based rather than credential-based approach, or even looking for candidates with solid foundational knowledge and the potential to learn and adapt.

Being responsive to changes in the job market and technology trends is crucial. As new technologies emerge and cybersecurity threats evolve, the demand for specific skills can shift significantly. Organizations must stay informed about these trends and proactively seek candidates with these emerging skill sets. This responsiveness also involves being aware of the broader job market dynamics, such as shifts in candidate preferences or the availability of talent in specific geographic regions or specializations. Adapting recruitment strategies to these market dynamics can help organizations stay competitive and attractive to potential candidates.

A culture that values continuous learning, flexibility, and adaptability is more likely to attract innovative and agile candidates. Demonstrating a commitment to staying at the forefront of technology and cybersecurity can make an organization particularly appealing to top talent. This culture should be reflected in its work practices and policies, recruitment messaging, and employer branding. By embracing change and promoting a culture of innovation, organizations can attract and retain professionals who are well-suited to thrive in cybersecurity.

Future-Proofing Cybersecurity Talent

Future-proofing the workforce is a strategic imperative in an industry as dynamic as cybersecurity. Anticipating future skill requirements is crucial for staying ahead of evolving cyber threats and technological advancements. Organizations must proactively identify the skills and competencies needed in the future, considering factors such as emerging technologies, threat landscapes, and industry trends. This foresight allows for establishing training and development programs that prepare cybersecurity talent for current challenges and future demands. By investing in ongoing education and skill development, organizations can ensure that their cybersecurity teams remain capable, adaptable, and equipped to handle new challenges as they arise.

Focusing on foundational skills that withstand technological changes is essential. While specific technical skills may evolve, certain foundational skills, such as critical thinking, problem solving, and the understanding of cybersecurity principles, remain consistently valuable. Emphasizing these core skills in training and development ensures that cybersecurity professionals have a solid base to build upon as they adapt to new technologies and methodologies. These skills enable professionals to understand and navigate the cybersecurity landscape, regardless of the specific tools or technologies used.

Balancing specialization with broad-based cybersecurity knowledge is another crucial aspect of future-proofing cybersecurity talent. While specialization in network security, incident response, or threat intelligence is valuable, a comprehensive understanding of the broader cybersecurity field is equally important. This balance ensures that professionals have a depth of knowledge in their specialized area and a broad understanding of how their specialization fits into the wider context of cybersecurity. It also prepares them to adapt more quickly to shifts within their area of expertise or to transition to different cybersecurity roles as needed. By fostering a specialized and broadly knowledgeable workforce, organizations can create a resilient and versatile cybersecurity team that is capable of responding to an ever-changing threat landscape.

Collaboration and Knowledge Sharing

In cybersecurity, characterized by rapidly evolving threats and technologies, collaboration and knowledge sharing are crucial to strengthening talent development and overall security posture. Encouraging collaboration within the cybersecurity community can involve creating forums, networks, or platforms where professionals can share insights, discuss challenges, and exchange ideas. Such collaboration can lead to a better understanding of emerging threats, developing innovative solutions, and sharing effective strategies. It also fosters a sense of community among cybersecurity professionals that is essential for mutual support and growth.

Sharing knowledge and best practices for talent development is another crucial aspect. Organizations can participate in industry conferences, workshops, and webinars to gain and impart knowledge. They can also contribute to professional publications and online communities. This sharing of knowledge not only helps in keeping the cybersecurity community informed and prepared but also contributes to the overall advancement of the field. It ensures that lessons learned and successes achieved in one area can benefit others facing similar challenges.

Building partnerships between industry, academia, and government is essential for a comprehensive approach to cybersecurity talent development. These partnerships can facilitate various collaborative initiatives such as research projects, internship programs, and curriculum development for cybersecurity education. Collaborations between academia and industry can ensure that educational programs are aligned with the practical needs of the industry, preparing students to enter the workforce with relevant skills. Partnerships with government agencies can provide insights into regulatory requirements, national security concerns, and opportunities for public-private cooperation in tackling significant cybersecurity challenges. Such multifaceted collaboration enhances talent development and contributes to a more cohesive and effective national and global cybersecurity infrastructure.

A

UTILIZING THE NIST NICE FRAMEWORK IN CYBERSECURITY HIRING

This appendix focuses on effectively incorporating the National Institute of Standards and Technology (NIST) National Initiative for Cybersecurity Education (NICE) Framework into cybersecurity hiring and workforce development. The NICE Framework provides a structured overview and common language for cybersecurity roles, which aids in standardizing roles across organizations. It is instrumental in enhancing educational and training programs by aligning them with industry needs. The framework includes various categories and specialty areas, along with a role-based approach with detailed descriptions and knowledge, skills, and abilities (KSAs) for each role—making it a valuable tool for job creation, ensuring role relevance, and customizing KSAs for organizational needs. Additionally, the framework guides career progression, aids in skill gap analysis, and supports the development of targeted training programs. It also enhances the interview and evaluation process by enabling framework-based interviewing, role-specific question development, and competency evaluation. The framework helps create personalized learning pathways and aids in tracking progress for continuous learning. Finally, integrating the NICE Framework into organizational strategy will support strategic workforce planning, talent attraction and retention, and aligning workforce capabilities with business objectives and industry changes.

INTRODUCTION TO THE NIST NICE FRAMEWORK

The NIST NICE Framework is a pivotal resource in cybersecurity workforce development, offering a structured overview and a common language for cybersecurity roles. Its objectives include categorizing and clearly defining various roles within the cybersecurity realm, which aids in standardizing these roles across organizations. This standardization is crucial for effective talent identification, recruitment, and retention. Additionally, the NICE Framework significantly enhances educational and training programs by providing guidelines for developing curricula and courses that align with the industry's evolving needs. This alignment ensures that training and education in cybersecurity are relevant, comprehensive, and directly applicable to the demands of the field.

OVERVIEW OF THE NICE FRAMEWORK

The NICE Framework, developed by the NIST in the United States, is a comprehensive guide designed to standardize and streamline cybersecurity education, training, and workforce development. This framework is vital for understanding and organizing the roles, competencies, and skills that are required in the cybersecurity domain.

The primary purpose of the NICE Framework is to provide a common language and systematic approach for managing cybersecurity workforce development. It is widely used by educators, employers, and policymakers to align cybersecurity education and training with industry needs, define professional requirements in cybersecurity roles, and establish clear career pathways in the field. The NICE Framework helps bridge the gap between the workforce's current capabilities and the industry's evolving needs by standardizing the terminology and skill sets required in cybersecurity.

The overall structure of the NICE Framework is organized into several key components:

1. **Categories:** These are broad groupings of standard cybersecurity functions. Categories provide a high-level view of the cybersecurity workforce and include areas such as *Operate and Maintain, Protect and Defend, Analyze,* and more.

2. **Specialty areas:** Within each category, specialty areas represent distinct areas of work within cybersecurity. Each specialty area focuses on specific tasks and roles, such as *Incident Response, Risk Management,* or *Software Assurance.*

3. **Work roles:** These are the most detailed groupings, defining specific roles within the cybersecurity workforce. Each work role includes a detailed description of tasks and responsibilities—providing a clear understanding of what is expected in various cybersecurity positions.

4. **KSAs:** For each work role, the NICE Framework outlines a list of specific knowledge, skills, and abilities required to perform the role effectively. These KSAs serve as a guide for individuals seeking to enter or advance in a cybersecurity career and for organizations looking to hire and train cybersecurity personnel.

The NICE Framework is a foundational tool for developing a skilled and capable cybersecurity workforce by providing this structured approach to categorizing and describing cybersecurity work. It is an essential guide for aligning educational programs with industry requirements, enhancing workforce planning and development, and improving the overall standards and capabilities of the cybersecurity profession.

FRAMEWORK OBJECTIVES

The NICE Framework has specific goals and aims in order to address critical challenges in the cybersecurity workforce. Its multifaceted objectives focus on standardization, workforce development, and aligning skills with industry needs.

One of the primary goals of the NICE Framework is to standardize cybersecurity education and work roles. Providing a comprehensive taxonomy of the skills, knowledge, and abilities needed in cybersecurity helps educational institutions develop curricula that are directly aligned with the industry's requirements. This standardization ensures that students and professionals are equipped with the relevant skills and knowledge that employers seek. Additionally, by defining specific work roles and associated competencies, the framework helps create a shared understanding and language for cybersecurity roles across different organizations and sectors.

The NICE Framework also aims to streamline developing, recruiting, and retaining cybersecurity talent. By clearly outlining career pathways and progression in cybersecurity, the framework aids individuals in navigating their career development. For employers, it serves as a guide to identify, recruit, and train employees with the necessary skills to fill specific cybersecurity roles. This leads to more effective workforce planning and talent management.

Furthermore, the NICE Framework plays a crucial role in aligning cybersecurity workforce capabilities with the industry's evolving demands. The dynamic framework is periodically updated to reflect technological changes, threats, and industry practices. This ensures that the skills and competencies defined in the framework remain relevant and up-to-date, thereby enabling the cybersecurity workforce to respond effectively to emerging challenges and technologies in the field.

Overall, the NICE Framework is vital for bridging the gap between the supply of skilled cybersecurity professionals and the demand for these skills in the marketplace. It supports the development of a robust, skilled, and adaptable cybersecurity workforce that is capable of meeting the complex challenges of today's digital world.

STANDARDIZING CYBERSECURITY ROLES

The NICE Framework is crucial in standardizing cybersecurity roles, which is fundamental in establishing a common language and expectations across the industry. By defining specific work roles and the associated KSAs that are required for each, the framework provides a clear and comprehensive guide to the various aspects of cybersecurity work. This standardization facilitates a shared understanding of what each role entails, which benefits employers and employees.

For employers, the standardization of roles means they can clearly articulate the requirements and expectations for each position, making it easier to identify suitable candidates during the hiring process. It also aids in structuring training and professional development programs to be aligned with specific role requirements. For employees and job seekers, the clear delineation of roles helps in understanding the career paths that are available in cybersecurity, the skills and qualifications required for each role, and how they can progress from one level to another within the field.

Another significant benefit of standardizing cybersecurity roles is facilitating more accessible communication and understanding across the industry. With a common framework in place, professionals across different organizations and sectors can communicate more effectively, having a mutual understanding of the roles and competencies involved. This common language is essential for collaborative efforts, such as industry-wide initiatives, cross-sector partnerships, and academic collaborations to advance cybersecurity education and workforce development.

The NICE Framework also supports the development of a skilled and versatile cybersecurity workforce. Clearly outlining the skills and knowledge needed for various roles guides individuals in their learning and development journeys, ensuring that they acquire the competencies in demand in the industry. This approach helps build a workforce that is not only skilled but also adaptable and capable of evolving with the changing landscape of cybersecurity threats and technologies. The standardization of roles, therefore, not only brings clarity and efficiency to workforce development but also contributes to the overall strengthening of cybersecurity capabilities across different organizations and sectors.

ENHANCING EDUCATIONAL AND TRAINING PROGRAMS

The NICE Framework significantly enhances educational and training programs in cybersecurity by providing a clear and comprehensive guideline for curriculum development and skills training. This framework is a valuable resource for educational institutions, helping them align their cybersecurity programs with industry requirements and workforce needs.

For educational institutions, the NICE Framework acts as a guide in curriculum development. It outlines the specific KSAs that are required for various roles within the cybersecurity domain. This information is crucial for educators to design courses and programs that are academically rigorous and practically relevant. By incorporating the competencies and work roles identified in the NICE Framework into their curriculum, educational institutions can ensure that their students are well-prepared for the demands of the cybersecurity workforce upon graduation.

Aligning training programs with industry needs is another critical area where the NICE Framework is instrumental. For organizations offering professional development and training programs in cybersecurity, the framework provides a detailed understanding of the current skills that are in demand in the industry. Training providers can use this information to tailor their offerings, ensuring that their programs help professionals develop the competencies that employers seek most. This alignment between training programs and industry needs is essential for addressing the skills gap in the cybersecurity sector.

Furthermore, the NICE Framework makes it easier for educational institutions and industry players to collaborate on initiatives such as internships, apprenticeships, joint research projects, and workforce development programs. These collaborations benefit both parties: they provide students and trainees with practical, hands-on experience, while giving employers access to a pool of talent trained in the specific skills they require. Such partnerships are crucial for building a robust and responsive cybersecurity workforce that can effectively meet the challenges of the digital age.

NAVIGATING THE NICE FRAMEWORK COMPONENTS

Navigating the NICE Framework involves comprehensively understanding its components to implement it in cybersecurity workforce development effectively. The framework is organized into various categories, each encompassing specific specialty areas that define the breadth of cybersecurity work. It adopts a role-based approach, providing detailed role descriptions that facilitate a clear understanding and communication of job functions in the cybersecurity domain. Central to this framework are the KSAs that are associated with each role, which are meticulously defined to align with the specific requirements and competencies needed in the field. This structured approach aids in creating precise job descriptions, training programs, and career development pathways, thereby ensuring alignment with the evolving needs of the cybersecurity industry.

UNDERSTANDING FRAMEWORK CATEGORIES

The NICE Framework categorizes the diverse aspects of cybersecurity work into several distinct categories, each representing a key area of function within the field. Understanding these categories is crucial for comprehending the full scope of cybersecurity roles and responsibilities. Each category encompasses specific activities and skill sets required in the cybersecurity domain.

Exploring the different categories defined in the framework involves looking at the high-level groupings of cybersecurity functions. The NICE Framework broadly classifies these functions such as:

- **Securely Provision:** This category involves conceptualizing, designing, and implementing secure IT systems. Roles in this category are typically focused on system architecture, software development, and risk management.
- **Operate and Maintain:** Focusing on the operation and maintenance of secure IT systems, this category includes roles that involve network administration, systems analysis, and cybersecurity operations.
- **Protect and Defend:** This category is centered around identifying, analyzing, and mitigating threats to IT systems. Roles under this grouping are typically concerned with incident response, threat analysis, and security monitoring.
- **Investigate:** This category deals with investigating cybersecurity events or crimes. Roles here encompass digital forensics, investigation analysis, and law enforcement activities related to cyber incidents.

- **Collect and Operate:** This category includes roles involved in collecting cybersecurity information and operating related collection systems.
- **Analyze:** In this category, the focus is on analyzing cybersecurity information to understand threats, vulnerabilities, and risks. Roles in analysis are crucial for strategic decision making and planning.
- **Oversight and Development:** This category involves establishing, managing, and governance of cybersecurity policies and strategies. It includes roles related to training, education, and policy development.

Each of these categories aligns with specific functions and tasks in cybersecurity, delineating clear areas of focus and expertise. Organizations can better structure their cybersecurity teams, define role responsibilities, and plan workforce development by examining how these categories relate to various cybersecurity functions. Additionally, individuals who are seeking to enter or advance in cybersecurity can use these categories to identify areas of interest and the specific skills they need to develop in order to follow their desired career path.

SPECIALTY AREAS WITHIN CATEGORIES

The NICE Framework further breaks down the broad categories of cybersecurity functions into more specific specialty areas. These specialty areas provide a detailed view of the diverse roles and responsibilities within the field of cybersecurity, each contributing uniquely to the overall cybersecurity ecosystem.

Delving into specific specialty areas involves exploring the various aspects of cybersecurity work that are categorized under each broad function. For instance:

- Under the **Securely Provision** category, specialty areas might include *"Risk Management,"* focusing on identifying and mitigating risks to IT systems, and *"Software Development,"* which is concerned with creating secure applications.
- In the **Operate and Maintain** category, specialties like *"Systems Administration,"* which is responsible for managing and ensuring the security of IT systems, and *"Network Services,"* which deals with the operation and maintenance of network systems, are critical.
- The **Protect and Defend** category includes critical areas such as *"Incident Response,"* where professionals manage and mitigate the impact of cybersecurity incidents, and *"Vulnerability Assessment and Management,"* focused on identifying and addressing system vulnerabilities.

- Within **Investigate**, specialties like *"Digital Forensics,"* which involves analyzing cybercrimes and extracting digital evidence, play a crucial role.
- The **Analyze** category encompasses *"Threat Analysis,"* where professionals evaluate and understand cyber threats, and *"Security Intelligence,"* which focuses on gathering and analyzing information to predict and prevent cyberattacks.

Understanding the significance of these specialty areas in the cybersecurity ecosystem is crucial. Each specialty area addresses a specific component of cybersecurity, contributing to the overall resilience and security of IT systems. For instance, while incident responders manage the aftermath of a cyberattack, threat analysts work proactively to identify potential threats before they materialize. Similarly, risk management professionals help craft strategies that reduce vulnerabilities, complementing the work of those in system administration who implement and maintain these strategies.

The delineation of these specialty areas helps organizations structure their cybersecurity teams effectively, ensuring that all aspects of cybersecurity are adequately covered. For individuals in cybersecurity, these specialty areas provide a roadmap for career development, allowing them to focus on and develop expertise in cybersecurity that aligns with their interests and career goals. This detailed structuring of the cybersecurity field into specialty areas ensures a comprehensive approach to protecting against and responding to cyber threats.

ROLE-BASED APPROACH

The NICE Framework adopts a role-based approach, identifying and analyzing distinct work roles within cybersecurity. Each work role is defined with specific responsibilities and required competencies, highlighting its importance in the broader cybersecurity ecosystem.

Analyzing the distinct work roles that are outlined in the framework involves delving into the specific tasks, skills, and knowledge that are required for each role. For example:

- **Cybersecurity analyst:** This role typically involves monitoring and analyzing cybersecurity threats, evaluating the security of systems and networks, and responding to incidents. The analyst plays a crucial part in identifying vulnerabilities and threats, thus protecting the organization from potential cyberattacks.

- **Incident responder:** People working in this capacity would be responsible for addressing and managing the aftermath of security breaches and cyberattacks. Their responsibilities include identifying the extent of the intrusion, mitigating the damage, and implementing strategies to prevent future incidents. This role is critical for minimizing the impact of attacks and restoring normal operations.
- **Security auditor:** The role of a security auditor is to focus on assessing and evaluating the effectiveness of security policies and systems. This role involves conducting audits, identifying security gaps, and recommending improvements. They are crucial in ensuring that the cybersecurity measures comply with regulatory standards and best practices.
- **Network security engineer:** A network security engineer specializes in protecting the organization's computer networks from threats. Responsibilities include designing secure network solutions, implementing security measures, and monitoring traffic for suspicious activity. This role is essential for safeguarding sensitive data and maintaining the integrity of the network infrastructure.
- **Cybersecurity manager/coordinator:** Anyone in this role would be responsible for overseeing the cybersecurity team and strategies. This role involves planning and implementing comprehensive cybersecurity measures, managing the team, and coordinating with other departments to ensure a cohesive security posture.

Each of these roles carries distinct responsibilities and requires specific skills and knowledge. Understanding the importance of each role helps in appreciating how they collectively contribute to an organization's cybersecurity defenses. Organizations can use this role-based approach to ensure that their cybersecurity teams are well-rounded and equipped to handle various aspects of cybersecurity. For professionals in the field, these roles provide a clear guide for career development, helping them focus on specific areas of interest and expertise within cybersecurity.

DETAILED ROLE DESCRIPTIONS

Providing in-depth descriptions of specific cybersecurity roles is crucial for clarity and understanding, especially in a complex and multifaceted field. These descriptions help delineate the scope, responsibilities, and skills required for each role, making it easier for individuals and organizations to understand their significance and how they fit into the broader cybersecurity landscape:

- **Cybersecurity analyst:** A cybersecurity analyst protects an organization's computer systems and networks. They monitor systems for unusual activities, analyze security breaches, and respond to incidents. They also play a crucial role in developing security policies and procedures. Their in-depth understanding of cybersecurity threats and their ability to analyze and interpret data are vital for detecting vulnerabilities and preventing potential security incidents.

- **Incident responder:** This role involves responding to and managing the aftermath of cyberattacks. Incident responders assess the damage caused by security breaches, contain the attack, and work on recovery processes. They are also involved in post-incident analysis to understand how the breach occurred, and they develop strategies to prevent future incidents. Their ability to act swiftly and effectively in the event of an attack is crucial for minimizing damage and maintaining organizational security.

- **Security auditor:** Security auditors conduct comprehensive reviews of an organization's information systems to ensure they comply with internal and external security standards and regulations. They evaluate security policies, procedures, and controls, identify vulnerabilities, and recommend enhancements. Their work is essential for ensuring ongoing compliance and identifying potential areas where security measures need strengthening.

- **Network security engineer:** This role safeguards an organization's network infrastructure. Network security engineers design and implement secure network solutions, manage firewalls, monitor network traffic for anomalies, and conduct regular security assessments. Their expertise is crucial for protecting sensitive data that is being transmitted across the network and preventing unauthorized access.

- **Cybersecurity manager/coordinator:** A cybersecurity manager or coordinator oversees the organization's security strategy and cybersecurity team. They are responsible for policy development, security planning, and coordinating the response to security incidents. They also play a crucial role in staff training and awareness programs. Leaders must have a broad understanding of cybersecurity principles and management skills to guide their teams and align cybersecurity strategies with business objectives.

Each of these roles plays a critical part in the cybersecurity ecosystem. They work in tandem to protect organizations from cyber threats, ensure compliance with security regulations, and maintain the integrity and confidentiality of information. Understanding these roles in detail helps structure an effective cybersecurity team and provides a career path for individuals looking to enter or advance in this field.

DEFINING KSAs

In the context of the NICE Framework and cybersecurity roles, KSAs are critical components that define the competencies required for each specific role. Understanding and detailing the KSAs is essential for individuals who are seeking to enter or advance in cybersecurity and organizations that are looking to hire the right talent:

- **Knowledge:** Knowledge refers to the theoretical understanding or factual information that an individual needs to perform a specific role. This might include knowledge of network architectures, understanding of cybersecurity principles, awareness of current threats and vulnerabilities, and familiarity with legal and regulatory requirements. Knowledge is typically gained through education, training, and continuous learning.
- **Skills:** Skills are the practical application of knowledge. They are the ability to perform tasks effectively and efficiently. In cybersecurity roles, this could include skills in threat analysis, proficiency in security tools and software, coding skills, or the ability to conduct digital forensics investigations. Skills are often developed through hands-on experience, practice, and formal training.
- **Abilities:** Abilities refer to the innate characteristics or talents that enable an individual to perform tasks. This might include analytical thinking, problem-solving ability, attention to detail, or working under pressure in cybersecurity. Abilities can be innate or developed over time through experience and practice.

Understanding how KSAs contribute to role proficiency is crucial. Combining the proper KSAs makes an individual proficient in cybersecurity. For example, a cybersecurity analyst needs the *knowledge* of security protocols, the *skill* to analyze security data, and the *ability* to identify patterns and anomalies. Together, these KSAs enable analysts to perform their roles effectively.

For individuals, understanding the KSAs that are associated with different cybersecurity roles can help guide their career development, informing decisions about education, training, and professional experiences. For organizations, clearly defining the KSAs needed for each role aids in creating accurate job descriptions, conducting effective recruitment, and developing targeted training programs to build a skilled cybersecurity workforce.

APPLICATION IN HIRING AND TRAINING

Utilizing KSAs to inform hiring decisions and training needs is a strategic approach in workforce development, particularly in the cybersecurity sector:

- **In hiring:** Employers can use the KSAs defined in the NICE Framework to create detailed and accurate job descriptions when filling cybersecurity roles. This helps attract candidates who are qualified and a good fit for the specific requirements of the role. During the recruitment process, KSAs serve as criteria for evaluating candidates. Employers can make more informed hiring decisions by assessing applicants against these specific KSA. This approach ensures that the selected candidates possess the right combination of expertise and competencies required for the role, thereby enhancing the effectiveness of the cybersecurity team.
- **In training needs analysis:** KSAs are invaluable in identifying training and development needs within an organization. Gaps can be identified by comparing the current KSAs of employees with those required for their roles or desired career progression. These gaps then inform the development of targeted training programs, workshops, and other educational initiatives. This ensures that training is relevant and tailored to the workforce's specific needs, thus enhancing the overall capabilities and preparedness of the cybersecurity team.

Leveraging KSAs for employee development and career progression involves a continuous process of assessment and growth:

- **For employee development:** KSAs provide a roadmap for individual employees to enhance their competencies. Employees can use the framework to identify areas for improvement or expansion of their skill set. This could involve seeking additional training certifications or taking on new projects that challenge their current abilities. By continually developing their KSAs, employees can increase their effectiveness in their current roles and prepare for more advanced responsibilities.
- **For career progression:** Understanding the KSAs that are associated with various roles within the NICE Framework enables employees to plan their career development strategically. For instance, an individual aiming to move from a technical role to a managerial position in

cybersecurity can identify the additional skills and knowledge needed for this transition and seek opportunities to acquire them. This proactive approach to career development benefits both the individual and the organization because it helps build a workforce that is skilled, versatile, and ready to meet future challenges.

In summary, effectively applying KSAs in hiring and training improves the cybersecurity team's immediate effectiveness and ensures its long-term resilience and adaptability in an ever-evolving field.

ALIGNING JOB REQUIREMENTS WITH THE NICE FRAMEWORK

Aligning job requirements with the NICE Framework involves utilizing the framework as a foundational tool for job creation in cybersecurity, thereby ensuring that each role is relevant and precise. This process includes integrating the KSAs outlined in the framework into job criteria, thus ensuring that the roles are precisely defined and aligned with industry standards. Additionally, there's an emphasis on customizing these KSAs to meet an organization's specific needs, allowing for the tailoring of roles to address unique organizational challenges and goals. This alignment facilitates effective and targeted hiring and ensures that the workforce is equipped with the necessary competencies to meet the evolving demands of the cybersecurity field.

UTILIZING THE FRAMEWORK FOR JOB CREATION

The NICE Framework is an invaluable tool for organizations crafting job descriptions for cybersecurity positions. By leveraging the detailed role descriptions provided by the framework, employers can ensure that job postings accurately reflect the responsibilities, skills, and knowledge that are required for specific positions in the field of cybersecurity:

- **Crafting job descriptions based on NICE Framework roles:** When creating job descriptions, the NICE Framework offers a comprehensive breakdown of roles categorized by specific KSAs. Employers can use these categories to define each role's core responsibilities and qualifications. For instance, a job description for a cybersecurity analyst can be developed by referring to the *Analyze* category in the framework, which details the requisite skills and knowledge for analysis-focused roles. This approach ensures that job descriptions are aligned with industry standards and expectations, making them more effective in attracting suitable candidates.

- **Ensuring comprehensive coverage of responsibilities and expectations:** Utilizing the NICE Framework ensures that job descriptions cover all critical aspects of the role. This includes not only technical competencies but also soft skills and general responsibilities. For example, a job description for a network security engineer can detail not only the technical skills in network defense strategies but also the ability to communicate effectively with other departments and to stay abreast of the latest technological developments. The framework's comprehensive approach helps set clear expectations for potential applicants, thereby enhancing the likelihood of finding candidates who are well-aligned with the role's requirements.

By accurately reflecting the scope of each role as outlined in the NICE Framework, organizations can create job descriptions that are clear, detailed, and tailored to attract the right talent. This alignment with the framework not only aids in efficient and effective recruitment but also ensures that the hired candidates are well-suited to meet the organization's cybersecurity needs.

ENSURING ROLE RELEVANCE AND CLARITY

In the dynamic field of cybersecurity, aligning job roles with current industry needs and standards is crucial for attracting the right talent and ensuring the effectiveness of the cybersecurity workforce. Utilizing frameworks like NICE helps maintain this alignment and relevance:

- **Aligning job roles with current industry needs and standards:** The cybersecurity landscape continually evolves, with new threats, technologies, and best practices emerging regularly. To ensure that job roles remain relevant and practical, they must be aligned with these current industry dynamics. Organizations can use the NICE Framework to regularly update and tailor job roles to reflect the latest industry needs and standards. For instance, if there's an increasing focus on cloud security in the industry, roles can be adjusted or created to address cloud security concerns, ensuring that the organization stays ahead of potential threats and keeps pace with technological advancements.
- **Providing clear and precise role outlines for potential candidates:** Clarity and precision in job descriptions are crucial to attracting suitable candidates. The NICE Framework's detailed breakdown of roles, categorized by specific KSAs, provides a solid foundation for crafting

clear job descriptions. Each role outline should comprehensively describe the responsibilities, required qualifications, expected competencies, and any unique aspects of the position. This clarity helps potential candidates to understand precisely what is expected in the role and assess their suitability for the position. It also aids in setting realistic expectations, reducing the likelihood of misunderstandings or misalignments between the role and the candidate's capabilities or expectations.

By ensuring role relevance and clarity, organizations can effectively attract and retain talent that is not only qualified but also well-matched to the specific needs of their cybersecurity operations. This approach contributes to building a robust, skilled, and responsive cybersecurity workforce capable of addressing the complex challenges in the field.

INTEGRATING KSAs INTO JOB CRITERIA

Incorporating KSAs into job criteria is crucial to creating effective job postings and descriptions in cybersecurity. By reflecting the required KSAs in job postings, employers can communicate the expectations and requirements of the role to potential candidates:

- **Reflecting the required KSAs in job postings and descriptions:** Utilizing the NICE Framework, employers can accurately detail the specific KSAs required for a particular cybersecurity role. This might include, for example, knowledge of specific cybersecurity protocols and standards, skills in using certain security tools and software, or the ability to analyze and respond to cyber threats. By explicitly listing these KSAs in the job description, candidates can better understand what is expected of them and self-assess their suitability for the role. It also helps streamline the recruitment process since matching candidates to job requirements becomes easier.
- **Using the NICE Framework to identify essential qualifications and skills:** The NICE Framework is a valuable tool for employers to identify the essential qualifications and skills needed for various cybersecurity roles. It helps distinguish between must-have and nice-to-have qualifications, focusing on the core competencies required for effective performance in the role. This clarity benefits the employer and the job seeker, ensuring that the recruitment process targets the right talent. Additionally, it aids in developing a more focused and efficient

interview process since interview questions and assessments can be tailored to evaluate the specific KSAs outlined in the job description.

By integrating KSAs into job criteria using the NICE Framework, organizations can enhance the quality of their recruitment process, ensuring that they attract and select candidates who are well-equipped to meet the demands of the cybersecurity roles they are filling. This approach improves the fit between the candidate and the role and contributes to building a more capable and effective cybersecurity workforce.

CUSTOMIZING KSAs FOR ORGANIZATION-SPECIFIC NEEDS

Adapting the NICE Framework's KSAs to suit specific organizational contexts is a critical step in tailoring cybersecurity roles to meet an individual organization's unique needs and challenges. While the NICE Framework provides a comprehensive and standardized set of KSAs for various cybersecurity roles, each organization may have specific requirements, culture, and strategic objectives that necessitate customization of these standards:

- **Adapting the NICE Framework KSAs to suit specific organizational contexts:** Organizations can start by reviewing the KSAs in the NICE Framework and modifying them to align with their specific operational environment and cybersecurity challenges. For instance, a company that heavily relies on cloud computing may place a greater emphasis on KSAs related to cloud security. Similarly, an organization in a heavily regulated industry might require additional KSAs about compliance and regulatory knowledge. This customization ensures that the workforce has the skills and knowledge that are most relevant to the organization's cybersecurity landscape.
- **Balancing standardized skills with unique company requirements:** While adhering to industry standards and best practices as outlined in the NICE Framework is essential, it is equally crucial to incorporate the organization's unique requirements into the cybersecurity roles. This balance can be achieved by maintaining the core KSAs that are universally recognized as essential for cybersecurity roles and then supplementing them with additional skills and knowledge that cater to specific organizational needs. For example, besides standard technical skills, an organization may also look for candidates with experience in specific sectors, familiarity with certain regulatory frameworks, or

proficiency in niche cybersecurity technologies that are particularly relevant to the company.

Customizing the KSAs not only aids in recruiting and developing talent that is well-suited to address the organization's specific cybersecurity challenges but also helps foster a workforce closely aligned with the organization's overall mission and strategic goals. This tailored approach to defining KSAs facilitates the development of a cybersecurity team that can effectively respond to the organization's unique security environment, thereby enhancing its overall cybersecurity posture.

UTILIZING THE NICE FRAMEWORK FOR CAREER PATHWAYS

Utilizing the NICE Framework for career pathways in cybersecurity involves a strategic approach to guided career progression, where the framework aids in setting clear goals and milestones for professionals. It enables a thorough analysis of skill gaps, identifying areas where individuals must develop to progress in their careers. This analysis is then used to design targeted training programs that are tailored to fill these gaps, thus ensuring that the training is highly relevant and practical. By aligning career progression with the structured guidance of the NICE Framework, organizations can create clear, attainable career paths for their employees, fostering professional growth and development that is in sync with the evolving needs of the cybersecurity industry.

GUIDED CAREER PROGRESSION

Guided career progression within cybersecurity, mainly when directed by the NICE Framework, offers a systematic approach to mapping potential career paths. This framework breaks down cybersecurity into specific roles, each with defined skills, knowledge, and abilities. For example, it delineates a path from an entry-level cybersecurity technician who is focusing on implementing basic security measures to a more advanced role like a cybersecurity analyst who is responsible for threat detection and response strategies. Using the NICE Framework, HR managers can show employees a clear progression route, emphasizing the incremental acquisition of skills and responsibilities. This helps create a transparent and achievable career ladder, where each rung represents a new set of competencies and a deeper understanding of the field.

Furthermore, the framework aids employees in comprehending their career trajectory within the complex and ever-evolving cybersecurity landscape. For instance, an employee beginning as a network security administrator can use the framework to understand the path toward becoming a network security architect. The NICE Framework outlines the necessary skills and qualifications for each role, helping employees identify the areas they need to develop. This guidance is invaluable for career planning, allowing employees to focus on targeted skill development and seek appropriate training opportunities. Such a guided approach not only empowers employees to take charge of their career progression but also aligns their personal growth with the organization's strategic needs, creating a workforce that is both skilled and motivated to advance within the cybersecurity domain.

SETTING GOALS AND MILESTONES

Developing clear objectives for career advancement involves establishing specific, measurable, achievable, relevant, and time-bound goals that align with the individual's career aspirations and the organization's needs. For instance, a cybersecurity professional in an entry-level position might aim to become a certified security analyst within two years. This goal is specific and time-bound and aligns with the individual's career trajectory and the organization's requirement for skilled analysts.

Identifying key milestones and skill development targets is equally crucial. Milestones serve as checkpoints in the journey toward achieving the larger objectives. They can be viewed as short-term goals that pave the way for career advancement. For example, a professional aiming for a role in cybersecurity management might set milestones such as completing a leadership training program or leading a small project team. Regarding skill development, targets could include mastering specific cybersecurity tools, gaining proficiency in a particular programming language, or understanding the latest compliance regulations. These targets should be clearly defined and must directly contribute to achieving the broader career objectives. By setting these milestones and skill development targets, professionals can ensure a structured and focused approach to career growth that facilitates continuous learning and development in cybersecurity.

SKILL GAP ANALYSIS

Skill gap analysis in cybersecurity is a critical process that involves assessing an employee's current skills against the desired competencies required for specific roles or career advancement. This analysis helps pinpoint the specific areas where an individual may need further development in order to meet the demands of their current role or to prepare for future roles. For instance, a cybersecurity professional might be proficient in incident response but may lack skills in risk assessment or data privacy regulations. By conducting a skill gap analysis, the organization can identify and address these areas of deficiency through targeted training or professional development opportunities.

Identifying areas for improvement and growth is a crucial outcome of the skill gap analysis. It is about addressing current shortcomings and preparing for future challenges and opportunities in the cybersecurity landscape. This might involve staying abreast of emerging technologies, such as artificial intelligence (AI) or blockchain, or developing soft skills, such as leadership and communication, which are increasingly crucial in higher-level cybersecurity roles. For example, an IT professional who is looking to transition into a cybersecurity analyst role may need to develop a deeper understanding of network security and threat intelligence. Identifying these areas for improvement allows individuals to focus their learning efforts more effectively and helps organizations tailor their training programs to build a more competent and versatile cybersecurity workforce.

TARGETED TRAINING PROGRAMS

Targeted training programs are essential in cybersecurity for addressing specific skill gaps that have been identified through skill gap analysis. Designing these training initiatives requires a focused approach where the content is tailored to meet employees' specific needs. For example, suppose a skill gap analysis reveals that a group of employees lacks expertise in cloud security. In that case, the organization can develop or source a training program focusing on cloud security technologies, best practices, and threat mitigation strategies. This targeted approach ensures that the training is relevant and practical and directly contributes to filling the identified skill gaps.

Aligning employee development with NICE Framework standards is another critical aspect of targeted training programs. The NICE Framework outlines the KSAs required for various cybersecurity roles. Training programs should be designed to align with these standards, ensuring that they address the organization's current needs and prepare employees for future roles and challenges in the cybersecurity landscape. For instance, if the NICE Framework highlights a growing need for skills in cybersecurity risk management, training programs can be developed to focus on this area—helping employees understand risk assessment methodologies, compliance requirements, and risk mitigation strategies. By aligning training initiatives with the NICE

Framework, organizations can ensure that their workforce development efforts align with industry standards and best practices, thereby leading to a more capable and proficient cybersecurity team.

ENHANCING THE INTERVIEW AND EVALUATION PROCESS

Enhancing the interview and evaluation process in cybersecurity hiring by using the NICE Framework involves adopting a framework-based interviewing approach. This method ensures that interviews are structured around the specific roles and competencies outlined in the framework, thus leading to the development of role-specific questions that accurately assess the required skills and knowledge. It also facilitates a thorough evaluation of a candidate's competencies, ensuring that they align with the defined KSAs for the role. Additionally, this approach allows for an assessment of the candidate's cultural and organizational fit, ensuring they have the technical skills required and align with the company's values and work environment. By incorporating the NICE Framework into the interview and evaluation process, organizations can make more informed and effective hiring decisions that contribute to building a competent and cohesive cybersecurity team.

FRAMEWORK-BASED INTERVIEWING

Structuring interview questions around framework-based interviewing is a strategic approach for assessing candidates in the cybersecurity domain. By formulating questions that are based on the NICE Framework roles and their associated KSAs, interviewers can ensure that their questions are relevant, comprehensive, and aligned with industry standards. For example, when interviewing for a cybersecurity analyst role, questions can be crafted to assess a candidate's proficiency in areas outlined by the NICE Framework for that role—such as their ability to analyze and interpret data, knowledge of cybersecurity threats, and experience with specific security tools and methodologies.

Ensuring a comprehensive assessment of candidate capabilities is crucial in this process. The interview should be designed to evaluate technical skills, soft skills, and other competencies that are critical for the role. This might include questions aimed at understanding a candidate's problem-solving abilities, their approach to continuous learning, and their ability to work collaboratively in a team. By structuring the interview in this way, organizations can gain a holistic view of the candidate's capabilities, ensuring that they are technically proficient and a good fit for the team and the broader organizational culture. Such a thorough assessment is critical to identifying candidates who are well-equipped to handle the challenges of a cybersecurity role and contribute effectively to the organization's cybersecurity efforts.

ROLE-SPECIFIC QUESTION DEVELOPMENT

Role-specific question development is crucial to structuring compelling interviews for cybersecurity positions. This approach involves tailoring interview questions to align with specific roles defined by the NICE Framework. By focusing on the unique requirements of each role, interviewers can craft questions that directly probe the candidate's suitability for the position. For instance, if interviewing for a role in incident response, questions might focus on the candidate's experience in handling cybersecurity breaches, their familiarity with incident response protocols, and their ability to work under pressure.

Focusing on relevant skills and experiences for each position ensures that the interview effectively assesses the candidate's proficiency in areas critical to the role. It is important to ask questions about their practical experiences, problem-solving skills, and specific technical competencies. For a cybersecurity risk management role, interview questions might concentrate on the candidate's experience with risk assessment tools, their understanding of compliance regulations, and their approach to developing risk mitigation strategies. This targeted approach allows the interviewer to understand the candidate's capabilities and experiences with the specific demands of the position, ensuring that the chosen candidate possesses the skills and knowledge essential for success in that role.

COMPETENCY EVALUATION

Competency evaluation in cybersecurity hiring involves a comprehensive assessment of candidates' skills and knowledge, mainly based on the criteria outlined in the NICE Framework. This evaluation method requires a systematic approach to determine whether candidates possess the competencies that have been outlined for specific cybersecurity roles. For example, when evaluating a candidate for a cybersecurity engineering position, the interviewer would assess technical skills such as proficiency in security software, understanding of network protocols, and experience with encryption technologies because these are critical competencies that are highlighted by the NICE Framework for such roles.

In addition to overall technical skills, assessing technical and soft skills that are pertinent to the role is equally crucial. Soft skills, including problem-solving abilities, communication skills, teamwork, and adaptability, are integral to the success of cybersecurity professionals. For instance, a candidate for a cybersecurity management role might be evaluated on leadership qualities, ability to communicate security policies effectively, and skill in managing cross-functional teams. These soft skills are essential for roles that require collaboration, strategic decision making, and the ability to handle high-pressure situations. By assessing a combination of technical expertise and soft skills, employers can ensure a well-rounded evaluation, selecting candidates who are technically competent and capable of thriving in the collaborative and dynamic environment of cybersecurity work.

CULTURAL AND ORGANIZATIONAL FIT

In the context of cultural and organizational fit, the NICE Framework can be instrumental in aligning candidate evaluations with the company's values and culture. When considering how candidates align with company values and culture, the NICE Framework's detailed role descriptions and competencies can serve as a reference point for what the organization values regarding skills, behaviors, and attitudes. For example, suppose a company prioritizes innovation and adaptability in its cybersecurity team. In that case, HR managers can use the NICE Framework to identify roles and competencies that emphasize these qualities, such as roles that require staying up-to-date with emerging technologies or adapting to changing cybersecurity threats.

Furthermore, the NICE Framework aids in balancing technical proficiency with interpersonal and team dynamics. It does so by providing a comprehensive view of each role, including the required technical skills and the soft skills and attributes that are necessary to excel in that role. For instance, a role that requires significant collaboration may list competencies in teamwork and communication as critical requirements. By using the NICE Framework as a guide, interviewers can develop questions and assessment criteria that evaluate these softer skills alongside technical abilities. This ensures a holistic assessment of candidates, where their ability to integrate into the team and contribute to the company culture is as important as their technical expertise. Thus, the NICE Framework becomes a valuable tool in ensuring that new hires are technically competent and a good fit for the organization's culture and values.

LEVERAGING THE NICE FRAMEWORK FOR CONTINUOUS LEARNING

Leveraging the NICE Framework for continuous learning in cybersecurity involves using the framework to drive training initiatives for creating personalized learning pathways tailored to individual roles and career aspirations. This approach focuses on ongoing skill enhancement, ensuring that professionals continually develop their competencies in alignment with evolving industry standards and requirements. By adopting a framework-driven training model, organizations can systematically address the dynamic nature of cybersecurity challenges, thereby keeping their workforce adept and responsive. Additionally, the framework facilitates tracking progress and achievements, enabling individuals and organizations to monitor learning outcomes and career development effectively. This structured approach to continuous learning ensures that the workforce remains up-to-date with the latest cybersecurity trends and technologies, thus fostering a culture of continuous improvement and professional growth.

FRAMEWORK-DRIVEN TRAINING

Framework-driven training, mainly using the NICE Framework, is an effective strategy for identifying and addressing training needs in the realm of cybersecurity. Utilizing the NICE Framework helps organizations precisely pinpoint their cybersecurity workforce's training requirements. This process involves mapping employees' current skills and competencies against the comprehensive list of KSAs outlined in the NICE Framework for various cybersecurity roles. For instance, if an analysis reveals a gap in advanced threat analysis skills among the team, this indicates a specific training need that can be directly addressed.

Once these training needs are identified, organizations can create or source training programs that are closely aligned with the identified KSAs and roles. This ensures that the training is highly relevant and tailored to fill the existing skill gaps. For example, suppose the NICE Framework indicates a need for proficiency in risk management for specific roles. In that case, the organization can develop or adopt training programs that are focused on risk assessment methodologies, compliance standards, and risk mitigation strategies. By aligning training initiatives with the NICE Framework, organizations ensure that their cybersecurity workforce is equipped with the latest skills and knowledge, directly contributing to enhanced cybersecurity capabilities and preparedness. This approach not only enhances the skill set of individual employees but also strengthens the organization's overall cybersecurity posture.

PERSONALIZED LEARNING PATHWAYS

Personalized learning pathways, developed per NICE Framework guidelines, are crucial in fostering a skilled and adaptable cybersecurity workforce. By creating individualized training plans for each employee, organizations can cater to their staff's specific needs and career aspirations while ensuring alignment with the broader skills and competencies outlined in the NICE Framework. For instance, an employee aiming to transition from a technical role to a cybersecurity management position would require a different training plan than someone focusing on technical expertise in areas like network security. These training plans can be tailored based on the individual's current skill level, the competencies required for the desired role per the NICE Framework, and personal career goals.

Encouraging self-directed learning and professional growth is also essential in these personalized learning pathways. Employees should be motivated to take charge of their learning journey by identifying areas where they want to expand their knowledge and skills. This could involve choosing specific certifications, workshops, or online courses that align with their interests and the NICE Framework's recommendations for their target role. By fostering a culture of self-directed learning, organizations empower their employees to continuously develop and stay abreast of the latest trends and technologies in cybersecurity. This approach benefits the individual in terms of career development and job satisfaction. It ensures that the organization has a continuously evolving and skilled cybersecurity team that is capable of meeting current and future challenges.

ONGOING SKILL ENHANCEMENT

Promoting continuous learning and upskilling is critical to ensuring that the cybersecurity workforce is adept at dealing with new challenges and technologies. This involves creating a work environment that values and encourages regular learning. Organizations can implement policies that allow time for learning during work hours, provide incentives for completing courses or obtaining certifications, and regularly communicate the importance of staying current with industry developments. For instance, an organization might encourage its cybersecurity team to regularly participate in workshops on the latest cybersecurity threats and mitigation strategies, thereby ensuring that their skills remain relevant and current.

Providing resources and support for employee skill development is also crucial. This can be achieved by offering access to training platforms, funding for professional courses or certifications, and opportunities to attend industry conferences and seminars. Mentorship programs can be established where more experienced employees guide others in their learning and career development. Additionally, organizations can create internal knowledge-sharing sessions where employees share insights and learn from recent training or projects. By investing in these resources and support systems, organizations not only enhance the capabilities of their cybersecurity team but also demonstrate a commitment to their employees' professional growth. This not only aids in skill development but also contributes to higher job satisfaction and retention rates.

TRACKING PROGRESS AND ACHIEVEMENTS

Tracking progress and achievements is vital to managing a cybersecurity workforce, especially when aligned with the NICE Framework standards. Monitoring employee progress involves regularly evaluating their skills and competencies against the benchmarks set by the NICE Framework. This can be done through periodic assessments, performance reviews, and tracking of training completions and certifications. For example, if an employee is working toward a role that requires expertise in cybersecurity risk analysis, their progress in acquiring relevant skills like risk assessment methodologies and proficiency in risk management tools can be tracked against the specific KSAs outlined in the NICE Framework for that role. This systematic approach helps identify areas where additional training may be needed and helps to plan future career development steps that align with the employee's aspirations and the organization's needs.

Recognizing and rewarding skill advancement and application is equally important in motivating employees and reinforcing the value of continuous learning. This can involve formal recognition programs, such as awards or special acknowledgments in company meetings, for employees who achieve significant milestones like earning a high-level certification or successfully leading a major cybersecurity project. Additionally, tangible rewards such as bonuses, promotions, or other incentives can be provided to those who demonstrate exceptional skill development and application in their roles. By acknowledging and rewarding these achievements, organizations motivate their staff and cultivate a culture of excellence and continuous improvement in their cybersecurity teams. This not only enhances the skills and capabilities of the individuals but also contributes to the overall strength and effectiveness of the cybersecurity workforce.

INTEGRATING THE NICE FRAMEWORK INTO ORGANIZATIONAL STRATEGY

Integrating the NICE Framework into an organization's strategy is critical for effective cybersecurity workforce planning. It serves as a foundation for strategic planning, ensuring that the workforce is aligned with current and future cybersecurity needs. This alignment helps attract and retain top talent since clear role definitions and career pathways that were outlined in the framework make the organization more appealing to professionals who are seeking growth and development. The framework also ensures that cybersecurity roles and training align with the organization's broader business objectives, which will enhance overall business resilience and capability. Furthermore, the NICE Framework's comprehensive structure allows organizations to adapt swiftly to industry changes and emerging trends, ensuring their cybersecurity workforce remains agile, skilled, and prepared to meet evolving threats and challenges. This strategic integration of the framework into organizational planning and operations is crucial for maintaining a robust, skilled, and adaptable cybersecurity team.

STRATEGIC WORKFORCE PLANNING

Integrating the NICE Framework into organizational strategy, particularly for enhancing recruitment and retention strategies, involves strategic workforce planning that aligns with the detailed guidelines of the framework. By incorporating the NICE Framework into recruitment strategies, organizations can more effectively identify the specific skills and competencies that are required for various cybersecurity roles. This alignment ensures that job postings, candidate evaluations, and interview processes are tailored to attract and assess individuals who meet the detailed KSAs outlined in the framework. For instance, if the NICE Framework emphasizes the need for skills in cloud security, recruitment efforts can be directed toward candidates with proven experience and qualifications in that area.

Ensuring the presence of a skilled and adaptable cybersecurity workforce goes hand in hand with retention strategies. Once employees are onboarded, the NICE Framework can be used as a continuous professional development and career progression guide. Organizations can significantly improve employee satisfaction and retention by offering clear pathways for growth and opportunities for skill enhancement that align with the NICE standards. This involves providing training and upskilling opportunities and recognizing and rewarding the application of new skills in line with the framework's competencies. An adaptable workforce is not only skilled in current cybersecurity practices—it is also prepared for future challenges and technological shifts, which is essential in the fast-evolving field of cybersecurity. Thus, organizations can build a robust, capable, and future-ready cybersecurity team by aligning recruitment and retention strategies with the NICE Framework.

ATTRACTING AND RETAINING TALENT

Attracting and retaining talent in cybersecurity can be significantly enhanced by leveraging the NICE Framework. To appeal to high-caliber candidates, organizations can showcase how their cybersecurity roles and career development opportunities align with the NICE Framework's well-respected and widely recognized standards. By advertising that they adhere to this framework in their role definitions, skill requirements, and career progression paths, organizations signal potential candidates that they are committed to best practices in cybersecurity and professional growth. This can particularly appeal to ambitious professionals who are seeking roles that offer clear, structured, and industry-aligned career advancement opportunities.

Using the NICE guidelines to foster a culture of professional development is also vital in retaining talent. Employees are more likely to stay with an organization that invests in their growth and provides clear pathways for advancement. By aligning employee training programs, performance evaluations, and career development initiatives with the NICE Framework, organizations create an environment where continuous learning and skill enhancement are encouraged and integral to the professional journey. This could involve implementing mentorship programs, offering support for obtaining certifications outlined in the NICE Framework, and providing opportunities for employees to engage in projects that allow them to apply and expand their skills. Such initiatives help build a workforce that is skilled and compliant with industry standards and deeply engaged and committed to the organization, thereby leading to higher retention rates and a more robust cybersecurity posture.

ALIGNING WITH BUSINESS OBJECTIVES

Aligning the cybersecurity workforce with business objectives is critical to integrating the NICE Framework into an organization's strategy. Ensuring that this alignment endures involves regularly reviewing and adjusting the cybersecurity team's goals and activities to match the broader organizational goals. This means that the cybersecurity team's skills, roles, and projects should directly support the company's mission, whether protecting customer data, ensuring compliance with industry regulations, or enabling secure digital transformation. For instance, if an organization's strategic goal is to expand its digital services, the cybersecurity team should have the skills and resources to secure these services effectively.

Utilizing the NICE Framework to support strategic business initiatives provides a structured approach to identifying the cybersecurity roles and competencies needed to support various business objectives. By aligning workforce development and training initiatives with the NICE Framework, organizations can ensure that their cybersecurity team possesses the right mix of skills and abilities to meet current and future business needs. For example, suppose a strategic business initiative involves migrating services to the cloud. In that case, the NICE Framework can guide the development of cloud security and risk management skills within the cybersecurity team. This alignment ensures that the cybersecurity workforce is proficient in their field and fully aligned and actively contributing to the organization's strategic objectives, thereby enhancing the overall effectiveness and competitiveness of the business.

ADAPTING TO INDUSTRY CHANGES

Remaining flexible and responsive to industry shifts is vital for organizations to maintain robust cybersecurity defenses. This flexibility involves staying informed about emerging threats, evolving technologies, and changes in regulatory landscapes. By being agile and adaptable, cybersecurity teams can swiftly adjust their strategies and tactics to counter new risks effectively. For instance, the rapid rise in remote work has necessitated a shift in focus toward securing remote access and protecting against increased phishing attacks, thus requiring cybersecurity teams to adapt quickly.

Continuously updating workforce strategies to stay ahead in cybersecurity is equally essential. This involves regularly reviewing and revising the cybersecurity team's skills, training programs, and recruitment criteria per the latest industry developments and best practices outlined in the NICE Framework. As new technologies and threats emerge, the framework can guide organizations in identifying the new skills and roles required to address these challenges. For example, with the increasing use of AI in cyberattacks, a workforce strategy might include upskilling team members in AI and machine learning to understand better and mitigate such threats. By continuously updating their strategies and ensuring their team is trained in the latest cybersecurity practices, organizations can protect against current threats and anticipate and prepare for future challenges, thereby keeping them at the forefront of cybersecurity innovation and defense.

B

DETAILED CYBER JOB POSITION LISTINGS

In the dynamic and ever-expanding field of cybersecurity, a wide range of specialized roles has emerged to address the diverse challenges and threats in the digital world. As organizations increasingly recognize the importance of robust cybersecurity measures, the demand for skilled professionals grows. To provide a clear understanding of the opportunities available in cybersecurity, a comprehensive list of 61 job roles has been compiled. These roles span various aspects of cybersecurity, from technical and analytical positions to management and strategic planning roles.

Each role in the list is accompanied by a brief description, typical qualifications required, and relevant certifications that can enhance a candidate's suitability for the position. It is important to note that while many of these roles traditionally require a college degree, the landscape of qualifications in the cybersecurity field is evolving. Due to the growing demand for cybersecurity professionals and the practical, hands-on nature of many entry-level cyber jobs, several companies are reevaluating the necessity of a college degree. Instead, there is an increasing focus on practical skills, hands-on training, and specific cybersecurity certifications.

This shift reflects a broader trend in the tech industry toward valuing demonstrated skills and real-world experience, potentially opening doors for individuals who have taken alternative educational paths, such as vocational training programs, boot camps, self-taught courses, or industry-specific certifications. As you explore the list of job roles, it is essential to consider this evolving perspective on qualifications and the various pathways that can lead to a successful career in cybersecurity.

Job Role	Description	Qualifications	Certs
Cybersecurity Specialist/ Technician	Implements and maintains security measures to protect systems and networks.	Bachelor's degree in IT or related field, experience in network and system security.	CompTIA Security+, CEH, SSCP
Cybersecurity Analyst	Monitors networks and systems for security breaches, analyzes threats, and reports incidents.	Bachelor's degree in cybersecurity or related field, experience in information security or network administration.	CompTIA CySA+, CEH, GCIH, CISSP
Cybersecurity Consultant	Provides expert advice on cybersecurity strategies and solutions to organizations.	Bachelor's degree in IT, extensive experience in cybersecurity, knowledge of various security frameworks.	CISSP, CISM, CEH, CCSP
Incident Responder	Manages the response to cybersecurity incidents, including mitigation and recovery.	Degree in cybersecurity, experience in incident handling, knowledge of forensic tools.	ECIH, CISSP-ISSMP, GCIH, CSIH
Vulnerability Assessment Analyst	Identifies and evaluates security vulnerabilities in systems and software.	Bachelor's degree in cybersecurity, experience with vulnerability assessment tools, understanding of network security.	CEH, CompTIA PenTest+, GPEN
Software Developer/ Engineer (Secure Software)	Develops secure software applications to minimize vulnerabilities.	Bachelor's degree in computer science or software engineering, knowledge of secure coding practices.	CSSLP, GWAPT, GSSP-JAVA, GSSP-.NET
Security Architect	Designs and implements secure network and system architectures.	Advanced degree in IT or cybersecurity, experience in security architecture, knowledge of risk management practices.	CISSP-ISSAP, SABSA, CISM
Cyber Defense Infrastructure Support Specialist	Maintains and supports the infrastructure required for cyber defense activities.	Bachelor's degree in IT, experience with network and security infrastructure, system administration skills.	CompTIA Security+, CCNA Security, CISSP

Continued

Job Role	Description	Qualifications	Certs
Identity and Access Manager	Manages systems and policies for ensuring proper identity and access control within an organization.	Bachelor's degree in IT, experience with identity management solutions, understanding of compliance requirements.	CISM, CIAM, CompTIA Security+
Risk Manager/ Analyst	Identifies potential cyber threats and develops strategies to mitigate risk.	Bachelor's degree in risk management or IT, experience in risk analysis, knowledge of cybersecurity and compliance.	CRISC, CISA, CISSP, CGEIT
Cyber Legal Advisor	Advises on legal aspects of cybersecurity, including compliance and regulatory issues.	Law degree, expertise in cyber law and data privacy regulations.	CIPP, CISSP, CIPM
Cyber Education and Training Specialist	Develops and delivers cybersecurity training and educational programs.	Degree in education or IT, experience in cybersecurity training.	CompTIA CTT+, CISSP, CEH
Cyber Policy and Strategy Planner	Develops policies and strategies for cybersecurity risk management and response.	Bachelor's degree in IT or related field, experience in policy development.	CISSP, CISM, CRISC
Cyber Operations Manager	Oversees daily operations of cybersecurity activities and teams.	Bachelor's or master's in IT or cybersecurity, management experience.	CISM, CISSP, CompTIA Security+
Data Analyst	Analyzes data to identify trends, threats, or anomalies relevant to cybersecurity.	Degree in data science or related field, experience in data analysis.	CompTIA Data+, CEH, CISSP
Network Operations Specialist	Manages and maintains network systems for security and efficiency.	Degree in network engineering or IT, experience in network operations.	CCNA, CompTIA Network+, JNCIA
Penetration Tester	Conducts simulated cyberattacks to test the security of systems.	Degree in cybersecurity, knowledge of penetration testing tools and techniques.	OSCP, CEH, LPT, GPEN

Continued

Job Role	Description	Qualifications	Certs
Cybercrime Investigator	Investigates cybercrimes by analyzing digital evidence and tracking activities.	Degree in criminal justice or IT, experience in digital investigations.	CFCE, CCE, EnCE, CISSP
Digital Forensics Analyst	Specializes in recovering and examining digital evidence for investigations.	Degree in digital forensics or IT, knowledge of legal procedures.	CHFI, GCFA, CCFP, GCFE
Chief Information Security Officer (CISO)	Leads and oversees the organization's overall cybersecurity strategy and implementation.	Advanced degree in IT, extensive experience in cybersecurity management.	CISSP, CISM, CGEIT, CCISO
IT Project Manager	Manages IT projects, particularly those related to cybersecurity, ensuring they meet objectives and timelines.	Bachelor's in IT or related field, project management experience.	PMP, CompTIA Project+, PRINCE2
Cybersecurity Engineer	Designs, implements, and oversees security systems to protect against cyber threats.	Bachelor's in cybersecurity or related field, experience in security system design.	CISSP, CEH, GSEC, CompTIA Security+
Systems Developer	Develops and maintains systems with a focus on improving security features.	Bachelor's degree in computer science or related field, coding and system development skills.	CompTIA Security+, CISSP, CSSLP
Cybersecurity Manager/ Administrator	Oversees cybersecurity strategies, policies, and teams within an organization.	Bachelor's or master's in cybersecurity, managerial experience.	CISM, CISSP, CompTIA Security+
Network Engineer	Designs, implements, and manages network infrastructure, ensuring security and efficiency.	Degree in network engineering or IT, experience in network management.	CCNA, CompTIA Network+, JNCIA

Continued

Job Role	Description	Qualifications	Certs
Systems Engineer	Integrates various IT systems, ensuring they work securely and efficiently together.	Bachelor's degree in systems engineering, IT, or related field.	CompTIA Security+, CISSP, CCNP
Cybersecurity Auditor	Conducts audits of cybersecurity policies and systems to ensure compliance and effectiveness.	Bachelor's in IT or related field, experience in auditing.	CISA, CISSP, ISO 27001 Lead Auditor
Cyber Instructor	Teaches cybersecurity concepts and skills in academic or professional settings.	Degree in education or IT, experience in cybersecurity.	CompTIA CTT+, CEH, CISSP
Cyber Workforce Developer and Manager	Focuses on developing and managing cybersecurity talent within an organization.	Bachelor's in HR, IT, or related field, experience in workforce development.	SHRM-CP, PHR, CompTIA Security+
Program/Project Manager and Acquisition Specialist	Manages programs and projects, specializing in procurement and acquisition in cybersecurity contexts.	Bachelor's degree, experience in project management and procurement.	PMP, CAPM, CPCM
Executive Cyber Leadership	Leads and defines the organization's cybersecurity strategy at the executive level.	Advanced degree in IT or business, extensive experience in cybersecurity leadership.	CISSP, CISM, CCISO, CGEIT
Secure Software Assessor	Evaluates software for security vulnerabilities and compliance with security standards.	Degree in computer science or IT, knowledge of secure software development practices.	CSSLP, GWAPT, CompTIA Security+
Security Control Assessor	Assesses and validates the effectiveness of security controls within IT systems.	Bachelor's in IT or related field, experience in IT security controls and audit.	CISA, CISSP, CRISC, CAP

Continued

Job Role	Description	Qualifications	Certs
System Testing and Evaluation Specialist	Tests and evaluates IT systems for security and performance, ensuring they meet specified requirements.	Degree in IT or related field, experience in system testing and evaluation.	CompTIA Security+, ISTQB, CEH
Research and Development Specialist	Conducts research and development focused on cybersecurity technologies and solutions.	Advanced degree in cybersecurity, IT, or related field, experience in research and development.	CISSP, CompTIA Security+, CEH
Systems Requirements Planner	Plans and defines the requirements for IT systems, focusing on security aspects.	Bachelor's degree in IT, experience in system design and requirements planning.	CompTIA Security+, PMP, CISSP
Cyber Defense Analyst	Analyzes information to identify and defend against cyber threats and vulnerabilities.	Bachelor's degree in cybersecurity, experience in threat analysis and cyber defense.	CompTIA CySA+, CEH, CISSP
Cyber Defense Incident Responder	Responds to and manages the aftermath of cyber incidents, including analysis and recovery efforts.	Degree in cybersecurity, experience in incident response and digital forensics.	ECIH, GCIH, CISSP-ISSMP, CSIH
Threat/Warning Analyst	Identifies and analyzes potential cyber threats, providing early warnings and threat intelligence.	Bachelor's in cybersecurity or related field, experience in threat intelligence and analysis.	CEH, CompTIA CySA+, CTIA, GCTI
Exploitation Analyst	Identifies vulnerabilities in systems and networks that could be exploited and provides insights for defense.	Bachelor's degree in IT or cybersecurity, experience in vulnerability analysis or penetration testing.	CEH, OSCP, GPEN, CompTIA PenTest+

Continued

Job Role	Description	Qualifications	Certs
All-Source Analyst	Integrates and analyzes data from various sources to assess cyber threats.	Degree in cybersecurity or related field, experience in data analysis and intelligence gathering.	CEH, CompTIA CySA+, GCTI
Mission Assessment Specialist	Evaluates cybersecurity missions and operations to determine effectiveness and suggest improvements.	Bachelor's in cybersecurity or related field, experience in operational planning and assessment.	PMP, CISSP, CompTIA Security+
Target Developer	Develops profiles and identifies targets in cyber operations for defensive or offensive strategies.	Degree in IT or cybersecurity, experience in threat analysis or offensive cyber operations.	CEH, OSCP, GPEN
Target Network Analyst	Analyzes network data to identify potential targets for cybersecurity operations.	Bachelor's in IT or cybersecurity, experience in network analysis and threat intelligence.	CompTIA Network+, CEH, CISSP
Cyber Operator	Conducts cyber operations based on specified objectives and targets.	Degree in cybersecurity, experience in cyber operations, offensive and defensive strategies.	CEH, OSCP, GPEN
Cyber Policy and Strategy Developer	Develops policies and strategies to guide cybersecurity practices and operations.	Advanced degree in cybersecurity or related field, experience in policy development and strategic planning.	CISSP, CISM, CRISC
Cyber Intelligence Planner	Plans and coordinates intelligence activities in the cybersecurity domain.	Bachelor's degree in IT or intelligence studies, experience in cybersecurity intelligence.	CEH, CompTIA CySA+, GCTI
Cyber Ops Planner	Develops plans for cybersecurity operations, considering threats and organizational objectives.	Bachelor's in cybersecurity, experience in operational planning and strategy.	CISSP, CompTIA Security+, CISM

Continued

Job Role	Description	Qualifications	Certs
Partner Integration Planner	Coordinates with external partners to align cybersecurity strategies and operations.	Degree in IT or related field, experience in partnership management and cybersecurity collaboration.	CISSP, CISM, CompTIA Security+
Communications Security (COMSEC) Manager	Manages and oversees the communications security aspects of an organization.	Bachelor's degree in IT or communications, experience with COMSEC policies and equipment.	CISSP, CompTIA Security+, CCNA Security
Cyber Defense Forensics Analyst	Analyzes digital evidence and supports investigations of cyber incidents.	Bachelor's in digital forensics or IT, experience in digital investigations.	CHFI, GCFA, GCFE, CCFP
Cyber Instructional Curriculum Developer	Develops educational content and curriculum for cybersecurity training programs.	Degree in education or IT, experience in curriculum design and cybersecurity knowledge.	CompTIA CTT+, CISSP, CEH
Cyber Instructor	Teaches and trains individuals in various aspects of cybersecurity.	Degree in education or IT, expertise in cybersecurity, teaching experience.	CompTIA CTT+, CEH, CISSP
Cyber Work Role Capability Developer	Focuses on developing and defining the capabilities and roles within cybersecurity workforces.	Bachelor's in HR or related field, experience in role development and cybersecurity.	SHRM-CP, PHR, CompTIA Security+
Information Systems Security Developer	Develops and implements security measures for information systems.	Bachelor's degree in IT or computer science, experience in system security.	CISSP, CompTIA Security+, CSSLP
Secure Software Developer	Specializes in creating software applications with a focus on security.	Bachelor's in computer science or software engineering, knowledge of secure coding practices.	CSSLP, GWAPT, GSSP-JAVA, GSSP-.NET

Continued

Job Role	Description	Qualifications	Certs
Security Architect	Designs secure network and system architectures to protect against cyber threats.	Advanced degree in IT or cybersecurity, experience in security architecture.	CISSP-ISSAP, SABSA, CISM
Cyber Defense Analyst	Analyzes information to identify and defend against cyber threats and vulnerabilities.	Bachelor's degree in cybersecurity, experience in threat analysis and cyber defense.	CompTIA CySA+, CEH, CISSP
Cyber Defense Infrastructure Support Specialist	Maintains and supports the infrastructure required for cyber defense activities.	Bachelor's degree in IT, experience with network and security infrastructure.	CompTIA Security+, CCNA Security, CISSP
Cyber Defense Auditor	Conducts audits of cybersecurity policies and systems to ensure compliance and effectiveness.	Bachelor's in IT or related field, experience in IT security controls and audit.	CISA, CISSP, ISO 27001 Lead Auditor
Information Systems Security Manager	Manages and oversees the security aspects of information systems within an organization.	Bachelor's or master's in IT or cybersecurity, management experience.	CISM, CISSP, CompTIA Security+

INDEX

Note: Page numbers followed by *f* and *t* refer to figures and tables, respectively.